Models of Confirmation
and Baptismal Affirmation

MODELS OF CONFIRMATION AND BAPTISMAL AFFIRMATION

Liturgical and Educational Issues and Designs

ROBERT L. BROWNING

AND

ROY A. REED

Religious Education Press
Birmingham, Alabama

Library of Congress Cataloging-in-Publication Data
Browning, Robert L.
    Models of confirmation and baptismal affirmation : liturgical and edu-
cational designs / Robert L. Browning and Roy A. Reed.
    Includes bibliographical references and indexes.
    ISBN 0-89135-097-7
    1. Confirmation.   2. Baptism—Reaffirmation of covenant.
3. Liturgics.   I. Reed, Roy A.   II. Title.
BV815.B75   1994
265'.2—dc20   94-24636
                                                                         CIP

Religious Education Press
5316 Meadow Brook Road
Birmingham, Alabama 35242
10 9 8 7 6 5 4 3 2

Religious Education Press publishes books exclusively in religious education
and in areas closely related to religious education. It is committed to enhanc-
ing and professionalizing religious education through the publication of
serious, significant, and scholarly works.

PUBLISHER TO THE PROFESSION

CONTENTS

PREFACE

Confirmation is an endeavor in the churches which naturally and acutely brings together the activity and concerns of religious education and liturgy. Today the activities of Christian-making in education, in exercise of faith, and in rite are matters under much scrutiny, undergoing serious rethinking and reform, involving considerable experimentation. Much of this is undertaken locally as individual congregations seek for some effective way to challenge, especially, youth to genuine Christian commitment and enculturate them in Christian faith. But denominations also are involved in efforts to bring whole families of Christian people to a thorough reconsideration of the matter of initiation into Christian faith.[1] All of this brings together a wide range of pastoral-theological-historical-liturgical-educational issues and strategies.

We were first confronted with new ideas about confirmation reading Max Thurian's book *Consecration of the Layman* which was published in French in 1957 and appeared in this country in English in 1963. Thurian used scriptural and historical evidence to argue that confirmation is part of baptism and has no meaning apart from the meaning of baptism. He used historical, theological, and pastoral data to argue for a new perspective on confirmation as repeatable and consecratory. He envisioned confirmation as indicating specific directions of a general ministry bestowed upon all Christians in baptism. His designation for the rite was confirmation/consecration. He actually preferred the term consecration, but thought that the word was preempted by its historic association with ordination.[2]

1

The understanding that confirmation is integral to baptism is now a commonplace that is part of all efforts to refresh thinking and practice patterns of Christian commitment in education and liturgy. The idea that confirmation is something repeatable in Christian commitment is having wide repercussions in the churches. It is something generally accepted as "baptismal renewal," even when not understood as confirmation itself.

Today, what to call this *sacrament* or *ordinance* is a question on the frontier of theological, liturgical, and educational thinking. The revised liturgy which appeared in 1978 in the *Lutheran Book of Worship* titled this service "Affirmation of Baptism," with the term "confirmation" relegated to a rubric.[3] The alternate United Methodist liturgy which appeared two years earlier (1976) retained the title of confirmation but added the term "renewal:" *A Service of Baptism, Confirmation, and Renewal.* In the introduction to the service the "confirming" section of the liturgy is described as "renewal of the baptismal covenant." What had been called confirmation is approached in these terms: "For those who have been baptized as infants or children, there is a significant first occurence of such renewal, commonly called 'confirmation'." [4] In *The Book of Common Worship* published in 1993 the Presbyterians titled what they have called confirmation, "Reaffirmation of the Baptismal Covenant." Six separate occasions for such renewal are indicated.[5]

Standing thus on shifting sands and wishing to speak about and to many different traditions we are hard pressed to know what language to use to describe what we are talking about. So we will use the assortment of terms now available: confirmation, affirmation of baptism, baptismal renewal, and some allusions to the subject and hope that you will forgive us if a particular description seems inappropriate to your tradition and experience.

Reasons for our study of confirmation or baptismal affirmation go well beyond the confusions mentioned above. At the local church level, church after church has experimented with fresh forms of religious education for confirmation and liturgical celebration in the hope that the young, especially, will find an exciting and authentic commitment to the Christian faith.

It was because of our awareness of denominational and local church efforts to understand and refocus confirmation that we decided to conduct a study not only of the biblical, theological, and historical foundations for confirmation but also the actual practices to be found in seven denominations where the rite has been an integral part of the initiation of the young. We studied denominational theological statements, curriculum resources, and from fifteen to twenty-five representative local churches within each denomination and their actual practices and self-understandings. The following denominations were studied: The Roman Catholic Church, the Episcopal Church, the Evangelical Lutheran Church of America, the United Methodist Church, the United Church of Christ, the Presbyterian Church, (U.S.A.), and the United Church of Canada. We did not include research from Orthodox churches because the Orthodox have continued the practice of unified initiation (baptism, chrism/confirmation, eucharist) in one liturgy. This omission should not denegrate the influence of Orthodox practice. Their faithfulness to ancient tradition is a strong influence in contemporary reform in many churches. Most of the ecclesiastical bodies we did study have expressed great concern to clarify and strengthen their understanding and practice of confirmation (affirmation of baptism or baptismal renewal). Most have had study commissions on the issues; several have designed new religious educational resources and approaches; some are still in the study phase.

In Part I we shall seek to open up a frank discussion of the varying models of confirmation we have found. We will also attempt to make sense out of the history of the concept and help us discern what the motivations for confirmation (or baptismal affirmation) have been and are today. We shall probe a central theological reality about confirmation: namely, that it is related intrinsically to baptism and that it is grounded in the empowerment that comes through the life-giving presence of God's Holy Spirit moving in and through the family and the faith community. We shall explore the potential of a fresh concept concerning confirmation: namely, that it is a *blessing* which comes to the lives of those who are surrounded by God's love within the faith community and symbolized and made real in and through the laying on of hands and anointing, and participation in the celebration of the eucharist. We shall show why it is theologically, psychologically and religious educationally sound to see confirmation as a part of the unified initiation, but a sacramental celebration which can and should be repeated at different times in life's pilgrimage when persons have new self-understandings and fresh and deeper commitments to the Christian faith and life.

In Part II we shall present the findings which have come as a result of our research into the understandings and practices of the seven denominations. We shall point out several major trends and their implications for the future of confirmation or baptismal affirmation.

In Part III we shall present our rationale for confirmation as a repeatable sacramental experience. We shall show: (1) why confirmation is strengthened when it is seen as a part of the unified initiation in infant baptism; (2) how it can be a significant statement of personal affirmation and strengthening of faith in late childhood; (3) how new understandings of faith development can make confirmation or affirmation of one's baptismal covenant a significant public celebration of fidelity in late adolescence; (4) how and why young adulthood may be *the* crucial time to critique and refine one's commitment to reaffirm and own one's faith, making a clear decision to become a part of the universal priesthood of all believers in some specific form of ministry through family, work, community, and world involvements; (5) why and how mid-life and older adult years will inevitably bring challenges and opportunities which will call for deeper self understandings, fresh visions of life's meaning and purpose, and reconfirmation of one's baptism and sense of vocation. At each of these stages on life's way, we will not only discuss the human needs present and the possible avenue for growth in faith but also the educational designs and liturgical celebrations which can strengthen persons so that they are spiritually centered and empowered to become blessings to others in our world.

In Part IV we will present guidelines for designing liturgical celebrations which correlate with the steps in the development of life in faith. We also will include original liturgies written by former and present students who have joined us in our journey of faith.

We have kept in mind the following audiences for this book: pastors, religious educators, liturgical leaders, parents, teachers, and mentors at the local church level, members of baptism or confirmation study commissions at the denominational level, professors and students in theological schools in the United States and throughout the world who are probing the core meanings of confirmation or baptismal affirmation as well as seeking fresh educational and liturgical approaches, and leaders of efforts to renew and deepen our liturgical and service life in the world. It is our hope that these chapters will stimulate dialogue, more research, fresh experimentation, and significant evidences of authentic and joyous commitment on the part of members of Christ's ministering body in our needy world.

We are especially grateful to many people who have cooperated with us in the research and writing phases of this project: Our thanks goes to all of the persons who helped us identify local church and judicatory leaders with whom we could have dialogue or from whom we received responses to our inventory (see appendix). Our special gratitude goes to William Schuyler of the Episcopal Church, John Gooch of the United Methodist Church, Ken Smith of the Evangelical Lutheran Church of America, Rodger Nishioka of the Presbyterian Church U.S.A., Art Kubick of the Roman Catholic Church, Thomas Dipko of the United Church of Christ and Yvonne Stewart and William Lord of the United Church of Canada. Our appreciation to many students in our courses on sacramentality, religious education, and liturgical life at The Methodist Theological School in Ohio, and to pastors, educators and lay leaders with whom we have tested ideas at countless seminars, workshops, and continuing education events. We are grateful for having been included in the study of such issues as we have worked with the study commissions of The United Methodist Church and The Evangelical Lutheran Church of America. We are thankful for the thoughtful assistance of Donald Mauck, Joanmarie Smith, Elaine Ramshaw, Edward Trimmer of the faculty of The Methodist Theological School in Ohio and for the support of the administrators of the school, President Norman Dewire, and Dean Frederick Tiffany. Our publisher, James Michael Lee, has given great encouragement and has evidenced keen awareness of the importance of the issues.

We are especially grateful to present and former students who have ventured forth to write liturgies for different occasions for baptismal affirmation throughout the life span. Our genuine gratitude goes to Kathryn Steen, graduate student in liturgical arts at Methodist Theological School in Ohio; Sue Ralph, pastor in West Salem, Ohio and director of Degrees of Freedom, a retreat house; Valerie Stultz, pastor of Trinity United Methodist Church in Orrville, Ohio; and Robert Klingler, pastor of the Sugar Grove-Chandlers Valley Circuit in western Pennsylvania. They have modeled in their innovative liturgies what we hope many others will attempt.

We are especially appreciative of the help of Datha Myers in the preparation of the manuscript. She has remained faithful in the midst of a very demanding schedule. We are indebted so much to so many who have opened their lives and, indeed, have been a blessing to us.

ROBERT L. BROWNING
ROY A. REED

Methodist Theological School in Ohio

NOTES

1. See the United Methodist study, *By Water and the Spirit*, (Nashville: Cokesbury, 1993) produced by a prestigious study committee for consideration by the church's General Conference. The publication is a study guide, as well as a statement of the text produced by the committee. Also see *The Confirmation Ministry Task Force Report* (The Evangelical Lutheran Church of America, 1993).
2. Max Thurian, *Consecration of the Layman* (Baltimore: Helicon, 1963).
3. *Lutheran Book of Worship* (Minneapolis: Augsburg, 1978), p. 198 ff.
4. *A Service of Baptism, Confirmation and Renewal* (Nashville: United Methodist Publishing House, 1976), p. 11.
5. *Book of Common Worship* (Louisville: Westminister/John Knox, 1993), pp. 431-488.

PART I

CONFIRMATION: PRESENT MODELS, PAST REALITIES, FUTURE DIRECTION

Chapter I

CURRENT MODELS OF CONFIRMATION

There is an insistence in the ecumenical community that the continuing confusion surrounding what we have traditionally called confirmation give way to clarity and fresh meaning. Looked at through the long lens of Christian history this insistence might seem to have scant possibility of fulfillment. Research and theological reflection concerning sacraments and "sacramentals" undertaken since the turn of the century affords more optimism.[1] There is increasing convergence of thought about Christian initiation and especially about what we have usually called "confirmation." Believing Tertullian's dictum that Christians are "made not born," most bodies of believers have had ample reasons to doubt their programs of Christian making. Shrinking numbers, distorted visions, shallow depth— many disappointments have motivated Christians to subject their patterns of invitation and initiation to intense scrutiny. Under this scrutiny "confirmation" came into focus as a particularly confusing and troubling element; just about everything concerning it is called into question. What to call it? Where did we get it? What does it mean? When do we do it? How do we do it?

Probably nothing is so indicative of the current confusion surrounding the confirming liturgy and education as the discussions about what to call it: Confirmation? Baptismal Renewal? Affirmation of baptism? Chrism? All of the above depending upon circumstances?

The term "confirmation" was first used by the French Councils of Riez and Orange in 439 and 441 to refer to the post-baptismal rite of hand laying.[2] Decisions of these local councils gave priests permission to anoint children they had baptized. Bishops were instructed to visit rural districts regularly to *confirm* these local baptisms by the laying on of hands. In a sermon on Pentecost Sunday in around 460 Bishop Faustus of Riez preached on this "confirmation" in terms that were to have immense influence on the history of the rite. Faustus stressed the importance of episcopal confirmation, claiming that it made those who received it more fully Christian. Confirmation imparted, he claimed, an additional strengthening of the Holy Spirit over its gift in baptism, where the Spirit was first imparted. This strengthening gave the Christian "warrior" added and needed power to fight and win life's battles with the world, the flesh, and the devil. At least a glimpse of the preparation for such an understanding is seen in a letter of Pope Innocent I to Decentius of Gubbio written in 416 in which the pontiff legitimized the independent post-baptismal anointing, giving it a pneumatic interpretation and basing its practice upon the hand laying depicted in Acts 8.[3]

Chrism, anointing with oil, and consignation, making the sign of the cross in the anointing, are the manifestations in the later church of the laying on of hands reported in Acts, and Hebrews, and alluded to in other New Testament passages. Anointing by the bishops was chiefly a tradition in the Western church, not practiced in the East. It spread gradually in the West and by mid fifth century needed some theological explanation both to justify its separation from baptism and to support its necessity and desirability.[4] The practice of episcopal confirmation spread gradually in the West until by the Middle Ages the gap between birth and baptism had narrowed to a few days or even hours while the time between baptism and confirmation had extended to several years. In the East, water bath, consignation and eucharist remained part of one initiation liturgy.

The Western practice of confirmation was upheld and greatly encouraged by the successful influence of the famous forgery perpetrated during the 800's known as the *Isadorian Decretals*. This was a collection of fabricated documents drawn up to defend the rights of diocesan bishops against archbishops and cardinals and to claim authority for papal supremacy. One decretal claimed that confirmation had a greater dignity and power than baptism because it was administered by a minister with a higher ecclesiastical office. This and other assertions concerning confirmation in the false decretals were given special amplification by Peter Lombard who relied upon them in the twelfth century to justify confirmation in his compendium of theology, *The Sentences*.[5] After about 1000 A D the rite of confirmation had already achieved an independent status as a sacrament performed by a bishop, done once, whose main feature was consignation with chrism. A foundation for a scholastic theology of confirmation had been laid.

Scholastic theologians of the Middle Ages had their own serious difficulties with confirmation. In them we hear forecasts of our present day problems. They followed sixth–century arguments about the necessity of confirmation but were disconcertingly aware that multitudes of Christians had never been confirmed. As thinkers who reasoned in Aristotelian categories they argued about what the scholastics called the *matter* of the sacrament.[6] Was it the laying on of hands described in the New Testament? If so, why was there no laying on of hands in the rite? Was the *matter* the anointing? Most thought that it was. What was the *form* of the sacrament? Was it the prayer asking the Holy Spirit to descend? Was it the anointing formula of words? And how was the sacrament instituted by Christ? The ending of Matthew's Gospel was clear enough about the command to baptize, but where is the command to confirm? If these difficulties were not enough, the medieval theologians had also to wonder about the special *character* said by the decretals and Peter Lombard to be imparted by confirmation. Of course, in theology one can count on disagreement and there were, even in the Scholastic period, theologians such as William of Auvergne (1180-1249) who denied that the Holy Spirit was bestowed in confirmation. Generally the Scholastics agreed with what Bishop Faustus had said in his sixth–century Pentecost sermon, that it was a "strengthening" which gave Christians the divine capacity to do what human nature otherwise could not do.[7] The medieval theology and practice of confirmation was canonized at the Council of Florence in 1439 which let Western Christians know finally and officially that in confirmation Christians grow in grace and are strengthened in faith. Alas, like many decisions in council, matters have not been settled. The Reformation sent many Western Christians on a quite different pilgrimage concerning confirmation, and in the twentieth century the liturgical movement has opened up all the old questions for everyone's investigation and consideration.[8] The practical problems of the church in the post-Constantinian era combined with clearer historical perspectives gained from better vantage points and improved historical tools have created a new situation for our images, understandings, and expectations of what we have traditionally called confirmation.

The models we attempt to portray in this chapter are not mutually exclusive; they overlap on one another. And they are models either now existing in the church or models which are logical possibilities deduced from current theological/pastoral discussion. We identify the following:

Overview of Various Models

1. *The sealing of the Holy Spirit.* The source of this image is the New Testament, especially in the Acts of the Apostles, and the evidence we have in the liturgical life of the church from at least the latter part of the second century where baptism by water and spirit was "sealed" in the laying on of hands or anointing with oil, leading on to first eucharist.

2. *The completion of infant baptism.* This generally is a ceremony with youth who have made a decision publicly to embrace the faith into which they were baptized and to "join the church."

3. *The ratification of a person's baptism.* After a rigorous period of religious instruction, and after careful examination of the individual's knowledge of the faith, the candidate makes an autonomous decision to be personally committed to it and is admitted in a public ceremony to full rights in the church.

4. *The affirmation of the baptismal covenant in adolescence or as renewal of covenant at any time during life's pilgrimage when an individual comes to new or deepened understandings and/or commitments in faith.* This model focuses upon baptism as the central sacrament which engrafts the person into the body of Christ, the ministering community. As persons move through life educational and liturgical opportunities to affirm and refocus this original "ordination" into the ministering community are needed. Unique life issues in adolescence, young adulthood, middle and older adulthood challenge individuals to deepen their self–understanding and their commitment to find fresh expressions of ministry.

5. *The blessing, following baptism, welcoming the new Christian into full communion in the church and at the Lord's table.* This model is prompted by Aidan Kavanagh's study, *Confirmation: Origins and Reform* (1988).[9] Kavanagh does not in fact present a theology or a liturgical model of confirmation as blessing. He does argue for the rite having its origins in episcopal post–baptismal blessing. For him the rite began and should regain its place as a modest ceremony of transition "from pool to table." This is a picture of confirmation as blessing.

6. *The separate sacrament which imparts the Holy Spirit and imprints a uniquely Christian character establishing identity and effective eternal*

salvation. The new "vitality" communicated in the sacrament strengthens the disciple to live in fidelity to the gospel. The sacrament must be administered by a bishop or a priest specially empowered to seal with the Holy Spirit.

7. *The repeatable sacrament, first experienced in the unified initiation through baptism, laying on of hands, and eucharist, for infants or adults.* The sacrament may be repeated at various times when the faith of the individual is in need of renewal and focus, whether in adolescence in regard to identity, or young adulthood relating to decisions about ministry through vocation, or middle adulthood in reference to changes in self-understanding or understanding of the faith, or in older adulthood relating to new forms of ministry made possible by retirement or redefinition of vocation. [This image is one which we as teachers and authors have pursued and developed in dialogue with many others. The image is relational and nonsubstantialistic and is based upon confidence in the spiritual power resident in the laity, the unique dynamism of God's Word, creating Christian community, mission, and the presence and potency of God's grace within the structure of the world itself.]

8. *The rite which symbolizes and celebrates "life in the Spirit," but is not itself a particular giving or receiving of the Holy Spirit.* In this image the renewal of baptism, or confirmation, is a rite secondary to the experience of receiving within one's heart and soul the gift of God's Spirit. The experience can come at any time in response to God's actions through others or in nature, through the symbols, sacraments, or rituals of the church which point to and celebrate God's grace in Christ and in creation. The important thing in life is the Spirit. A rite can celebrate life in the Spirit, but the celebration itself does not necessarily correspond to a personal openness to receive God's spiritual empowerment. The Spirit gift and the openness to receive it can take place in many settings. It can happen in the hearing of the Good News, as one surrenders in trust to the validity and power of the message; it can happen in response to the incarnation of God's love in the self-giving of a member of Christ's body. The rite of laying on hands, anointing with oil, or signing with the cross may be used to symbolize such empowerment and wholeness.

In this study we shall attempt to sort out and interrelate the images described above. In so doing we shall make our own evaluations concerning strengths and weaknesses in the various views. We shall begin these considerations with an expanded discussion of the models depicted above.

1. *The Sealing of the Holy Spirit*

The idea of confirmation is rooted in the New Testament stories about the gift of the Holy Spirit coming into the lives of those who responded to God's good news in Jesus and the symbolization of this gift, or the gesture which conveyed it in the laying on of hands described by Luke in the Acts of the Apostles. There has been and is now considerable confusion in the church about how God's gift of Spirit comes to people. This is true because the account in the New Testament of the gift is itself confusing, in part contradictory and incomplete. One pattern is described in Acts 9 where, after receiving the gift of Spirit when Ananias laid hands upon him, Paul was baptized. In this sequence confrontation with the living Christ and reception of the Holy Spirit are a prelude to baptism. In the description of Pentecost in Acts 2 a different sequence is indicated. Believers are exhorted to repent and be baptized so that then they would receive the gift of the Holy Spirit. They were then given instruction and shared together in the eucharist.

A different pattern yet is described in Acts 8. The apostle Philip had preached, healed, and baptized many Samaritans. Apostles from Jerusalem heard about this and that the Samaritans had not yet received the Holy Spirit. So Peter and John "laid their hands on them and they received the Holy Spirit." (Acts 8:17). Here is evidence of a delayed "confirmation" which has been a much cited precedent in the Western church. Baptism is here thought to be inadequate without the laying on of hands. This has been for many Christians a perfect proof-text for the "apostolic" role of a bishop in the rites of Christian initiation. In Acts 19 the laying on of hands occurs directly following baptism. Paul encounters disciples in Corinth who understood themselves to have been baptized into John's baptism. Paul baptizes them "in the name of Jesus," and he laid his hands upon them and they received the gift of the Holy Spirit.

So there is ample room for confusion about the gift of the Spirit within the book of *Acts*, the primary scriptural source of the concept of confirmation. In some cases the Spirit precedes baptism as people responded to the good news of Christ, as with St. Paul. In other cases baptism itself appears to be the occasion for the gift of the Spirit, as at Pentecost. In another case the Holy Spirit was imparted well after baptism by apostles through whom the Spirit was channeled, as in Acts 8. And in Acts 19 we see the Holy Spirit was received apparently immediately following baptism. Nothing in the New Testament outside of Acts helps us to clear up this confusion. There are many references to Spirit gift, such as those of

Paul; and other indications of hand laying in the letters to Timothy (I Timothy 4:14; 5:22; II Timothy 1:6) and in Hebrews (Hebrews 6:1-4); and reference to the "seal" of the Holy Spirit (Ephesians 1:13). None of these "instances" provides enough clues to enable us to put together a New Testament picture of Christian initiation.

Outside the New Testament the pieces of a picture of Christian initiation are incomplete to help us put the puzzle together until into the third century. There are hints of a rite of chrism already in the second century, such as the phrase from Theophilus of Antioch, writing in about the year 180: "We, therefore, are called Christians on this account, because we are anointed with the oil of God."[10] There are some references to rites of hand laying in Irenaeus in *Adversus Haeresies*,[11] and some gnostic writings, but no clear evidence of any rite of initiation beyond water baptism. In the third century the picture clarifies. From many sources, Tertullian, Cyprian, Hippolytus, Origen, and others, we see an image, not of separate rites, but of one rite of initiation involving water-bath, chrism, and eucharist. What later came to be called "confirmation" does not appear in these early sources to be an independent rite—or second sacrament—but the bishop's anointing of each of the newly baptized with holy oil.[12]

Most scholars assume that the hand-laying ceremony, mainly as anointing and with consignation,[13] began to be common practice in the later part of the second century. Prior to that time, generally, if not universally, *baptism* was in water and Spirit, as the dialogue between Jesus and Nicodemus in John 3:5 implies. A similar implication is lodged in Jesus' words in Acts 1:5, where in his post-resurrection words to the disciples he asked them to stay in Jerusalem and wait for the promise of God: "This, he said, is what you have heard from me; for John baptized with water, but you will be *baptized* with the Holy Spirit not many days from now." Many scholars of this history, believe that water-baptism itself was a baptism of Spirit and that in the post–apostolic age the entire rite of initiation was understood in its essence as a Spirit event.[14] In his comprehensive study of confirmation, Gerard Austin further concluded that the unified rite of initiation which had been well established apparently by the third century (baptism, chrism, eucharist) was undermined because of a tendency to subordinate Spirit to water, to "refer all the activity of the Spirit to what happens in the sacrament of baptism."[15] Austin concludes: "This unfortunate subordination of Spirit to water had disastrous results: it boxed in the activity of the Spirit, limiting it to certain isolated ritual moments; it impoverished the water-rite, cutting it off from its other ritual components such as anointing, hand-laying and so on, and ultimately it led to the disintegration of a once-unified rite of initiation."[16] This is probably an overstatement but doubtless a factor in the disintegration of the initiation liturgy.

Gerard Austin argues further with the assumption in Acts 8:17 that Peter and John had to lay hands on the Samaritans to impart the Holy Spirit after they had been baptized by Philip. How could the Samaritans have believed and been baptized if the gift of the Holy Spirit had not been present in their lives, he wonders. Was not the response of faith a gift of the Spirit? Austin agrees with other scholars who have concluded that far from denoting a separation of baptism and confirmation, in this case the laying on of hands was a device used by Luke to assert that the Spirit is channeled through the church, represented by the college of the twelve apostles in Jerusalem.[17]

At any rate, by the third century the picture we have of Christian initiation is of a single rite with three symbolic/ceremonial moments. In some pictures there is a pre– rather than a post-baptismal anointing, as in the Syrian church, or both a pre– and a post-baptismal anointing. The rapid and vast expansion of the church, and the practice of baptizing infants, forced the function of baptizing to be extended to presbyters. In the West, the bishops could not entirely let go of their role in initiation, and by 416 Pope Innocent I is trying to bless an administrative claim on authority arguing that sealing with chrism could only be administered by a bishop, since bishops alone had the power to impart the Holy Spirit. Luke must have smiled from his place in eternity because Innocent based his argument on Acts 8:17.

The split among baptism, confirmation, and eucharist was further widened as eucharist gradually was separated from baptism and confirmation. Infants received the eucharistic cup well into the thirteenth century, when laity were allowed only to receive the bread. Infants had received the cup only from the tenth century onward. This meant that from the thirteenth century infants were left with no communion at all. An action of the Fourth Lateran Council in 1215 declared that communion was not obligatory for children until they reached years of discretion. And in 1563 a decision of the Council of Trent stated that infants did not need the eucharist because they could not lose their baptismal grace until the age of discretion. These kinds of decisions completed the disintegration of the unified rite of initiation.

Reformation leaders largely reinforced the disintegration of the unified baptismal rite. They saw confirmation as a personal claiming of the baptismal faith after study and public examination.[18] Only in the twentieth century are we possessed of reasonably accurate pictures of liturgical practice in the earliest years of the church and have discovered the significance of the unified initiation and the anchoring of the anointing, or laying on of hands in the one rite of water and the Spirit with full inclusion into the body of Christ celebrated by the Supper of the Lord.

2. *The Completion of Infant Baptism and "Joining" the Church*

This image is the one most common among Protestant churches which practice infant baptism. While many see infant baptism as entrance into belonging in the church family, many do not. In the United Methodist Church, for instance, a baptized infant has had the status of "preparatory member." The oxymoronic dimensions of that title seemingly bothered few until recently. United Methodists recently have had a study commission examining their understandings and practices of initiation. While some United Methodists have made serious effort to distinguish confirmation education from membership education, the tradition in the denomination has maintained the perspective that confirmation was the climax to a period of intensive preparation—based upon general preparation in family, church school and corporate worship—which brought young adolescents into "full membership" in the church. This approach to affirmation of baptism/confirmation is, in general, a contribution of Reformation conceptions about Christian initiation. While many Protestants, like the Lutherans and Presbyterians have been emphasizing *affirmation of baptism* either in new liturgy or in supplemental liturgy, the "joining the church" concept still dominates the thinking of many. Episcopalians often speak of "confirmed members," a phrase which puts confirmation at the apex of initiation even though the laying on of hands and or anointing are part of their liturgy of baptism.

Like the United Methodists the Evangelical Lutheran Church in America has been involved in a major study of confirmation. The new Lutheran thinking emphasizes confirmation more as celebration of God's grace and the affirmation of baptism and less as public examination and declaration of faith. (See Chapter V) Already in 1979 a joint commission of Lutherans attempted a clarification about confirmation which declared that, "on the practice of confirmation . . . great care must be taken that confirmation neither implies joining the church nor overshadows baptism. It is an affirmation of baptism, a way of saying 'Yes' to baptism. It is not therefore an unrepeatable, once-for-all act but something that can be done at several points in one's life."[19] Such thinking is typical of many Protestants working in the churches today to reform and revise the theology and liturgy of Christian initiation. Such thinking is not itself prompted by inclinations to ecumenicity, but in its commonness across denominations it is ecumenical; and it is generated out of historical research, theological inquiry, and pastoral pondering that in schools, scholarly organizations, and pastoral associations is decidedly ecumenical.[20]

3. *Ratification of Baptism after Intensive Preparation, Examination or Evaluation, and Public Commitment*

This image is similar to the one previous, but it emphasizes more the individual decision for baptismal commitment. Historically, the primary emphasis here was often on public examination of faith and a preparation which involved memorization of confessional formulas and sometimes specified answers to catechetical questions asked by a confirming pastor or bishop. Current ratification approaches are much less cognitive and more relational. The image is generally associated with Lutheran, Anglican, or Presbyterian/Reformed churches, although it is a pattern being adopted by many Catholics, especially in its more relational forms. Churches coming out of the Reformation are moving away from this model, especially as it involves the public examination of faith. This public performance is increasingly viewed as too cognitive and perfunctory. More personal, communal, affectional, pilgrimage, and lifestyle images are modifying rituals which previously stressed correct belief and allegiance to approved church practice and authority.

The strength of the traditional Reformation ratification model was its emphasis on the importance of the human response in confirmation. The simplistic comparison often observed was that in confirmation Protestants celebrated the human response whereas Catholics the divine activity of Spirit. In the contemporary revisions, these opposites are moving toward one another in theological understanding and in liturgy. Some Catholic dioceses have instituted confirmation programs involving features of the ratification model primarily because they are seeking to retain youth in the church or are seeking a confirmation pattern that will keep youth challenged and engaged.

A study by Paul Turner of Catholic and Reformation confirmation patterns describes this movement by some Catholics toward a more traditionally Protestant model. He has examined Catholic confirmation programs of Milwaukee, Indianapolis, Phoenix, San Bernardino, and other places and observed more emphasis being placed upon mature, personal, free response and affirmation of the baptismal faith than upon the gift of the Holy Spirit.[21] Turner observed that while some Catholics have adopted features of the characteristic Protestant confirmation, Lutherans and other Protestants are including laying on of hands or anointing in their new liturgies. Turner appreciates the ecumenical convergence, but believes that the essential meaning of confirmation is compromised if the primary emphasis is not upon the movement of the Holy Spirit in individual life and in the church.

Art Kubick, a Catholic religious educator, has distinguished three major schools of thought about confirmation in the Roman church: unitive, ratification, and canonical. The *unitive* school advocated adult baptism in the unified initiation with water baptism followed immediately by confirmation through laying on of hands and anointing, followed by eucharist. In this model, infants are enrolled in a catechumenate and initiated later after religious education through baptism, confirmation, and eucharist.

The *canonical* school formally affirms the practice of a unified initiation even though it does not approve the combining of baptism, confirmation, and eucharist for infants as the Orthodox church does. Most canon lawyers interpret the unity to mean that children are baptized as infants, are prepared for and celebrate first communion around age seven, and then are confirmed sooner or later, depending upon diocesan policy.

In the *ratification* model the sequence of initiation would involve baptism as an infant, first communion around age seven and confirmation during middle to late adolescence when human commitment is more an autonomous response. Kubick believes that the dominant direction in Catholicism today is toward this ratification model. The three elements of the unified initiation are present but their sequence has been changed to make human response in commitment the climax of the initiation process. The ratification school sees confirmation, thus, as a sacrament of autonomous affirmation of faith which is "an initiation sacrament; . . . the end of a long catechetical process bracketed by infant baptism and confirmation; . . . a sacrament that commissions a person for carrying out the mission of the public church; . . . an opening for youth and adults to the leadings of the Spirit; a remembering and reactivating of the fundamental sacrament of baptism within the church community."[22]

At a time when many Protestants are unhappy about their own ratify-ing programs of confirmation because they focus upon young adoles-cents who interpret confirmation as graduation from study and permission to be adult-like in their behavior and attend church if they feel like it, some Catholics are being attracted to their own version of the ratification model. By moving confirmation to late adolescence (age 14-18) many Catholics believe that they are having more success with less attrition of youth involved in the confirming programs. It is not yet clear if these programs in fact will result in more mature decisions to affirm baptism and be committed to the mission of the church in the world.

4. *Confirmation as "Affirmation of Baptism" or Baptismal Renewal*

In this model confirmation is an affirmation of one's baptismal covenant. The term, affirmation, is replacing confirmation as a term and a concept. The emphasis here is on the person's response to God's grace in Christ. The *Affirm* Series of the Evangelical Lutheran Church of America takes this approach.[23] Likewise, the United Methodist Church is moving in this direction. In the new study document on baptism a rec-ommendation is made for a change from the use of the term "Confirmation" to the term "Affirmation of Baptismal Covenant." The new position changes in a significant way the meaning of both baptism and con-firmation. Previously, United Methodist infants were baptized and made "preparatory members" of the church until confirmation at which time they "joined the church," being confirmed and strengthened in the faith. The new statement says, that "at some point in the growth process there should be a special preparation for this event of Profession of The Faith Into Which We Were Baptized, focusing on one's understanding of one's self and one's personal appropriation of the Christian faith, spiritual disci-plines, and discipleship. Since baptism includes us in the body of Christ, the Church, this process should not be understood as preparation for Church membership. Instead, it is a special time for experiencing, reflect-ing on, growing in, and sharing God's grace. This provides the context and opportunity to make a public profession of faith in Jesus Christ and com-mitment to Christian discipleship. It is a time when the youth consciously embraces Christian vocation, the priesthood of all believers, in which she or he was included in baptism. Once this response has been con-sciously made, the young woman or man should participate in a special rite celebrating this event.[24]

Several other denominations are moving in this direction as well, espe-cially the United Church of Christ, the Episcopal Church, the United

Church of Canada, and the Presbyterian Church. In all of these patterns we see an affirmation of one's baptism on the part of the adolescent or adult with their personal commitment being emphasized within the context of a spirit–filled faith community which confirms and supports the person affirming his or her faith. In some communities such as the Episcopal and Roman Catholic, the emphasis on the Holy Spirit is stronger and is symbolized by the presence of the bishop as the confirming minister. In several faith communities the increasing presence and involvement of sponsors and family members reveal the much stronger relational theology behind the changes.[25] In all but the Roman Catholic and Orthodox patterns confirmation is not seen as a sacrament. Rather baptism and communion are the two sacraments with confirmation (as Affirmation of Baptism) seen as a rite or ordinance with power to symbolize important personal response on the part of the candidate and corporate support on the part of the faith community.

5. *Confirmation as a Blessing and Recommitment*

The potential of the idea that confirmation (or baptismal renewal) is a creative and religiously meaningful way to extend God's blessing upon each of us during our lifetime of self giving and mutual ministry is a novel suggestion based upon recent research.

As we have noted, Aidan Kavanagh, in his book, maintains that he and others have in the past misinterpreted the meaning of confirmation in the early church. Kavanagh believes that in the *Apostolic Tradition* (c. 215) the prayers and laying on of hands, administered by the bishop were not a bestowal of the Holy Spirit on the newly baptized but, rather, a *dismissal liturgy* and a *blessing* of the neophyte as he or she left the baptismal service and prepared to receive Holy Communion.[26] The privilege was reserved for only those who had made the complete pilgrimage of the catechumen or the dismissal of those who were still catechumens and could not take communion. The dismissal or *missa* became so important that it later was the name used for the eucharist itself.

Kavanagh traces the movement of the ceremony from the prayers and laying on of hands after baptism as a dismissal and blessing to the later interpretation that these words and actions invoked and brought the seal of the Holy Spirit to the candidate in a way different from baptism. Kavanagh makes no radical liturgical recommendations out of his "discovery." He believes that the initiation should be threefold (baptism, confirmation, and eucharist). And he believes baptism (in water and the Spirit) is the non-repeatable centerpiece with confirmation largely as a bridge to eucharist which completes the engrafting of the person into the body of Christ.

We believe that the idea of confirmation as blessing has intriguing possibility as a rationale for confirmation. Blessing is a much neglected category in scriptural study and theology. Whatever else confirmation might be, it intends to draw us into faith in Christ and into God's "economy" of blessing.

6. *Confirmation as a One-time Sacrament which Imprints a Character Uniquely Christian in Terms of One's Identity and Eternal Salvation*

As we have maintained, the history of confirmation is clearer today than ever before. As we have seen in discussions of previous images confirmation as a separate sacrament did not appear until the third and fourth centuries and usually as a part of the unified initiation. Because of the strong emphasis which increasingly was made on the imparting of the Holy Spirit through the laying on of hands, anointing with oil or signing of the cross on the forehead only by a bishop, the importance of this part of the unified initiation was magnified. As we have noted we see this increased emphasis in Tertullian's *De Baptismo* (Circa 200), in *Apostolic Tradition* (Circa 215) and in the letters from Pope Innocent I to Decentius, Bishop of Gubbo, in 416 and in the general practice of the church.

Pope Innocent's letter is worth underscoring because it established a pattern which was a precursor of the inauguration of confirmation as a separate sacrament which imparted the Holy Spirit in a unique way beyond baptism. He said, "Concerning the consignation of infants, it is clear that this should not be done by any but the bishop. For presbyters, although they are priests, have not attained the highest rank of the pontificate. The right of bishops alone to seal and to deliver the Spirit the Paraclete is proved not only by the custom of the church but also by the reading in the Acts of the Apostles which tells how Peter and John were directed to deliver the Holy Spirit to people who were already baptized. For it is permissible for a presbyter, either in the absence of a bishop, or when they baptize in his presence, to anoint the baptized with chrism, but only with such as has been consecrated by the bishop; and even then they are not to sign the brow with that oil, for that is reserved to bishops alone when they deliver the Spirit the Paraclete."[27]

This image gained acceptance as a pattern of preparation especially as the catechumenate ended in the fifth and sixth centuries and after the expansion of the church into rural areas away from urban centers where bishops tended to reside. This demographic fact brought about the inevitable separation of the baptism by presbyters from the much later confirmation by bishops or chorebishops who in their travels sought to reach all those baptized however many years it took.[28]

It was not until Thomas Aquinas in the thirteenth century that we find a systematic theological defense of confirmation as a sacrament which, like baptism and holy orders, imprints a character which is a "certain kind of participation in the priesthood of Christ." Gerard Austin reminds us that Aquinas lacked the knowledge we have today about how confirmation had been a part of the unified initiation. Therefore Aquinas' view has been etched into the consciousness of leaders for centuries. It was the image of confirmation as a separate sacrament which was a one-time strengthening by the Holy Spirit "for activity that is different from that for which power is given in baptism. For in baptism power is received for performing those things which pertain to one's own salvation in so far as one lives for oneself. In confirmation a person receives power for engaging in the spiritual battle against the enemies of the faith."[29]

This view was reinforced in the Council of Trent (1545-1563) and in many other statements until Vatican II when there was a recognition that confirmation was one part of the whole of Christian initiation.[30] The emphasis on the strengthening of the Holy Spirit in order to spread the faith by word and deed is still present. The constant factor in this somewhat unfortunate history is the emphasis on the sacramental nature of confirmation whenever it takes place.

Protestants such as Luther, Zwingli, Calvin, and others rejected confirmation as a separate sacrament not because they understood that it was originally a part of the unified initiation but because they rejected the basic understanding of the nature of sacrament implied.[31] The substantialistic interpretation was rejected and along with it the seven sacraments in favor of the two: baptism and communion.[32] This rejection of the seven sacraments was unfortunate because it has taken over 400 years for the churches to move to a view of sacramentality which may allow Protestants to see and affirm the sacramental power of the other five liturgical acts and for the Roman Catholic Church to be open to a relational instead of a substantialistic view of the nature of the sacraments. We wish to maintain the sacramental nature of confirmation in our model, without an emphasis on confirmation as a one-time sacrament which imprints an indelible character. Rather, we wish to develop the concept that confirmation or affirmation of one's baptismal faith is a sacrament, relationally grounded in the unified initiation and repeatable at different points in life when there are changes in one's self-understanding and commitment to be in ministry in and through the body of Christ. While this pattern is implied in several of the above images, most Protestant understandings and practices do not see confirmation as a sacrament. We believe this reservation is wrongly anchored in substantialistic assumptions which are waning and are unnecessary in our understanding of sacramentality.

7. *Confirmation or Affirmation of Baptism as a Repeatable Sacrament*

The sacrament is experienced first in the unified initiation (baptism, hand-laying or anointing, eucharist); it can and should subsequently be repeated. We take this position because of our concept of sacrament and our view of the human need for periods of reassessment and recommitment in the normal life cycle.

Much previous understanding of confirmation as sacrament has seen it as a substantialistic imparting of the Holy Spirit to the already baptized and a strengthening of the faithful for service. As such it is traditionally seen as a one-time event. The idea that confirmation is repeatable is genuinely innovative but by no means an unknown idea in contemporary, ecumenical conversation about the rite as liturgy or as a program of education.

The only way this position can be held with integrity is within a redefinition of the nature of sacrament. Such a redefinition has been taking place ecumenically, and includes contributions from Protestant, Catholic, and Orthodox theologians. This has been referred to as "the quiet revolution in sacramental understanding and practice" in our previous book.[33] The quiet revolution concerning sacraments and sacramentality involves, in part, a movement away from substantialistic understanding where God's grace is imparted or withheld by those who have the power to channel that spiritual power, and toward a relational understanding. A relational view sees God's grace present in the world and interpersonally in the church in the dynamic of a loving, caring, forgiving, justice-seeking body of Christ. This reality is pointed to and participated in when the signs of God's kingdom are shared and made visible in particular sacraments. These events of participation in Christ, the primordial sacrament, are as few or many as a body of Christ may designate. In the tradition they are variously, baptism, confirmation, eucharist, marriage, reconciliation, ordination, consecration of laity for ministry, healing and wholeness in life and death, and the forgotten sacrament of servanthood, footwashing. All of these gestures of commitment make Christ's love visible in human life, not, we think, in an automatic or mechanistic way. They are authentic only as they create and celebrate real love, forgiveness, commitment, healing, etc., in a personal and a social interaction.

In this sacramental understanding, confirmation can stand as a sacrament, which, like the eucharist, can and should be repeated when the faith of the person is tested, stretched, and matured as experiences of life unfold. To see confirmation or affirmation of baptism as a sacrament deepens the understanding and experience of the rite and preparation for it as a genuine celebration of and commitment to the reception of God's grace and guidance in the call to ministries of the body of Christ.

In the presentation of this perspective, we will make every effort to deal honestly with other models, identifying positive aspects as we seek to develop and exhibit a model of confirmation/affirmation of baptism considerably more developed than we have previously delineated.

8. *Confirmation as a Rite which Symbolizes and Celebrates "Life in the Spirit" but Cannot Be Equated with a Particular Giving or Receiving of the Holy Spirit*

In this view confirmation is a necessary reality for every person because it is identified as the conscious reception of God's grace through the Holy Spirit and through the lively faith of the recipient. Therefore, while the signs of the personal experience of receiving God's Holy Spirit, the laying on of the hands or the anointing with oil, are positive rituals they do not in any sense "guarantee" the desired reality. Theodore Jungkuntz articulates this point of view when he maintains that Jesus himself had many confirmations of his call to ministry beyond his baptism by John. These confirmations sharpened and refocused his awareness of his mission and of God's Spirit empowering him to fulfill that mission. He cites the transfiguration (Matthew 17:1-8), Gethsemane (Matthew 26:30-35), and others.[34]

Likewise, the apostles were "baptized in the sense of clear response to Jesus when 'they left their nets and followed him'" (Mark 1:17-18). Such a response was later confirmed especially at Pentecost when they experienced the empowerment of the Holy Spirit. This experience was an actual confirmation, "a visible and audible manifestation of their own adoptive call as 'sons of God'," (Acts 2:32-33) and an 'anointing' and public commissioning for their apostolic ministry (Acts 2:33, 43). And it was repeatable (Acts 4:5-13, 23-25).[35]

In this perspective it is God who does the confirming through the Holy Spirit. This experience is a result of God's action and the human response of faith. II Corinthians 1:20-22 says it well: "For in him [Christ] everyone of God's promises is a 'Yes'. For this reason it is through him that we say the 'Amen' to the glory of God. But it is God who establishes (confirms) us with you in Christ and has anointed us, by putting his seal upon us and giving us his Spirit in our hearts as a first installment." The human response of "Amen" opens the door to God's sealing and anointing through the Spirit. The New Testament points to the importance of the human "Amen." In I Peter 1:10 we see the central focus of such an experience of affirmation. "Therefore, brothers and sisters, be all the more eager to confirm your call and election for if you do this, you will never stumble."

While baptism is both in water *and spirit*, the seal and guarantee of God's empowerment of the person is a gift of the Holy Spirit to those who respond in faith. As persons we do not control when the awareness of that gift will take place. The confirmation by the Holy Spirit is that for which we prepare and pray but for which we must finally wait (Acts 1:4). Therefore, Jungkuntz believes that all of the struggles about the efficacy of the signs, laying on of hands, anointing with oil, or the signing with the cross on the forehead, are off target.

Jungkuntz concludes: "It certainly need be no departure from the faith to give ritual expression to these concepts. However, when the reality which is signified is not experienced except by way of the ritual and not by way of a subjective, personal encounter with the presence and working of the Holy Spirit, then we know the church is losing its faith and its nerve, being no longer able to 'wait for the promise'"[36] Such rituals are not the guarantee of the presence of the Spirit. The guarantee is finally God's gift in response to our authentic faith.

It is our belief that ritual expression has genuine spiritual power when seen as an intrinsic extension of a spirit-filled community of faith, a community in which God's spirit of acceptance, love, trust, forgiveness, judgment, and justice are incarnated even as Christ was the incarnation of God's love for the world. While we agree that there can be no perfect correlation between the ritual action and the movement of the Spirit or any absolute correlation between the outward public affirmation of one's baptism and the inner subjective surrender and openness to God's presence, we see real spiritual power in such public affirmations in the community of faith. We shall return to this issue in Chapter III and in our suggestions for educational and liturgical designs in Parts III and IV.

NOTES

1. The literature is extensive, we recommend especially the following:
   Gerard Austin, *The Rite of Confirmation: Anointing with the Spirit* (New York: Pueblo, 1985).
   Henri Bourgeois, *On Becoming Christian: Christian Initiation and its Sacraments* (Mystic, Conn: Twenty-Third Publications, 1985).
   Robert Browning and Roy Reed, *The Sacraments in Religious Education and Liturgy* (Birmingham, Ala.: Religious Education Press, 1985).
   Bernard Cooke, *Sacraments and Sacramentality* (Mystic, Conn.: Twenty-Third Publications, 1983).
   Charles Davis, *Sacraments of Initiation* (New York: Sheed and Ward, 1964).
   J. D. C. Fisher, *Confirmation Then and Now* (London, SPCK, 1978).
   John Gallen, ed., *Made Not Born* (Notre Dame, Ind.: University of Notre Dame Press, 1976).
   Robert Jenson, *Visible Words* (Philadelphia: Fortress, 1978).
   Urban T. Holmes, *Confirmation: The Celebration of Maturity in Christ* (New York: Seabury, 1975).
   Aidan Kavanagh, *Confirmation: Origins and Reform* (New York: Pueblo, 1988).
   Thomas A. Marsh, *Gift of Community: Baptism and Confirmation* (Wilmington, Del.: Michael Glazier, 1984).
   Joseph Martos, *Doors to the Sacred* (Garden City, N.Y.: Doubleday, 1981).
   Max Thurian, *Consecration of the Layman* (Baltimore: Helicon, 1963).
   Kenan B. Osborne, *The Christian Sacraments of Initiation* (New York: Paulist, 1987).
   Mark Searle, *Christening: The Making of Christians* (Collegeville, Minn.: Liturgical Press, 1980).
   Mark Searle, ed., *Alternative Futures for Worship: Baptism and Confirmation* (Collegeville, Minn.: Liturgical Press, 1987).
   Alexander Schmemann, *Sacraments and Orthodoxy* (New York: Herder and Herder, 1965). Reprinted as *For the Life of the World.*
   Paul Turner, *Confirmation: The Baby in Solomon's Court* (New York: Paulist, 1993).
   Geoffrey Wainwright, *Christian Initiation* (Atlanta: John Knox, 1969).
2. Frank C. Quinn, "Theology of Confirmation," in *The New Dictionary of Sacramental Worship*, ed. Peter E. Fink (Collegeville, Minn.: Liturgical Press, 1990), p. 277 ff.
3. J. D. C. Fisher, *Confirmation Then and Now* (London: SPCK, 1978), p. 133.
4. Martos, *Doors to the Sacred*, p. 211 ff.
5. Quinn, in *The New Dictionary of Sacramental Worship*, p. 278 ff.
6. Medieval philosophers followed Aristotle in understanding *matter* as the stuff underlying all natural existence before it is determined and actualized by *form*.
7. Martos, *Doors to the Sacred*, p. 214f.; Fisher, *Confirmation*, p. 133 ff.
8. Thurian, *Consecration of the Layman* (Baltimore: Helicon, 1963); Turner, *Confirmation: The Baby in Solomon's Court*; Searle, ed., *Alternative Futures for Worship*; Jenson, *Visible Words*; Arthur J. Kubick, *Confirming the Faith of Adolescents* (New York: Paulist Press, 1991); Leonel L. Mitchell, *Initiation in the Churches* (Washington: Pastoral Press, 1991); Austin, *The Rite of Confirmation*; Julia Upton, *A Church for the Next Generation* (Collegeville, Minn.: Liturgical Press, 1990); William J. Bausch, *A New Look at the Sacraments* (Notre Dame, Ind.: Fides/Claretian, 1977); Kavanagh, *Confirmation: Origins and Reform*; Osborne, *The Christian Sacraments of Initiation*; William R. Myers, ed., *Becoming-Belonging: A Practical Design for Confirmation* (Cleveland: United Church Press, 1993).

9. Kavanagh, *Confirmation: Origins and Reform.*
10. Fisher, *Confirmation Then and Now*, p. 27.
11. Ibid., p. 21.
12. Joseph Jungmann, *The Early Liturgy* (Notre Dame, Ind.: University of Notre Dame Press, 1959), pp. 74-86; E. C. Whitaker, *Documents of the Baptismal Liturgy* (London: SPCK, 1970), pp. 2-20; James F. White, *Documents of Christian Worship* (Louisville: Westminster/John Knox, 1992), pp. 148-156; Herman Wegman, *Christian Worship in East and West* (New York: Pueblo, 1985), pp. 34-40.
13. See Tertullian's homily on baptism, James F. White, *Documents of Christian Worship* (Louisville: Westminster/John Knox, 1992), p. 149. Sealing by making the sign of the cross, generally on the forehead.
14. Aidan Kavanagh, *The Shape of Baptism: The Rite of Christian Initiation* (New York: Pueblo, 1978), pp. 15-23.
15. Austin, *The Rite of Confirmation*, pp. 5-15.
16. Ibid., p. 5.
17. Ibid., p. 7.; see Reginald Fuller, "Christian Initiation in the New Testament," in *Made Not Born*, p. 14.
18. Paul Turner, *The Meaning and Practice of Confirmation: Perspectives From a Sixteenth Century Controversy* (New York: Peter Lang, 1987).
19. *Affirm Planning Guide* (Minneapolis: Augsburg, 1984), pp. 84-89.
20. See Laurence H. Stookey, *Baptism: Christ's Act in the Church* (Nashville: Abingdon, 1982), pp. 75-79; Craig Cox, "Rethinking Confirmation: Possible Ways," in *Confirming the Faith of Adolescents*, pp. 165-177; Bausch, *A New Look at the Sacraments*, pp. 111-126.
21. Paul Turner, *The Meaning and Practices of Confirmation: Perspectives From a Sixteenth Century Controversy* (New York: Peter Lang, 1987), p. 319.
22. Arthur J. Kubick, *Confirmation Notes: Current Developments, PACE* 29 (New York, 1986).
23. *Affirm Planning Guide* (Minneapolis: Augsburg, 1984), p. 84.
24. "By Water and the Spirit: A Study of the Proposed United Methodist Understanding of Baptism" in *Faith and Mission*, The General Conferences of the United Methodist Church. Vol I., February 20, 1992, Nashville, Tenn. p. 258.
25. Browning and Reed, *The Sacraments in Religious Education and Liturgy.*
26. Kavanagh, *Confirmation: Origins and Reform.*
27. J. Neuner and J. Dupuis, *The Christian Faith in the Documents of the Catholic Church* (Staten Island, N.Y.: Alba House, 1982), p. 387.
28. See Austin, *The Rite of Confirmation*, p. 27 for a fine history of the development of confirmation as separate sacrament.
29. Thomas Aquinas, *Summa Theologiae III*, Vol. 57, Blackfriars in conjunction with McGraw Hill Book Co. (New York) and Egre & Spottiswood (London), 1975.
30. Turner, *Confirmation: The Baby in Solomon's Court*, pp. 5-18.
31. Martin Luther, "The Pagan Servitude of the Church," in *Martin Luther: Selections from His Writings*, ed. John Dillenberger (New York: Doubleday, 1961), p. 124ff.
32. See Browning and Reed, *The Sacraments in Religious Education and Liturgy*, Chapter 1.
33. Ibid.
34. Theodore R. Jungkuntz, *Confirmation and the Charismata* (New York: University Press of America, 1983).
35. Ibid., pp. 3-5.
36. Ibid., p. 21.

Chapter II

MAJOR TRENDS IN LITURGY AND RELIGIOUS EDUCATION AND THEIR IMPACT ON CONFIRMATION AND BAPTISMAL AFFIRMATION

Reconsideration of the practice and meaning of what has been called confirmation is motivated by many influences. Chief among these, as we have indicated, is the pastoral concern which raises questions about the adequacy of our way of Christian-making and is forcing a new look at many sides of the relation between initiation and evangelism. All the processes of initiation are crucial to the way we invite and claim, because they lie at the center of the making of commitment. For Christians, problems about baptism/confirmation are always symptoms of problems about evangelism and its relation to religious education and liturgy.

It is important to pause in our discussion of past, present, and possible future models to identify major liturgical and religious education trends which are influencing ecumenical and denominational efforts to develop fresh understandings and practices concerning confirmation or baptismal affirmation. As we unfold the following liturgical and religious education trends the reader is invited to join us in making connections with recent developments in specific church settings. We will seek to illustrate how these more general trends have found expression in confirmation or baptismal affirmation, to some degree in this chapter but especially in Parts II, III, and IV.

Liturgical Trends

1. *Ambiguities of New Testament evidence.*

Fresh thinking about pastoral aspects of Christian initiation is enabled, if indeed not forced, by the growing consensus that there is no clear and consistent pattern of a liturgy of initiation in the New Testament. Not all scholars agree,[1] but most historians and theologians concerned with such matters see attempts to found a practice of Christian initiation solely upon an original New Testament model as futile.[2]

As we have already indicated the two texts commonly used to authenticate a scriptural sacrament of confirmation are Acts 8, where Peter and John laid hands upon Samaritans, and Acts 19, where Paul laid hands upon disciples at Ephesus. What is clear in these passages and others in Acts is that Luke relates the symbolic action of the laying on of hands to the gift of the Holy Spirit. If there was any normal means whereby this was done, Luke does not make it clear. The gentile household of Cornelius received the Holy Spirit before water baptism (Acts 10:44-48), and indeed St. Paul also received the Holy Spirit before baptism (Acts 9:17-19). Moreover, one needs to recognize that while most of the reference in the New Testament to the laying on of hands concerns *ministry* or *mission,* most do not specify the gift of the Holy Spirit.

Clearly in the New Testament baptism becomes the gateway to belonging in the church, and baptism is joined in meaning to the forgiveness of sins and the gift of the Holy Spirit (Acts 2:38-42). What part the laying on of hands played is unclear. Luke indicates that it is a sign of the gift of the Spirit and probably its effect as well. This identification is not self–evident in the rest of the New Testament. If this was universal practice, for instance, it seems strange that Paul makes no reference to it, and that it is not specified in the pastoral epistles or in the Gospel of John.

The attempt to separate the symbolic acts of washing and hand-laying and identify them with the related meanings correspondingly of forgiveness of sins and Spirit gift breaks down in the face of the use of water as a symbol of Spirit. In John 7:37-39, for instance: "Let anyone who is thirsty come to me, and let the one who believes in me drink. As the scripture has said, 'Out of the believer's heart shall flow rivers of living water.' Now he said this about the Spirit." This image is perpetuated in common patristic attitudes which see the water of the font as itself sanctified through the power of prayer, and having sanctifying power.[3] It may be that the pattern of apostolic action in initiation ritual described by

Luke had more to do with the need to promote the authority of the apostles in baptism rather than with common ritual practice in Luke's church.
    2. *Baptism as the real focus for conversion and commitment.*
    A second result of historical and theological work which influences a pastoral reconsideration of the Christian initiation, especially of "confirmation," is the conclusion that baptism is properly the real focal point for conversion and commitment. This is a judgment hard for many Christians to make who have traditionally practiced infant baptism. Infants do not seem appropriate subjects of conversion and commitment. In the light of this contradiction the powerful baptism of the New Testament which could cancel damning pasts and grant new life with the gift of Spirit from Godself eventually was denatured by the addition of a later sacrament which had power to give in fullness what baptism conveyed only "prematurely."
    The result of this evolution is that in the tradition of infant baptism, the practice of confirmation becomes a demeaning of baptism. The concentration of attention has been upon the nurture of confirmands bringing them "to respond to God's grace, openly to confess their faith, and to lead a Christian life."[4] So it is that one United Methodist bishop, reacting to the attempt of many within the denomination to afford baptism a primary position, complained that such persons were confusing baptism with faith. Seen in the light of the way we initiate Christians and "do" baptism, such a judgment is understandable. Seen in a New Testament light such a view is absurd. The attempt to bring the church to a practice of baptism which makes it integral to Christian witness and to the response of faith is an attempt to be faithful to scripture.[5]
    The gospel story begins with baptism; indeed, with the baptizing of John which is called by Mark, "The beginning of the good news of Jesus Christ, the Son of God." The meaning of baptism established at Pentecost in the preaching of Peter, namely that it is for the forgiveness of sins and the gift of the Holy Spirit, is already forecast in the baptism of Jesus by John. John's baptism was for "repentance and the forgiveness of sins". Moved by John's symbolic actions, Jesus "saw the heavens torn apart and the Spirit descending like a dove on him."[6] The New Testament presents the baptism of the believers as a recapitulation of the powerful commitment experience of Jesus. The earliest disciples brought new believers into the faith doing for them what John had done in baptism, calling to repentance and forgiveness, and adding a phrase which became a confession, "in Jesus' name," and adding the blessing of Spirit gift. If

this invitation to initiation in the second chapter of Acts does not specify and establish a liturgy, it does establish a "genetic code" of themes of initiation which persist in the body of Christ. It is clear that they are themes of conversion and commitment.

Probably no text is so revealing of the dimension of conversion and commitment attached to baptism by the early church than the confrontation between Jesus and the sons of Zebedee described in the tenth chapter of Mark. James and John want to sit at Jesus' side in glory. His question to their question images baptism: "Are you able to drink the cup that I drink or be baptized with the baptism that I am baptized with?" Many questions have been raised about this passage and not a few scholars doubt its dominical authenticity. What cannot be doubted is the image it conveys about the New Testament church's understanding and practice of baptism. The baptism of the believers does recapitulate the baptism of the master and the meaning of baptism is nothing strictly ceremonial or conceptual. It is the dynamic of commitment.

The apostle Paul, the principal theologian of baptism in the New Testament, also understands the symbol as recapitulation in the disciple of the faithfulness of Christ. Saving faith for Paul is participation in the pattern of faith lived out by God's revelation: "Do you not know that all of us who have been baptized into Christ Jesus were baptized into his death? Therefore we have been buried with him by baptism into death, so that, just as Christ was raised from the dead by the glory of the Father, so we too might walk in newness of life."[7]

Matthew's gospel ends with the challenge to Christian-making and pictures the human response to the call to discipleship and to baptism as synonymous: "Go therefore and make disciples of all nations, baptizing them. . . ." (Matthew 28:19)

If we conclude, in faithfulness to scripture, that baptism should be a central focus in our Christian-making whereby we comprehend and express our conversion and commitment, then the theology and practice of Christian initiation for most Christians will need fundamental revision.

3. *Confirmation: part of the baptismal gift.*

A revision of Christian initiation is prompted in the third place by historical and theological research which supports the conclusion that the seal of the Spirit, which we have called confirmation, is inseparably part of baptism itself. In the immediate post-apostolic age there was no rite called confirmation. The hand-laying and sealing with oil came immediately after water baptism and were regarded as integral parts of the sacrament of baptism. Chrism, which early became an aspect of hand-laying and hand-laying itself were generally identified with Spirit gift. In this the early pastoral theologians followed the practice set forth in Acts. This is generally the case in the early church, although we cannot identify the practice as a universal development. The Syrian church, for instance, had no rite of anointing following water baptism but rather a prebaptismal anointing which had more the flavor of exorcism than Spirit gift.[8]

When water baptism and hand-laying became separated in the Western church the reasons were administrative rather than theological. Bishops could not handle the expanded role of baptizing in a rapidly growing church, and they would not let go of the role. They settled for "confirming" at a later convenient time, what presbyters had done at an earlier appropriate time. The understanding about this, worked out by at least the early fifth century, was that the confirming was a completing/strengthening which equipped the Christian with Spirit power to enable a faithful life.

No such bifurcation of the initiation rite took place in the church of the East. In the Eastern church the unity of the rite was maintained at the expense of the role of the bishops. The Western church sacrificed the unity of the rite to the participation of the bishop. In practice, and in understanding, the hand-laying sacrament which evolved in the West had nothing to do with the ideas about confirmation current in the church today, such as personal commitment, consecration of the laity, or understanding the essentials of the Christian life.

Modern scholarship has pointed out the logic and the illogic in this evolution.[9] Prominent in the illogic of the rupture of the initiation rite is the diminishing of baptism itself and the obscuring of the rich baptismal imagery and understanding of the New Testament and early church. The separation of water baptism and hand-laying has confused our conception of baptism and left us with a second-stage sacrament/sacramental/ordinance which is at once part of the baptismal reality, yet distinct from it with separate purposes and effects. Does it confer the Holy Spirit? Does it strengthen Christians for faithful life as soldiers of Christ? Does it celebrate Christian maturity and commitment?

There is a growing consensus for the conclusion that whether we consider confirmation a sacrament or not it must be viewed as part of the baptismal gift. There is increasing support for the position that the laying on of hands, as seen in Acts or in the post–apostolic church, is a confirmation of baptism rather than a confirmation of the baptized, and that what we have called confirmation is not something that completes baptism, but is an integral part of it.[10]

4. *Need for a liturgy of commitment.*

Whatever conclusions we may draw out of history or theology about Christian rites of initiation are finally important only as they are relevant to pastoral concerns. No revision or reform of initiation rites is thinkable that does not place conversion and commitment in their center. Rejoining the water bath and the laying on of hands into a single rite of belonging is useless as a gesture to an "authentic" history. Rejoining these ritual symbols will be a powerful positive reform if the revision helps us join elements which necessarily belong together in the dynamic of Christian faith: the freedom of forgiveness and the blessing of new life in the Spirit. Such a revision is also a call to embrace a radically altered view of the significance and meaning of religious education in the process.

Any revision which unites the rites of water bath and hand-laying is a particular problem for those Christian traditions which allow the baptism of infants. In these traditions the element of personal commitment is identified with the "postponed" rite of hand-laying. In the revisions being either proposed or adopted in the churches which celebrate confirmation there is clear difference between Protestant and Roman Catholic approaches.

Protestants in general are adapting the model for confirmation contemplated in the 1960's by Max Thurian to which we referred earlier, where the laying on of hands becomes an action which is repeatable and appropriate for particular occasions of commitment involving individuals, groups, or entire congregations. The ritual of hand-laying is returned to the baptismal rite as an essential element and is a dimension of that rite which is repeatable rather than separate from it and particular, as a one-time confirmation. As one would expect, the revisions of the Protestant churches are various. There seem to be at least two common elements, however. In all cases, the ritual of laying on of hands is returned to the baptismal rite and the terminology used for a subsequent rite is changed, either outright into "Renewal of Baptism," or "Affirmation of the Baptismal Covenant," or in some combination such as the titles found in the *Book of Worship* of the United Church of Christ, "Confirmation: Affirmation of Baptism" and "Reception of Members: Affirmation of Baptism."[11]

The liturgy of the United Church of Christ makes no provision nor mention of a continuing function beyond "confirmation" for the service of hand-laying. Other Protestant liturgies stress the repeatability of the rite. The Presbyterian *Book of Worship* goes so far as to specify the occasions for the "Reaffirmation of Baptism" and provides appropriate individual liturgies: "public profession of faith," "those uniting with a congregation," "for a congregation," "marking occasions of growth in faith," "in pastoral counseling."[12] Most revisions or proposals simply allow for the rite to be repeated without specifying or even suggesting occasions. The Episcopal and Lutheran rites, while repeatable, specify that one of these remain a designated "confirmation" functioning in the usual Reformation understanding as a conclusion to the process of initiation. In actual practice, the repeating of the Affirmation of Baptism is just beginning to increase in those denominations. Among some Protestants, the renewal of baptism in what is in fact a repeated rite of "confirmation" is becoming rather common. This is the case among United Methodists, whose official liturgy is not very clear about "baptismal renewal," but where the practice has been popularized and spread by various organizations within the church.

With Catholics, suggestions for reform are different. So far, a repeatable "confirmation," while explored, has not been seriously considered. The sacrament remains separate and unrepeatable. Hand-laying has been returned to the sacrament of baptism as an "anointing after baptism." The text spoken by the celebrant reads:

> The God of power and Father of our Lord Jesus Christ
> > has freed you from sin
> > and brought you to new life
> > through water and the Holy Spirit.
> He now anoints you with the chrism of salvation
> > so that united with his people
> > you may remain forever a member of Christ
> > who is Priest, Prophet and King.[13]

The text used by the bishop later in confirming reads, "be sealed with the gift of the Holy Spirit."[14] Exactly what the Holy Spirit does in "sealing" that is different from what the Holy Spirit does in bringing one "to new life" is less than clear to many. At any rate the sacrament is separate from baptism, though the action of anointing accomplished in baptism is repeated in confirmation. The sacrament is understood to convey an indelible "character." This is "characterized" in the *Catholic Constitution* explaining the new rite as, "the inexpressible gift, the Holy Spirit himself, by whom they are endowed with special strength. Moreover, having been signed with the character of this sacrament, they are more closely bound to the church and they are more strictly obliged to spread and defend the faith, both by word and deed, as true witnesses of Christ."[15]

In spite of such stalwart defenses of traditional Western confirmation there are voices within Catholicism which speak for the reuniting of water baptism and the laying on of hands in one sacrament of initiation, and for reforms which will promote authentic conversion and commitment. One line of advocacy promotes a return to adult baptism, or at least a commitment to an understanding and practice of baptism which affirms the baptism of adults as normative in the church. Such a view allows infant baptism, but sees it as derivative and is committed to move away from it. Such a position has been articulated especially by Aidan Kavanagh. Kavanagh argues that the "spirit and principle" of adult initiation are in fact what are operative in other rites of initiation and as such "subordinate" any other rites.[16] It is unclear what this "reform" has amounted to. Obviously infant baptism is still alive and well in Catholicism. On the other hand the *Rite of Christian Initiation of Adults* (RCIA) has proved to be a powerful instrument of reform in many Catholic parishes. For instance, the new rite and the catechumenal process involved becomes a religious education system of great significance. In the liturgy it does unite water baptism, laying on of hands and anointing with chrism. The catechumenate whose several steps point toward the final liturgy of inclusion is a workshop of commitment. The impact of the RCIA upon Catholicism as a whole ought to be in large measure an underlining of adult commitment powerfully expressed in a unified liturgy of initiation. The final effect of the new rite and the revitalization it has wrought could conceivably be a normalization of adult baptism in the church. That day does not appear. It could, in time, appear.

William Bausch who has written one of the best reforming surveys of sacramental thought and practice, suggests the possibility of new liturgy for initiation when he observes that "some liturgists have suggested that we really ought to rejoin the whole initiation rite again—baptism, confirmation, and eucharist—and then invent some other paraliturgical service that, at meaningful moments of people's lives restate the commitment made at baptism."[17] Bausch does not develop this idea. What he does suggest is that pastors and others should "raise questions about baptism,

promote a strong catechesis surrounding it and. . . . perhaps restore the catechumenate to prepare for it; for baptizing indiscriminately is as harmful
to confirmation as it is the baptism itself."[18]

This judgment has troubled many, such as Julia Upton who maintains
that "indiscriminate infant baptism persists because there is no other pastoral alternative."[19] Upton advocates the solution of a catechumenate for
children. She finds it a "scandalous inconsistency" that the church baptizes children and ignores them until they reach school age. "With the possibility of a catechumenate, the decision of whether or not to have their
child baptized could more realistically be returned to the parents. Children
in the catechumenate would be able to have a more personal understanding of how the faith is lived by contact with members of the catechumenal community. At the time of this baptism they would be able to
make an unencumbered decision of their own in a ritual which would
give dramatic testimony to their commitment."[20]

Upton sees her model for such a catechumenate in some of the educational programs already in pastoral practice and points out that the
RCIA provides rites for initiating children of catechetical age. We have
not heard her ideas promoted in a Protestant context, but they well might
be.

5. *The Eucharist as the climactic moment of Christian initiation.*

From the earliest witness in the Ante-Nicene church—the *Didache*,
Justin, and Tertullian onward–it is clear that the supper of the Lord was
the climax toward which the catechumenate and all liturgies of Christian
initiation moved. There is much to wonder about in the glimpses of initiation in scripture and early church. There is little doubt about the role of
eucharist. Those who were included in the family of the Lord were invited immediately to the table of the Lord. The unction and hand-laying
ceremonies were a "transitional rite to the celebration of the actual confirmation of baptism, the eucharist."[21]

Much has been written about the relative roles of the Holy Spirit in the
water rite and the hand-laying or unction. Not much has been made of the
role of the Spirit in initiation in the climactic celebration of eucharist.
This connection is vitally important for two reasons. A personal reason:
In the supper of the Lord we receive Jesus Christ, as a presence mediat-
ed to us personally and individually by the Holy Spirit of God. And a
communal reason: In the banquet of thanksgiving we are joined in the
body of Christ to every other Christian in one Spirit.

The unified initiation which joins water bath, hand laying, and or anointing, and eucharist is from at least the late second century a connected pattern of the Christian enculturation and celebration of inclusion. It is a model which an increasing number of Christians believe to be adequate for their time.

6. *The communal nature of Christian initiation.*

We have just identified the Lord's supper as a moment of particular insight in Christian initiation about the communal nature of the church and of the events of initiation. This experience and understanding is worth dwelling upon for its own sake. Christian initiation is certainly about the gift of the Holy Spirit, and the Holy Spirit is a community endowment. The description of the movement of Spirit power at Pentecost which Luke portrays in Acts 2 or Paul's evocation of many gifts but one Spirit in I Corinthians 12, or John's description of Christ's Spirit-blessing upon the apostles in the twentieth chapter of the fourth gospel are all pictures showing that to receive the gift of the Holy Spirit is to become members of a Spirit-filled people. The New Testament evidence tells us that the recipient of the Spirit is never the isolated individual, but the individuals in community. The recipient of the Spirit is primarily the church, and converts receive the gift of the Spirit by becoming part of the Spirit-filled people. This is an understanding which probably cannot be underlined enough in our age of isolation and alienation. Faith itself, and the act of Christ in bestowing faith as a gift of the Holy Spirit, can never be separated from church.

7. *The independence of the Holy Spirit.*

It is probably fair to say that theology has progressively registered increasing awareness of the radical independence of God. Or to put it another way, Christians in general seem less and less impressed with the power of our incantations to command God or effect the movements of God's Holy Spirit. When it comes to belief, to commitment, Paul's judgment that no one can say "Jesus is Lord" except by the Holy Spirit (I Corinthians 12:3) is widely acknowledged. So also is the judgment expressed by Joseph Martos in his excellent study of sacraments, that "the Holy Spirit, the spirit of God . . . cannot be confined to a single set ritual. . . . In the words of John's gospel . . . (it) . . . blows where it wills."[22]

What are called substantialistic understandings in liturgy, the belief that things are as the words of our liturgies say they are when the authorized person says the authorized word, are increasingly called into question. In liturgy this means that more and more people see our sacraments as celebration of what God has done and is doing without assuming that our words and gestures call down God's presence and actions. This means that liturgy is enabling rather than automatic. It means that we are always concerned with questions of authenticity and commitment, never taking these things for granted. It means that liturgy is pictured as the rich soil for God's planting and nourishing rather than a provided garden-filled green house.

There is temptation here in two directions: the extremes of always knowing what to do and never knowing what to do. If we no longer believe that our liturgies "work" automatically, we do have reason to have trust in the tradition, to explore its richness of meaning, of ceremonial-gestural action, of effect in life. We have reason to trust the scriptural imagery in our patterns of initiation, the liturgy based upon them, and the vitality of God's Spirit in the life of God's people.

Religious Education Trends

As we approach the end of the twentieth century we can look back and discern several major trends in the theories and practices of religious education which have already or are in the process of influencing patterns of preparation for confirmation or baptismal affirmation. These trends came out of the work of major religious education theorists, the decisions of ecumenical groups and denominations regarding the foundations for the church's educational ministry, studies of the relationship between religious education and liturgy, and research on human and faith development. The trends, of course, overlap and are in creative tension at times.

   1. *The movement from religious education for assent to right beliefs to a religious education that interrelates beliefs and a quest for truth that can be integrated with all of life.*

The word "catechism" symbolizes the nature of a religious education which was aimed at imparting knowledge about and assent to the fundamental teachings concerning the Christian faith. Over time, denominations hammered out their own doctrinal positions concerning sin, salvation, Christ, the Bible, the church, human nature, and destiny. Education for commitment to and membership in the body of Christ was often conceived of in terms of exposure to, memorization of, and assent to these great beliefs. Preparation for baptism as adults or confirmation as children or youth was especially seen in such terms.

There is a refreshing emphasis today on the importance of religious instruction concerning core beliefs in order for individuals to know from where they have come and who they are in respect to the faith community's values and identity. However, such instruction should focus on the quest for truth, always entertaining the "why?" questions, encouraging internalization, testing, refinement, and honest decision making. Sara Little gives a positive interpretation of the religious instruction model, agreeing with Thomas Green that "teaching is the process of dealing with subject matter in such a way as to enable students to assess the truth of the same in terms of their own frames of reference."[23] She underscores the importance of the thinking process in order that persons will be able to understand their beliefs and relate their beliefs to their wider responses in faith, that they will be able to come to decisions about their core beliefs on which they will base their everyday actions. Such a positive approach to religious instruction fits very well with what is happening in many confirmation curricula and classes today often led by pastoral and lay teams. There is a movement away from right answers to understanding and sharing meanings within the faith community in order to move out beyond the community.

James Michael Lee, whose trilogy of writings[24] defines a major version of the religious instruction model, emphasizes the crucial nature of clear instructional objectives in relation to a wide range of religious contents leading not to cognitive learning alone but to Christian behavior and a Christian lifestyle. Lee honors the quest for clear thinking about religious issues, especially to counteract a sentimentality which sometimes puts a religion of the warm heart over against the religion of the mind. He maintains that there should be no separation of heart and mind. He makes a significant contribution in his detailed discussions of the many other kinds of content beyond the cognitive. He helps us identify the importance of affective content (the positive or negative feelings present in the learning situation), verbal content (all linguistic elements used in the teaching-learning interaction), nonverbal content (all other-than-linguistic elements present), unconscious content (depth psychological content-internal communication with the self and communication between teachers and learners at the unconscious level), and lifestyle content (the overall pattern of a person's activities, the way a person organizes his or her self-system and lives out life). Such a broadened and deepened view of religious instruction has been helpful in moving confirmation education away from rote learning and recitation of right belief to an approach that has clear objectives in terms of lifestyle, behavior, feelings, and the central understandings and beliefs of the Christian faith. It is the objective that all these levels will be present and interacting "at an intensely personal level."[25]

2. *Moving from a theory-practice approach to a praxis approach in which theory and practice are in ongoing interaction.*

In the theory to practice pattern the approach often was to start with the theological and/or biblical insight and then seek to apply it to the life of the learner, or, in some cases it started with the felt needs of the learner and then went to the biblical or theological norm for help in meeting the needs. This theory to practice approach was captured in the ecumenical effort of sixteen denominations to develop a basic philosophy of Christian education in the late 1950's and early 1960's. The result was the publication of *The Church's Educational Ministry: A Curriculum Plan*. The study yielded a guiding principle, called the principle of intersection between the gospel and life issues of the learner. Five learning tasks were designed to bring about this intersection. These were:

(1) Listening with growing alertness to the gospel and responding in faith and love.

(2) Exploring the whole field of relationships in light of the gospel.

(3) Discovering meaning and value in the field of relationships in the light of the gospel.

(4) Appropriating personally the meaning and value discovered in the field of relationships in the light of the gospel.

(5) Assuming personal and social responsibility in light of the gospel.[26]

This approach was very influential in respect to all teaching/learning activities of the cooperating churches, including confirmation education designs. This emphasis moved confirmation programs strongly in the direction of the intersection of the gospel, as the good news about God's unconditional love through Christ for all people, with the actual life issues of adolescents and adults for whom confirmation programs were designed.

The emphases on "listening with growing alertness to the gospel" came out of the critique of the Religious Education movement during and after World War II.[27] The belief that children could be nurtured within the family and the church to grow up never knowing when they were not Christian was sharply contested as being too optimistic about human nature. Theorists such as D. Campbell Wyckoff[28] and Randolph Crump Miller,[29] while committed to the importance of education through relationships within the family and the church, called for deeper exposure to core theological understandings of the Christian faith. Such challenges became very influential in the Cooperative Curriculum Project and indirectly in confirmation programs coming out of the participating denominations.

There is a movement today toward a theory of Christian Religious Education that is grounded in praxis which recognizes that both theory and practice are always present in our actions. It is not possible to come to life without presuppositions, without prior "theories" through which we see and interpret the meaning of our daily actions as individuals or as a society. Such an approach is changing significantly the way Christian Religious Education is conceived and carried out. Thomas Groome's shared Christian praxis model has stimulated such a shift and has become very influential ecumenically as well as within the Roman Catholic community out of which he comes.[30] The difference between his five steps and the five learning tasks coming out of the Cooperative Curriculum Project are revelatory of the changes that are taking place in Christian religious education in general and in baptismal and confirmation education in particular. The five steps are called movements because there are many sub-steps within each movement which make the teaching-learning experience dynamic, personal, flexible, genuinely corporate and decision/action oriented.

Movement 1, Naming/Expressing Present Action, invites all participants to name what is going on in their lives around a generative theme or an engaging symbol coming out of the Christian Story and Vision in interaction with life. Participants are invited to express what is going on in their lives or in society, how they perceive praxis, how they feel about it. What are the operative values, meanings and beliefs in the present actions under investigation or discussion? They can talk about, symbolize, act out in drama, dance, music, or art what is happening to them. Each person is to own his or her picture of the meanings, questions, concerns he or she has about present actions. Participants are invited to express their perceptions to at least one other person, but are never forced to do so. Individual differences in learning style are to be respected.

Movement 2, Critical Reflection on Present Action, encourages participants to come to a critical consciousness concerning the assumptions, reasons for, prejudices behind, problems with present actions. It also invites participants to begin to share their own life "stories" and "visions" with other members of the learning group. Their sharing should be honest, passionate, rather than dispassionate analysis. The latter could make the learning community too "heady" and less related to feelings and hopes people actually have.

Movement 3, Making Accessible Christian Story and Vision, is the time for sharing the great Christian Story and Vision, but in direct relation to the issues which have emerged in naming and reflecting on the present actions of those in the learning/serving community of faith. This sharing is the primary responsibility of the educator, but all are invited to share the Story and Vision as they have known and experienced it. The educator especially employs a "hermeneutic of retrieval" in skillfully reclaiming and making accessible in creative and engaging forms the specific stories and visions coming out of the great Story of God's self-revelation and will, through such themes as creation, covenant, Christ, and church as recorded in scripture and history. The educator is encouraged to employ a "hermeneutic of suspicion" in order to help the group look at possible distortions in the past or present understandings of the texts, for instance, how Christian churches supported slavery at certain times in history but finally were able to see the inconsistency of such a stance through the Christian understanding of love and justice. Finally, Movement 3 invites participants to construct more adequate understandings of the Christian Story/Vision for our day in relation to present praxis.

Movement 4, Dialectical Hermeneutic Between the Story and the Participants' Stories, asks the participants to enter into dialogue concerning the meaning of the faith community's Story for the stories coming out of the lives of the participants. Also, group members ask how their unique stories respond to, affirm, push beyond the Story/Vision coming out of Movement 3. The sharing should be critical in the sense that honest positive and negative expressions are freely invited without judgment from the educator. Participants again may use speech, art, journaling, movement, role-playing, and other methods to appropriate the Christian Story/Vision for their own stories and self-understanding.

Movement 5, Decision/Response for Lived Christian Faith, goes back to the "present action" and invites participants to come to decisions about their behavior, their actions. The effort, of course, is to maintain some consistency between the central affirmation about life coming out of the Christian Story/Vision and the problems, issues, feelings, and concerns about present actions in which the participants are engaged. The hope is "to make a particular choice for a faith-filled Christian praxis and to form participants' identity and character as agents of God's reign; that is, to promote conation, wisdom, and ongoing conversion in Christian faith."[31]

We have paused to set forth Groome's approach at this point because several interpreters whom we quote later in our book refer to this shared Christian praxis approach in reference to the need for moments of preparation for and celebration of ongoing conversion through confirmation as a repeatable experience or via baptismal affirmation throughout the stages of faith. (See Part III)

A comparison of Groome's five movements with the Cooperative Curriculum Project's five stages reveals some interesting similarities and differences. For instance, in Groome's model it is important to start with present action (praxis) in which theory and practice are interactive rather than with the gospel, as the Cooperative Curriculum Project does. Groome's model invites honest sharing of issues related to present actions and the evoking of the sharing of present stories and visions in order to get inside the real world of participants and to discern where they are, how the gospel has or has not penetrated their worlds. Then when persons are open and ready for the sharing of the great Christian Story and Vision, via many faith stories and visions from scripture, history and God's present encounters, the educator and the learners can be more profoundly engaged sympathetically and critically in the process. The Cooperative Curriculum Project, and Groome's model both call for intersection of gospel and life. Both call for decision making at a personal and social level. Both recognize that the steps or movements need not be strictly sequential. However, shared Christian praxis is an action-reflection-action model while the earlier model was more theory to practice in pattern. An illustration of how Groome's model is influencing confirmation education is the common practice of designing an intensive period of sharing, often in a retreat format, as the beginning event in confirmation or baptismal affirmation programs. This is designed to help participants identify what they are doing in their daily lives and what their stories and visions about the meaning of life really are as revealed in their actions. (See the new Presbyterian Confirmation program design in Chapter V.)

3. *The movement beyond a nurture model of religious education toward a faith development perspective.*

"Nurture into Christ-like living," as we have previously described this model,[32] was and is a very important emphasis. To nurture is to pay attention to the profound human needs of the learner and to surround him or her with all of the qualities of life which will bring forth growth and personal and social fulfillment. There is recognition that it is not enough to teach the great Christian beliefs cognitively. There must be an incorporation of God's love, trust, acceptance, and justice in the lives of parents, teachers, and peers if the learner is to internalize the Christian lifestyle and incorporate Christian values in daily decisions. Most current approaches to Christian education would not want to lose this emphasis. Nurture images are anchored in scripture and have been reinforced and refocused by such persons as Pestalozzi and Froebel in the seventeenth and eighteenth centuries, Bushnell in the nineteenth century, several twentieth–century educators,[33] and various ecumenical and denominational efforts. The nurture model often placed a strong emphasis upon religious nurture during childhood and adolescence on the assumption that personality formation and a sense of direction for life are crucial at these times.

While nurture approaches emphasized growth and development throughout the life span, it was not until the seminal work of James Fowler concerning the nature and the stages of faith that the developmental perspective became even more important. Fowler's research discovered that the final three stages of faith development are adult. In fact, deep ownership of faith seldom takes place prior to young adulthood (Stage IV Individuative-Reflective Faith); moreover the more profound wrestling with the implications of faith and the ability to come to a clear commitment to the Christian faith, while remaining open to how God works through the lives of all of the human family, is most often associated with middle adulthood (Stage V Conjunctive Faith).

Fowler's final stage of faith development is seldom reached before older adulthood (Stage VI - Universalizing Faith). This final stage brings persons to a call for a radical love and justice for all persons and nature, with a willingness to risk putting such a faith to work in the difficult arenas of personal, social, and political life. Fowler does not see faith development as a straight–line movement. It is dynamic and a struggle for all. The "aha" experiences which take place often are similar to conversion experiences and what he calls recapitulations of previous stages.[34] This means that Christian religious education is a lifelong process and that there normally will be several times when reassessment and recommitment should take place. It is such a theoretical framework which is behind our belief that confirmation or baptismal affirmation should be seen as a repeatable experience. (See Part III) Fowler's work has been widely critiqued.[35] Other developmental models have emerged with genuine potential.[36]

    4. *The movement away from schooling as the primary strategy for Christian education toward a congregational or community of faith*

approach inside of which schooling in various forms will still have an important place.

The Religious Education movement, starting with the formation of the Religious Education Association in 1903, sought to up-grade the Sunday School in quality of leadership training, curriculum, and church-home cooperation. Closely graded curriculum resources resulted with attention to insights from biblical scholarship and personal and social ramifications of the Christian faith. The schooling model has been the pre-supposition behind much curricular experimentation during this century. Because of this major emphasis, confirmation education has most often followed the schooling paradigm with classes, homework requirements, recitation, and even examinations. The current trend is to redesign baptismal and confirmation education with a much stronger emphasis on participation within the whole life of the community of faith, in its worship, mutual ministries, and outreach into the wider world, with a view not only to individual decisions to affirm faith privately but also to affirm the power of the faith community to influence public issues in our society. The whole understanding of the sacraments has taken on a strong corporate meaning. Christ lives not through the institution of grace via clergy but through the faith community which becomes the ministering community of love to those who are members and to those beyond the community.

Such a strategy was articulated early by C. Ellis Nelson (1967) in his discussion of the power of the community of faith to engender faith response.[37] Nelson has crowned his long career with his most recent attempt to develop more fully the community of faith approach and to set forth the details of such a strategy.[38] He sets a much wider framework for Christian religious education with the formation of a congregational Central Study Group (CSG). This group's purpose is to develop approaches to the edification of the whole congregation and through the interrelating of learning, worshiping, and serving for all of the participants. This is done in order for the congregation to realize its power to form and transform individual lives and also the life of the congregation in its ministry in the world.[39]

This wider stance is well delineated by Charles Foster, John Westerhoff, and William Willimon and in our own work. Foster highlights the importance of *participation* and *mediation*. Persons grow in faith and commitment through this much wider participation. However, such congregational participation can result in a closed system in which the church family becomes too ingrown. Mediation is a corrective, because it calls for the congregation to develop its identity and to mediate between the congregational members and the public issues and concerns at any given time.[40] Westerhoff and Willimon have shown how participation in the sacramental life from birth to death within the faith community has great power to form and transform. Again, this is not a rejection of what happens in schooling experiences. It places these experiences within a process of participation in the wider life of the church community which has the possibility to nurture and challenge persons to grow and engage in ministry.[41] Our own work has underscored the power of the community of faith, in its education and liturgical life, to form and transform persons throughout life. We have sought to develop a model of sacramentality which is relational and alive spiritually in the body of Christ. It is an approach in which all are ordained in baptism for lifelong ministry and nurtured through participation in a rich range of ministering activities, with several opportunities to reassess, reformulate, and publicly celebrate fresh expressions of commitment throughout life.[42] It is in dialogue with this movement that many of the recommendations in this book have been given birth.

   5. *The movement from a split between liturgy and religious education to an approach which brings liturgy and religious education together as partners.*

Such cooperation can take place without destroying a certain healthy creative tension between liturgy and education. Liturgical life is rich with stories, images, symbols, signs, and relationships of significance which are powerful educators of participants concerning the core meanings and purposes of the Christian faith. Of course, education prior to such experiences can greatly enhance liturgical celebrations. Educational reflections upon liturgical high points (such as baptism during the Easter Vigil) can and should take place after the celebrations, helping participants understand and put into personal and corporate frames of reference what they have experienced. However, Christian religious education should also help persons develop a critical consciousness about both the authenticity of the liturgies and the religious educational designs. It is such critical consciousness which helps us evaluate and revitalize our religious life. Erik Erikson has helped us understand how easy it is for our ritual life to become automatic, wooden, and dead. When this happens education's task is to help us discern why our rituals have become detached from our real life issues. When we make these discoveries we are in a better

position to develop fresh liturgical approaches which more fully capture
the good news of God's love and grace in the midst of our lives.
Reritualization is a natural result.[43] A new catechesis is emerging, especially within the Roman Catholic Church in its *Rite of Christian Initiation
of Adults*. This catechesis model moves away from the schooling/teacher-
centered approach to a socialization model related to initiation. The new
rite of initiation brings together religious education and liturgy with
power and integrity. Catechesis' goal is "growth in commitment," not
only "growth in understanding." It reaches fulfillment in "worship and
action for justice" not only in "mastery in an intellectual sense." It presumes a conversational approach: that participants stand within a circle
of faith "rather than a commitment to disciplined inquiry," and is a cousin
to "celebration" rather than "study." The catechumenal approach has a style
which is "a way of 'walking along' with people" rather than "a way of
studying." It escapes the feeling of obligation because it "can only occur
in an ambience of freedom."[44] James Dunning, one of the major leaders
of the revolution in catechesis within the Roman Catholic community,
made the above comparison in an attempt to underscore the power of
the interrelation of catechesis and sacramental celebration. Fortunately,
he goes on to quote Mary Boys' criticism. "Boys notes, 'What seems to
be missing in catechetical theory (and here is a clue to education as a
political activity) is any sense of critical ecclesiology. Contemporary catechesis seems to account only for the process of being socialized into a
believing community."[45] Boys wisely recognizes the need for the development of a critical consciousness, which is a central task of a con-
structive religious education in interaction with sacramental and liturgical celebrations of commitment.

It is our thesis that profound and engaging educational and liturgical
experiences can and should take place with parents, sponsors, and the
congregation prior to, during, and after infant baptism, prior to, during,
and after eucharist, before, during, and in a continuing way through life
in regard to confirmation or baptismal affirmation. This same dynamic
should be present in marriage celebrations, the ordination of clergy, or the
consecration of lay persons for the universal priesthood, and at other
points throughout life.[46] Such an approach is an undergirding assumption for our interrelating religious education and liturgy in respect to
confirmation or baptismal affirmation from infant baptism on to the celebration of fresh commitment to Christian vocation on the part of young,
middle, and older adults within the faith community. (See Parts III and IV)

6. *A movement toward the integration of religious education and spirituality.*

It is not so much that these two approaches were split from one
another in the past. It is more that spiritual growth was either assumed
to be a part of religious education or it was thought to be related to
worship and personal devotion. Somehow it was seen as the responsibility of the church rather than of religious education.

Spirituality is being seen as a celebration of God's ongoing creation in
each of our lives, as an affirmation of the whole person, physically, sex-
ually, socially, interpersonally, morally. Older images of spirituality were
often related to decisions to separate ourselves from the sensual, from personal feelings or from touching, seeing, and hearing others. Instead we
were to reject human temptations and relate to God. Such views have
been replaced by fresh images. Commenting on the meaning of this new
awakening Maria Harris asserts that it calls "people to be responsible; to
be alert in their senses to everything surrounding them, to see fully with
their eyes and hear fully with their ears. Thus having come alive, they
could then learn to acknowledge creation as the great gift it is, and themselves at its center, dancing and singing ancient words, 'Glory, glory,
glory; Holy, holy, holy.' In doing that, they break through to their own spirituality."[47] Harris, an excellent religious educator, suggests a rich array of
approaches to awakening, centering, self–discovery and discovery of
God's spirit in our midst, meditating, praying, questioning, journaling,
mourning, transforming, giving birth to new realities, bonding with others, and naming ourselves before God. Such a joyful, life-affirming spirituality, with its many spiritual disciplines, is being integrated into
Christian religious education of persons at all levels of life. Commenting
on the great spiritual leader, Thomas Merton, Basil Pennington concludes that Merton was both a great spiritual guide and a great religious
educator. "Merton was able to constantly hold life in the context of joy -
its true content - because each day he heard in the gospels the proclamation of the good news and in his prayer he experienced the all-affirm-
ing, creative love of God at the ground of his being, in each one of his
brothers and sisters, and at the heart of the whole creation."[48]

Such a positive spirituality has potential for enriching our approach
to confirmation or baptismal affirmation in education and liturgical
celebration. Some of the more promising designs employ imaginative,
existential reflections upon scriptural stories in relation to stories of
the participants, training in meditation, prayer, journaling, the writing

of liturgies which reflect the life of the group, and other patterns.

Finally there is reason to believe that God's spirit of love and truth is present in the caring, loving, and forgiving communities of learning and living which form around baptismal preparation for parents and sponsors, or confirmation education for youth or adults. Clearly, the Spirit of God calls us to interrelate religious education and liturgical celebrations, recognizing that worshipful moments in which God is met take place in our learning experiences and that rich liturgical life is itself a powerful educator of the human spirit.

NOTES

1. Thomas A. Marsh, *Gift of Community: Baptism and Confirmation* (Wilmington, Del.: Michael Glazier, 1984).
2. G. R. Beasley-Murray, *Baptism in the New Testament* (Grand Rapids, Mich.: Eerdmans, 1962). G. W. H. Lampe, *The Seal of the Spirit* (London: Longmans, Green, 1951). Concerning confirmation see J. D. C. Fisher, *Confirmation Then and Now* (London: SPCK, 1978), pp. 1-3: and Gerard Austin, *The Rite of Confirmation: Anointing with the Spirit* (New York: Pueblo, 1985), pp. 6-9.
3. E. C. Whitaker, cf., *Documents of the Baptismal Liturgy* (London: SPCK, 1970), p. 7.
4. *The Book of Services* (Nashville: United Methodist Publishing House, 1985), p. 55.
5. This point has been made in countless studies: We list these few as particularly convincing: Laurence H. Stookey, *Baptism, Christ's Act in the Church* (Nashville: Abingdon, 1982); Kenan B. Osborne, *The Christian Sacraments of Initiation: Baptism, Confirmation, Eucharist* (New York: Paulist, 1987); Max Thurian, *Consecration of the Layman* (Baltimore: Helicon, 1963); Kilian McDonnell and George T. Montague, *Christian Initiation and Baptism in the Holy Spirit* (Collegeville, Minn.: Michael Glazier/Liturgical Press, 1991).
6. Mark 1:4-11
7. Romans 6:3-4
8. Thomas M. Finn, *Early Christian Baptism and the Catechumenate: West and East Syria* (Collegeville, Minn: Liturgical Press, 1992), pp. 18-22.
9. Nathan D. Mitchell, "Dissolution of the Rite of Christian Initiation," in *Made Not Born*, ed. John Gallen (Notre Dame, Ind.: University of Notre Dame Press, 1976), pp. 50-82.
10. Leonel L. Mitchell, *Initiation and the Churches* (Washington, D.C.: Pastoral Press, 1991), pp. 195-207.
11. *Book of Worship: United Church of Christ* (New York: UCC Office for Church Life and Leadership, 1986), p. 127.
12. *Book of Common Worship* (Louisville: Westminster/John Knox Press, 1993), pp. 446-488. The liturgies are together titled, "Reaffirmation of the Baptismal Covenant."
13. *The Rites* (New York: Pueblo, 1988), p. 416.
14. Ibid., p. 491.
15. Ibid., p. 474.
16. Aidan Kavanagh, *The Shape of Baptism* (New York: Pueblo, 1978), p. 109 ff.
17. William J. Bausch, *A New Look at the Sacraments* (Notre Dame: Fides/Claretian, 1977), p. 107.

18. Ibid., p. 108.
19. Julia Upton, *A Church for the Next Generation* (Collegeville, Minn.: Liturgical Press, 1990), p. 74.
20. Ibid., p. 75.
21. Frank C. Quinn, "Theology of Confirmation," in *The New Dictionary of Sacramental Worship* (Collegeville, Minn.: Liturgical Press, 1990), p. 283.
22. Joseph Martos, *Doors to the Sacred* (New York: Doubleday, 1981), p. 229.
23. Sara Little, "Religious Instruction," in *Contemporary Approaches to Christian Education*, ed. Jack L. Seymour and Donald E. Miller (Nashville: Abingdon Press, 1982) p. 39.
24. See James Michael Lee's three books, *The Shape of Religious Instruction: A Social Science Approach* (Birmingham, Ala.: Religious Education Press, 1971); *The Flow of Religious Instruction* (Birmingham, Ala.: Religious Education Press, 1973); and *The Content of Religious Instruction* (Birmingham, Ala: Religious Education Press, 1985).
25. Lee, *The Content of Religious Instruction*, p. 743.
26. *A Design for Teaching-Learning* (St. Louis: Bethany Press, 1967), p. 33.
27. This critique was contained in a report, *Christian Education Today* (Chicago: International Council of Religious Education, 1945), chaired by Luther A. Weigle of Yale Divinity School.
28. D. Campbell Wyckoff, *The Gospel and Christian Education* (Philadelphia: Westminster, 1959).
29. Randolph Crump Miller, *The Clue to Christian Education* (New York: Charles Scribner's Sons, 1950).
30. See Thomas H. Groome, *Christian Religious Education: Sharing Our Story and Vision* (San Francisco: Harper & Row, 1980). Groome's work has also made a significant contribution to the rebirth of practical theology as a discipline. Also see Don S. Browning, *Fundamental Practical Theology* (Minneapolis: Fortress, 1991).
31. Thomas Groome, *Sharing Faith: A Comprehensive Approach to Religious Education and Pastoral Ministry: The Way of Shared Praxis* (San Francisco: HarperSan Francisco, 1991), p. 292. Also, see the writings of Paulo Freire who made a signal contribution with his emphasis on praxis in religious education.
32. See Robert L. Browning and Roy A. Reed, *The Sacraments in Religious Education and Liturgy* (Birmingham, Ala.: Religious Education Press, 1985).
33. Horace Bushnell, *Christian Nurture* (New Haven: Yale University Press, 1967). Also, see Harold W. Burgess, *An Invitation to Religious Education* (Birmingham, Ala.: Religious Education Press, 1975). His Chapter III on The Social-Cultural Approach gives a sound history of this model, referring to the contributions of religious education leaders such as George Albert Coe, William Clayton Bower, Sophia Fahs, Ernest Chave, Wayne Rood, and others. Also, see Didier-Jacques Piveteau and J. T. Dillon, *Resurgence of Religious Instruction* (Birmingham, Ala.: Religious Education Press, 1977) for a good analysis of the Nurture Model with particular attention to the work of Wayne Rood ("On Nurturing Christians") and John H. Westerhoff III and his emphasis on the socialization of persons into faith and a catechesis of nurture into which baptism and confirmation education and celebrations fit (*Will Our Children Have Faith?*, 1976) and *Generation to Generation* with Gwen Neville (1974).
34. James W. Fowler, *Stages of Faith* (San Francisco: Harper & Row, 1981), p. 290.
35. Craig Dykstra and Sharon Parks, eds., *Faith Development and Fowler* (Birmingham, Ala.: Religious Education Press, 1986). Also Kenneth Stokes, ed., Faith *Development in the Adult Life Cycle* (New York: Sadlier, 1982).

36. See Jack L. Seymour and Donald E. Miller, *Contemporary Approaches to Christian Education* (Nashville: Abingdon, 1982), Chapter 4 on the Developmental Approach, pp. 73-102. See Gabriel Moran, Religious Education Development (Minneapolis: Winston Press, 1983) for a unique paradigm. Also, see Romney Mosley, "Education and Human Development in the Likeness of Christ," in *Theological Approaches to Christian Education*, ed. Jack L. Seymour and Donald E. Miller (Nashville: Abingdon Press, 1990), pp. 146-162, for a psychological and theological analysis.

37. C. Ellis Nelson, *Where Faith Begins* (Richmond: John Knox Press, 1967).

38. C. Ellis Nelson, *How Faith Matures* (Louisville: Westminster/John Knox Press, 1989) pp. 204-230.

39. See C. Ellis Nelson, ed., *Congregations: Their Power to Form and Transform* (Atlanta: John Knox Press, 1988). Also, see Richard Robert Osmer, *A Teachable Spirit: Recovering the Teaching Office of the Church* (Louisville: Westminster/John Knox Press, 1990). Osmer makes a strong case for the teaching office not only of the pastor but of the whole congregation/denomination/wider church. His thoughts correlate well with C. Ellis Nelson's Congregational Strategy.

40. Charles R. Foster, "Education in the Quest For the Church," in *Theological Approaches to Christian Education*, pp. 99-101.

41. See John H. Westerhoff III and William H. Willimon, *Liturgy and Learning Through the Life Cycle* (New York: Seabury, 1980).

42. Robert L. Browning and Roy A. Reed, *The Sacraments in Religious Education and Liturgy: An Ecumenical Model* (Birmingham, Ala.: Religious Education Press, 1985), pp. 119-137. Also see Robert L. Browning, "A Sacramental Approach to Inclusion and Depth of Commitment" in *Congregations: Their Power to Form and Transform*, and Robert L. Browning, "The Pastor as a Sacramentally Grounded Religious Educator," in Robert L. Browning, ed., *The Pastor As Religious Educator* (Birmingham, Ala.: Religious Education Press, 1989).

43. See Erik H. Erikson, *Toy and Reasons: Stages in the Ritualization of Experience* (New York: Norton, 1977), p. 115.

44. James B. Dunning, *Echoing God's Word: Formation for Catechists and Homilists in a Catechumenal Church* (Arlington: The North American Forum on the Catechumenate, 1993) p. 42.

45. Ibid., p. 44.

46. This thesis is fully developed in Browning and Reed, *The Sacraments in Religious Education and Liturgy*. It is also well developed by Marianne Sawicki in "Tradition and Sacramental Education" in *Theological Approaches to Christian Education*, pp. 43-62. Sawicki takes a different position about confirmation than we do. However, her work is an important contribution to the ongoing dialogue.

47. Maria Harris, *Dance of the Spirit: The Seven Steps of Women's Spirituality* (New York: Bantam Books, 1989) p. 6.

48. M. Basil Pennington, "Western Contemplative Spirituality and the Religious Educator," in *The Spirituality of the Religious Educator*, ed. James Michael Lee (Birmingham, Ala.: Religious Education Press, 1985), p. 123. (See an excellent discussion of "Spirituality as life" by Joanmarie Smith; also see Smith's "The Spiritual Education of God's People" in *The Pastor As Religious Educator*, pp. 107-125). She concludes with a fine bibliography of books and resources for children and youth, mid-life and old age, families, and for journaling and spiritual direction. Also see Mary Elizabeth Moore, "Meeting in the Silence: Meditation as the Center of Congregational Life" in *Congregations: Their Power to Form and Transform*, pp. 141-165. She relates spirituality to Christian religious education with imagination and integrity.

Chapter III

CONFIRMATION AS SPIRIT GIFT

The relation of Holy Spirit to the second act of initiation, confirmation, has always been both obvious and obscure. It is obvious because it is the "laying on of hands" half of the initiation rite and this gesture is a sign—scriptural and traditional—of Spirit gift. It is obscure because the relation and/or difference between the Spirit gift received in baptism and that received in confirmation has always been a matter of confusion and controversy. The ambiguity about what is obvious and what is obscure is but part of the result of the dismemberment of the initiation rite in the Western church. When the parts of the rite are rejoined as a whole liturgy including the laying on of hands or anointing, then this sign, repeated once or many times, ceases to be a gesture separate from baptism representing a new or different gift. There is Spirit gift. This grace offered in Christ's church and its movement in our spirits is something that can happen many times.

Baptism and its renewal in individual human lives and in the church, through confirmation or affirmation of baptism, is an action of the Holy Spirit. Such an assertion makes some Christians very uneasy. They hear in it the fiat of a sacerdotal absolutism which many reject. That statement, however, is not based upon authoritarian dictate in the church but upon the New Testament. Baptism is not presented in the New Testament as a grace machine run by an authorized and empowered clergy, but as something God does. St. Paul puts it this way: "For in one Spirit we were all baptized into one body—Jews or Greeks, slave or free—and we were all made to drink of one Spirit" (I Corinthians 12:13).

For Paul, having the Spirit is the *sine qua non* of Christian life. "You are in the Spirit, since the Spirit of God dwells in you: Anyone who does not have the Spirit of Christ does not belong to him" (Romans 8:9). Since having the Spirit is an irrepressible liveliness of Christian identity, it is unthinkable that the activity of Christians in initiating new followers of Christ could fail to be a celebration of the Gift of Spirit. Becoming a Christian means becoming united to Christ and again, as St. Paul puts it, "anyone united to the Lord becomes one spirit with him" (I Corinthians 7:17). What is absolutely clear about the image of baptism we can construct from New Testament references, whether from Paul's correspondence or from Jesus' questions to James and John in the synoptics, "Can you be baptized with the baptism with which I am baptized?" (Mark 10:39), is that our earliest ancestors in Christian faith understood baptism as *life*. When they speak of baptism they do not describe or prescribe a ritual procedure. They describe the life of faith. If we heed the New Testament evidence, and if we understand initiation in Christian faith as marked by baptism, then baptism, in the nature of the case, must be a sign among us of Spirit blessing and Spirit life.

There is no picture of what the liturgy of baptism was like at Pentecost. Nobody seemed to care enough about the "how" to write it down and preserve it. There is much more information about the "why." Peter is very specific in his Pentecostal sermon: "Repent and be baptized every one of you in the name of Jesus Christ so that your sins may be forgiven; and you will receive the gift of the Holy Spirit" (Acts 2:37-38). Baptism is adopting the name of Jesus Christ; it is repentance for evils and the discovery of freedom in forgiveness and a new life in a life-giving Spirit. Peter refers to all of this as a "promise" of God addressed to everyone: "For the promise is for you, for your children, and for all who are far away, everyone whom the Lord our God calls" (Acts 2:39). Few modern disciples are in doubt that the "Lord our God" calls all. Few are in doubt about themselves possessing no special key to, or power over, the ways of God's Holy Spirit. We are not guarantors of the Spirit. Our role as disciples is to tell the story and announce and live out the promise and receive into communion all who respond. This is what we celebrate through the signs of the promise in baptism with the water cleansing and the blessing in laying on of hands. Beyond that our job is to nurture the tender shoots of Christian life and to trust that God will gift with the promised Holy Spirit all who hear and answer the call. Beyond these things the disciple cannot go because not even apostolic faithfulness can control God or God's grace; and the Holy Spirit is God. The Spirit comes, we believe, as a gift both from "Father" and "Son," but the Spirit is Godself. The Spirit is free, as tradition attests, it "blows where it chooses, and you hear the sound of it, but you do not know where it comes from or where it goes" (John 3:8). Our experience affirms this understanding. Our pastoral efforts to share or bestow Spirit obviously do not always succeed. This is clear in the results. What can be done is invite and prepare and nurture in a way that, in itself, is a channel of the Holy Spirit. Religious education, therefore, within the family and in the wider church family can be an incarnation of God's life–giving Spirit. Such a reality can then be recognized and celebrated in the liturgy. The ancient prayer is still our prayer: "O come, Creator Spirit come, and make within our souls thy home." The church and her ministers cannot command the Spirit. We can pray. We can celebrate the Spirit gift. We can discover openness to the Spirit gift. We can make invitation, even be an invitation. We cannot command.

The liturgies of all Christian peoples reflect this understanding. Confirming United Methodists pray that "The Holy Spirit work within you, that having been born of water and the Spirit you may live as faithful disciples of Jesus Christ."[1] Presbyterians pray, "O Lord, uphold *name* by your Holy Spirit. Daily increase in *him, her* your gifts of grace: the spirit of wisdom and understanding, the spirit of counsel and might, the spirit of knowledge and the fear of the Lord, the spirit of joy in your presence, both now and forever."[2] Pastors in the United Church of Christ pray, "O God, in the grace of Jesus Christ you have accepted this your servant *name* through the water of baptism. Nourish in (her/him) the power of your Holy Spirit that (she/he) may serve you in the world."[3] Catholics pray, "Let us pray to our Father that he will pour out the Holy Spirit to strengthen his sons and daughters with his gifts and anoint them to be more like Christ the Son of God."[4]

The texts of all Christian liturgies of initiation acknowledge that the gift of the Holy Spirit is a gift of God. Baptism indeed is no human act. The Spirit birth, as John tells us in the third chapter of his gospel, is "from above." The first Christians were manifestly aware that they were living under the governing power of the Spirit.

How to think of this has not been without its difficulties. Paul's emphasis upon baptism as into Christ's death and resurrection has sometimes diminished our understanding of baptism as an event of Spirit. Also

Peter's speech in Acts 2 where he invites believers into baptism in Christ's name and promises the gifts of the Holy Spirit can set up some confusion about the roles of Christ and the Holy Spirit in baptism. The characteristic way in which theologians put Christ and Spirit together is to understand that "the Son is sent in the power of the Spirit, and the Spirit is sent through the risen Christ,"[5] and to recognize that it is the Spirit moving in human life which brings about commitment to Jesus Christ. "No one can say 'Jesus is Lord,' except by the Holy Spirit" (I Corinthians 12:3). Jesus' ministry begins in his own baptism in water and Spirit, and the risen Christ bestows the Spirit-gift upon the church, something as intimate to Jesus as his own breathing (John 20:22), and something as much a part of God as truth and continuing presence (John 15:26-16:12).

The language of Mark 10:38-40 surely reflects the baptismal understanding and practice of the nascent church. Jesus' questions to the disciples about being baptized with his baptism demonstrate the extent to which these first Christians saw baptism as the ministry of faithfulness to the kingdom. Whatever they did as ritual is unclear; we have a few clues, but no picture. It is clear that their image of baptism was of living faith. The Jesus of their dedication was a man of God's Spirit, a man with prophetic gifts: "Here is my servant, whom I have chosen, my beloved, with whom my soul is well pleased. I will put my Spirit upon him" (Matthew 12:15-21). To become Christian followers of the Way, was to be baptized into the *name* of Jesus (Acts 2:38) and become a people of the Spirit, the Spirit of Christ. The baptism of believers was a recapitulation of the baptism of Jesus in the Jordan (Mark 10:38-40; Romans 6:1-11; Colossians 2:12-13). Followers came to Jesus in repentance seeking forgiveness of sins. They found the freedom of forgiveness and a dynamic new agapic life in the life-giving spirit of Jesus.

Trying to understand the relative roles of Christ and the Holy Spirit in our baptismal faith it is helpful to realize as Jürgen Moltmann points out that, as the New Testament tells the story, Spirit and Christ have a shared history. Jesus is anointed by the Holy Spirit at his baptism in the Jordan (Mark 1:10). His public ministry is under the sign of the Spirit (Luke 4:14; 18, etc.). The Spirit leads and drives him on his way (Mark 1:12). He is blessed by God's Spirit with prophetic gifts (Matthew 12:15-21). Jesus' signs and wonders are perceived as Spirit empowered (Luke 4:1,14). In the Spirit he offers himself up for death on the cross (Hebrew 9:14). God raised him from death in the power of the Spirit (Romans 8:11), and has exalted him to be a life-giving Spirit (I Corinthians 15:45). Events of

Jesus' life, death, and resurrection are seen in the New Testament as formed by the Spirit.[6]

It is the conviction of the New Testament writers, such as Paul, and of later Christian witnesses that our human encounter with the Jesus of this story is Spirit imparting, and that in a paradoxical and circular way it is this Spirit that brings about commitment to Christ, that it is the Holy Spirit that reveals, glorifies, and completes the Lordship of Christ in believers.[7] So Paul can say in Romans 8:9, that whoever does not have the Spirit of Christ cannot belong to him. Spirit and Christ have a mutual and interdependent history in our life of faith.

This relatedness of Spirit and Christ is a primary image in the gospel portrayal of the baptism of Jesus. Jesus is "announced" as Luke puts it, as one whom "God anointed with the Holy Spirit and with power" (Acts 10:38). This image is recapitulated at Pentecost describing a relationship every bit as real and necessary for the Christian community as for Christ. Spirit gift is God's promise for those "called," as Luke puts it, "for you, for your children, and for those who are far away, everyone whom the Lord our God calls" (Acts 3:39).

The model of Jesus' baptism as a paradigm for the meaning of baptism itself is usually not the primary theme in church teaching about the sacrament. The pauline image of dying and rising, or the johannine image of new birth tend to predominate. Jesus' question to disciples James and John, "Can you be baptized with the baptism with which I am baptized?" (Mark 10:38), was a question about his impending fate on the cross, but it was obviously also a question about the meaning of his own baptism and its power. Inherent in the question is the conclusion that the lives of the disciples, the followers, are shaped by the life of the master. In Jesus' evocation of his own baptism he projects an image of Spirit empowerment in the pilgrimage of faithfulness. Implied in his question and in the answer he himself gives to his own question (Mark 10:38-45) is the affirmation that all baptism is into Jesus' baptism and that the baptized will be gifted with the Spirit and led by the Spirit. It is important to affirm about baptism, that it is the Christ sign of Spirit empowerment. The *reality* of baptism as Spirit power cannot come through magic, or through potent incantations or guaranteed gestures. Disciples, as we have written, can tell the story; they can pray in Spirit invitation. Disciples can also *prepare*. A great deal of the life of faith as disciples of Jesus is the *advent* task of being ready, of planning, teaching, caring, of being open to the gift of the Spirit. Our life together as church is the life of being called out (ekklesia) to get ready, to allow the gifts of Spirit to flow through us and to act with Spirit guidance, power and blessing. This is not magic, it is not theological formula; it is the Spirit's inspiration *among* a people baptized in Christ Jesus.

The promise of baptism announced at Pentecost prepares disciples to do for penitents in baptism what John the Baptist did now in Jesus' name, and with Spirit blessing. These additions to John's baptism of repentance and forgiveness are, of course, momentous. The addition of the name of Jesus creates a people of the name, baptized not alone for the sake of a coming kingdom, but into the life of the one who is the King, whose Lordship is a way in the world. The addition of Spirit gift creates a people of special blessing, a people gifted with power "from above," and power deep within, which creates life new and generates gifts for specific tasks in the church and the world. Identity in the name of Jesus and Spirit gift are different sides of one reality, the baptized reality of discipleship to one whose ministry began under the sign of baptism in water and the Holy Spirit.

There are some, by now classic, distortions in the understanding of Spirit-gift common among many Christians. The perception of Spirit gift as primarily emotional and personal is a serious distortion of the picture of this gift which we discover in the New Testament. Spirit-gift is indeed not simply defined, but it is not an abstraction. Holy Spirit was not "doctrine" for these early Christians but powerful personal experience. It was personal experience not so much as private emotion, but as tasks, ministries, different jobs to be done (I Corinthians 12); as insight, illumination, and the urgings of prayer (Romans 8, Letters of John); and as attributes of character (Galatians 5). Such "gifts" were experienced as available God-power, not as something static, but as a renewing gift (Titus 3), a "developing" gift. In the variety of New Testament testimony about this Spirit gift the emphasis is upon acting for God and not upon personal feelings. Furthermore, the gift of the Holy Spirit is seen more as a public than a private event. The Holy Spirit comes alive within the church, as in the Pentecost drama, more as communal liturgy than private piety. Such an observation does not denigrate the personal piety of the great mystics or other exemplars of prayer, but reminds us, out of the sources of our faith understanding and experience, that Holy Spirit is the presence and power of God *among* us as well as *within* us. Our life together as Christians deeply depends upon this insight. The most powerful testimony to this understanding is found in the New Testament.

What we find there informs us that the Holy Spirit is found in the face of our brothers and sisters in Christ. We might even say that the Holy Spirit is the One without whom I would not have a brother or sister in Christ. The enlivening Spirit of God so graphically represented at Jesus' baptism as a special gift in his life, is also the special gift of all who name the name of Jesus as their Sovereign and Savior. It is the Spirit's illuminating and inspiring companionship that binds Christians together in love and sends them in ministry to a desperate and needy world.[8]

While it is not possible to coerce or capture God's Holy Spirit, it is crucial to remember that the church is seen as a people of this Spirit and that this Spirit gift is not something to hoard, but to share.[9] Faithful members of Christ's body cannot capture the Spirit, but it can possess them. A people so gifted are powered by a graceful power. The creation of signs of this grace in the church and in the world is something necessary in order that this Spirit blessing will be confirmed again and again as Christians rediscover God's working in fellowship and God's calling to service in the world. This is an affirmation of baptism which can and should be repeated and a continuing quest to know what it can mean to be baptized with the baptism with which Jesus is baptized.

NOTES

1. *The United Methodist Book of Worship* (Nashville: The United Methodist Publishing House, 1992), p. 92.
2. *Book of Common Worship* (Louisville: Westminster/John Knox, 1993), p. 444.
3. *The Book of Worship: United Church of Christ* (New York: U.C.C. Office for Church Life and Leadership, 1986), p. 152.
4. *The Rite of the Catholic Church, Volume IA, Initiation* (New York: Pueblo, 1988), p. 490.
5. Jürgen Moltmann, *The Church in the Power of the Spirit* (New York: Harper & Row, 1977), p. 321.
6. Ibid., p. 236.
7. Ives M. J. Congar, *The Word and the Spirit* (London: Geoffrey Chapman, 1986), pp. 15-41. See also: George Moberly, *The Administration of the Holy Spirit in the Body of Christ* (Oxford & London: James Parker, 1868), Bampton Lectures.
8. Joseph Haroutunian, *God With Us* (Philadelphia: Westminster, 1965), pp. 62-83.
9. See Rachel Henderlite's classic book, *The Holy Spirit in Christian Education* (Philadelphia: Westminster, 1964) for an analysis of the three extremes most often found in Christian education at the local level. (1) The Spirit of God is primarily an immanent principle working through the natural processes; (2) The Spirit is totally transcendent and incomprehensible (so, developing a Christian education program is problematic); (3) The words of the Spirit of God are confined within the Bible and the task of Christian education is to teach that book. Henderlite calls for a more dynamic view of the Holy Spirit in Christian education. She up-dates her

views in her section on the Holy Spirit in *Harper's Encyclopedia of Religious Education*, ed. Iris V. Cully and Kendig Brubaker Cully (San Francisco: Harper & Row, 1990), pp. 312-313. Also see James Michael Lee, *The Flow of Religious Education: A Social Science Approach* (Birmingham, Ala.: Religious Education Press, 1973), pp. 174-180. Lee analyzes and rejects what he terms "The Blow Theory" of religious education. His critique is a challenge to all attempts in the name of the Holy Spirit to be amorphous concerning our goals and processes in religious education.

Chapter IV

CONFIRMATION AS BLESSING

When we look back at the experiences in our lives we know very clearly when we have been blessed. We can name persons and events that have shaped our lives for the good. Certain experiences have filled our profound need for affirmation of who we are and of what we can become. These experiences are most often incarnations of unearned love and acceptance or models of integrity, truth and justice. Such experiences have projected images of the meaning and purpose of life itself and have become the seedbed for our faith in ourselves, others and God.

We need not only the blessing of parents and family members but also the blessing of a community in which our faith is anchored and confirmed. One friend said, "I was blessed by parents who loved me enough to say yes to me as a person while also saying no to some of my behavior and attitudes. There was no big gap between what they said they believed about life and the way they lived." This same person also said, "And, I was blessed by growing up in a church where the pastor and people affirmed me for raising questions and seeking to put my Christian beliefs together with ideas to which I was exposed in other areas of my life. For instance, when I went to college and took religion and philosophy courses where I had to think critically about my faith, I was not upset inside as some of my friends were. It all seemed natural and normal. I was really blessed by being in a church family which encouraged honest thought along with a warm piety." Such statements point to a quality of life and faith which can be and should be a central meaning for confirmation.

Confirmation experiences should be a blessing for the person as well

as for the community of faith, whether the confirmation is a part of the unified initiation, is seen as a separate rite or sacrament, or is seen as a
repeatable rite or sacrament. The quality of blessing should shine through
the entire experience so that when looking back the person of faith can say
with integrity, "I was blessed by being a part of a family and a church that
made possible . . ." Every person, of course, will finish the statement in
a unique way.

A Possible Origin of Confirmation as Blessing

Some recent research concerning the origin of confirmation has concluded that the ritual associated with it was probably a blessing of the bishop at the time the catechumens were being dismissed prior to the celebration of the eucharist or a blessing by the bishop of those who had just
been baptized in preparation for their first communion. Aidan Kavanagh
in his earlier studies interpreted this laying on of hands and anointing
by the bishop, such as reported in the *Apostolic Tradition*, allegedly by
Hippolytus (c. 215), as a sealing with the Holy Spirit. In his most recent
work he maintains that this ritual action was not a separate imparting of
the Holy Spirit beyond that already a part of baptism itself. The structure
of the baptismal liturgy was baptism by water *and Spirit*, the blessing
by the bishop was a dismissal prior to the eucharist. In this view baptism and eucharist are central sacraments with confirmation or consignation as a transitional blessing or *missa* before communion. This was so
highly developed during the catechumenate period that the eucharist
itself became known as the *missa* and unfortunately was attended by
fewer and fewer persons due to a misinterpretation of who could and
should be present.

Kavanagh does not emphasize for contemporary liturgy the aspect
of blessing which he found in the origin of confirmation. Rather, he
presents the history of the misinterpretation, emphasizes baptism and
eucharist as primary sacraments, but continues to affirm the unified initiation by the priest, and first eucharist especially for adults and children
of catechetical age, and possibly for infants as the Orthodox always
have. Kavanagh does not favor but recognizes the practice of confirmation, followed by first communion, for those who were baptized as
infants. He believes that the preconciliar position should be maintained
in such cases, namely, that "confirmation must be celebrated by a bishop or a presbyter delegated by him, often after the candidates have

already begun to receive communion."[1]

Confirmation as blessing by God, the faith community and the family should have a relational quality which is empowering and substantial. It is not, however, to be seen as a substantialistic imparting of the Holy Spirit by a bishop or by a priest or minister. Kavanagh seems not to be able to free himself from such assumptions even though he asserts that baptism, eucharist, as well as confirmation are "'analogies' produced by the Christian story from the beginning."[2] The "substantial" nature of confirmation is the *quality of the relationships engendered* between the confirmed and the ecclesia (the wider church) and the ecclesiola (the small church which is the family). This depth relationship is what is being celebrated in confirmation understood as blessing. Such a position is well developed in the thought of Claus Westermann in his classic study *Blessing in the Bible and the Life of the Church.*

The Biblical Base for Blessing

Westermann sees two main themes in the biblical witness: deliverance and blessing. He believes that God's deliverance through the Exodus and the covenant, and through the intervention in Christ, is given much stronger emphasis than God's ongoing blessing which is a consistent presence in all of life. These two themes show up in two main ways: epiphanies and theophanies. *Epiphanies* are God's coming in liberating, delivering, revealing, judging, intervening to bring salvation or wholeness back to life. *Theophanies* are blessings which God gives in creation and ongoing recreation. Through God's presence at all times life is seen as holy in every aspect. God's presence can be found in the growth of the soul of each person. As each person shares love, faith, hope, a sense of justice and inner and outer peace the soul of the person giving blessings grows as well as the soul of the person being blessed. "The vital power, without which no living being can exist, the Israelites called *berakhah*, blessing."[3]

The act of blessing means giving an identity. This identity is sacred and fundamental to self-affirmation and the discovery of one's purpose and destiny in life. Sometimes, as the Bible describes often, the identity is a new one as seen in the Abram/Abraham or Sarai/Sarah stories or in the Saul/Paul saga. Blessing also was a part of the early vision as God called Abram to go out in faith not knowing where he was going in order to become a blessing to all the families on the face of the earth (Genesis 12:3). From Abraham forward there is the persistent vision of God's continuing presence to empower persons to live faithfully as sons and daughters of God and to bless one another. This was seen in the Old Testament blessings of fathers to sons and mothers to sons and daughters.

Confirmation as blessing, whether as a part of baptismal celebration or as a rite of passage at the different stages of life, has great potential for strengthening both the sense of identity and the relationships of love and trust. It also conveys the sense of the manifestation of God's living Spirit as persons become aware of God's moving and living presence in their lives.

Westermann unpacks the history of the misunderstanding of blessing as something magical along with the misperception that certain persons were given the power to bless (bishops, priests) while others did not possess such power. Westermann maintains that: "Blessing is concerned with people throughout their lives, with their birth and maturity, with the union of man and woman and the birth of children, with aging and death. The message of the gospel encounters a person somewhere in his or her life, and then it is not only the before and after that are important. . . . God's bestowal of blessing is concerned with the whole of human life. It is for this reason that the blessing which accompanies a person throughout life and is bestowed at certain points in the special rites of the church finds its necessary significance."[4]

Westermann believes blessing is the authentic element in all the rites of the church—baptism, confirmation, marriage, burial, anniversaries. Blessing and proclamations of God's deliverance need to be interrelated and focused. Proclamation should be focused—not just in general. "It needs to be related to blessings of individuals—infants, boys and girls, husband and wives, the elderly, at the point of death. Deliverance and blessing must be together."[5]

We agree with Westermann's underscoring of the need in a mass society for faith to be personal and a genuine incarnation of love and justice within the family and the body of Christ, into which children, youth or adults are engrafted in baptism and in which they are strengthened and empowered for ministry and mission through the increasingly clear identity they find in confirmation and baptismal renewal experiences throughout life. Confirmation as blessing is related profoundly to the empowerment of God's Holy Spirit brought into reality by the incarnation of God's love in Christ and in each of our lives as extensions of the body of Christ to one another and to the whole of creation. The one who blesses gives something of his or her own soul just as God gives of

God's eternal and abiding love in ongoing creation and redemption. Blessing which is genuine moves us beyond the family, beyond even the security and warmth of the church family, out to the wider family of God with its many misunderstandings, divergent symbol systems, and hurts as well as its surprising visions of God's grace and peace which break through these divisions. As we help persons find their unique identities and their unique ministries through the blessing of confirmation we are helping them move out to strengthen the sense of God's universal family.

Blessing and the Sacramental Nature of Life

Blessing is anchored in an understanding of the sacramental nature of all of life. There should be no absolute split between the sacred and the profane. Unfortunately, the history of blessing has been plagued by this implied split. There has been a tendency to see blessing as a force which would take persons or things away from the grasp of the evil one and put them within God's influence. Thomas Simons, in his study of blessing calls for a thorough-going review and purification of such demonological concepts. He states, "The view that the world is held captive by the power of the evil one hardly corresponds to the first creation account of Genesis, whose author believes that in spite of the experience of evil, all things come from God's hand *good*."[6] Simons seeks to reclaim this more unified conception of creation by calling attention to the Eastern church's view of blessing which is much more wholistic and positive. Such a perspective "is expressed in the fundamental conception that blessings, and, for that matter, all the sacramentals and sacraments focus on the relation of the world to the Body of Christ and on the wonderful experience of the Cosmic Christ in the most varied situations in life. Blessing urges itself upon the church as its mission and task arising out of the eucharist that is at its very heart."[7]

Blessing: A Gift All Can Give

Just as there should be no sacred/secular split there should be no split between the clergy and laity in respect to who can bestow blessing. Many lay Christians think that only clergy, especially bishops, have the power to bless others by their words or actions. Such a view has made blessing an occasional or special experience rather than a mundane, everyday experience which can impregnate all of life with meaning, wholeness, and vision.

There is a movement to reclaim the potential of "the universal priesthood of all believers" in all Christian communities. This means that parents, teachers, and members of the body of Christ all have the power to bless one another as they become channels of God's grace, love, and truth in their words and attitudes. Simon urges clergy to highlight for laity the rich potential of the "office of blessing" because its practice in respect to the concerns of family life, the use of possessions and food can contribute greatly to the sanctification of all of life. The theme of blessing God and blessing humanity comes from many sources. We see it in the early liturgies and in early understandings of eucharistic life.[8]

Laity and clergy as equally empowered members of the body of Christ have rich possibilities for becoming actual, living blessings, incarnations of God's full life of shalom within the eucharistic life of the family, the church family, and the wider family of God. Such a view is further grounded in the belief that the world itself is a sacrament of God's presence. So what we do as couples preparing for children, what we do at the birth of our children, how we support and nurture children to find meaning and purpose in life, how we bind or free them to become their best selves and embrace a vocation of caring and ministry beyond themselves, can all become occasions for blessing not only our children and families but indirectly "all the families on the face of the earth." God is at the center of blessing but we are active participants in God's blessing as we become channels of God's Holy Spirit in our daily lives. Such active participation takes place in the everyday rituals of life in feeding, clothing, talking, sheltering, nurturing, playing, disciplining, etc. These deep–running everyday rituals are those through which we communicate our visions of reality, our life-giving, spirit-filled relationship of love, or our fear and mistrust. Those fundamental rituals in the family are focused and enhanced by the great faith stories and sacraments of the church which become the motivating and empowering centers of meaning and purpose for the visions of reality we carry with us wherever we go and in whatever we do. The great sacramental experiences of baptism, confirmation, and eucharist then become the primary paradigms for blessing children, youth, and adults and giving them a vision of their meaning, purpose and eternal destiny in life's pilgrimage. It is not enough, however, to project such a positive picture of the potential of sacramental blessing. We must "put teeth" in such an approach by providing educational and liturgical guidelines, optional experiences, and resources for parents, liturgical leaders, and participants. Such approaches should start with family life education and marriage preparation. Such redirection and liturgical celebrations should become concrete and focused for young couples as they prepare for their first child and as the congregation joins them in preparations for infant baptism or the dedication or enrollment of their child as a catechumen.

The Blessing of Confirmation as a Repeatable Sacrament

We see the importance of infant baptism in this unified initiation where confirmation is a repeatable element. In the preparation of parents and congregations for infant baptism we have several opportunities for blessing the child and for recognizing and celebrating God's presence in all of the processes of life in the family: a safe and loving prenatal life leading to the birth; of child development and the stages of human and faith development; the recognition by the parents and the congregation of the reciprocal relationships needed to surround the child with support, acceptance, and nurture; the celebration of the child's engrafting fully into the body of Christ in baptism; the entering into a covenantal relationship between the parents, the congregation, and God to bring up the child to be a blessing to all.

This process of blessing and empowerment is represented in the educational and liturgical steps which the church is beginning to make available to parents. These steps give the infant an identity as a child of God, as a child of a particular human community, and his or her family, as well as an identity as an important member of the body of Christ in mutual ministry from baptism onward.

As Myron Madden has asserted, the giving of the name to the child should symbolize all of these important relationships and should be the first blessing given by parents to their child. The name projects an identity for the child, and the process of naming can be the occasion for projecting hopes and aspirations which can be freeing and rewarding or a burden to bear.

In this process we most profoundly want to bless our children with a positive self-image and a deep acceptance and love which is unearned yet empowering. Madden correctly says that we can go through life looking for blessing we may not have received from our parents. The blessing we most want and need is to know inside that we are accepted and loved for ourselves because we exist not because of what we have done to prove our worth. Early acceptance, love and affirmation are blessings on which children can build a productive life. The achievement should be a freeing and fulfilling response to acceptance by parents, others, and God rather than a troubled attempt to earn acceptance, love, and affirmation.[9] Madden wisely sees this process of identity building as empowerment for the child. The naming, the engrafting of the child into the faith community, accepting the child and projecting images of meaning and ministry are ways of building a sense of self and a sense of power to influence others and to be someone of significance in life. As we mature we often seek power in nonproductive ways. What we need and want is "power that is related to who we are (our being). This is the kind of power that is a real blessing—not related to what others have granted us . . . this kind of power is important but it should be built on personal identity before God and acceptance of that identity."[10] When our power is so grounded we are not so intent on having power over others. We see in Jesus one who sought to give the kind of power that comes when we meet genuine human needs. This is the kind of power which blesses and affirms others. The absence of identity and the absence of a sense of personal empowerment lead us into the way of evil manipulations where we seek identity and power in patterns that hurt others and ourselves.

The rituals which the faith community is beginning to recover or to innovate have possibility for identity, empowerment, and blessing. In a variation of the historic catechumenate program for adults a fresh approach has been developed for parents and the congregation around the birth of a child and the child's engrafting into the body of Christ through infant baptism.

The approach involves home visitations of the expecting couple with a series of rituals: 1. *Before birth* after communication and prayer with the parents to be and the beginning of counseling and learning about the elements essential for a healthy birth and a healthy child. 2. A *rite of baptismal intent* before the congregation with a sponsor who personifies the link between the couple and the wider church. 3. A *ritual after the birth* in the hospital or at home along with a plan to enroll the child for baptism and thanking God for the joys of this new life, with discussion concerning the role of parents as the first teachers of faith in the family which becomes the nursery of faith. 4. The *ritual after death* if there is a miscarriage or still birth at which time pastoral care of the couple is essential along with care from the congregation. 5. The *rite of enrollment* at which time the child is named and enrolled for baptism, with parents committing themselves before the congregation to become the child's first community of faith. 6. The *prayer before baptism* to ask God's blessing on the coming event and to prepare the family and the congregation to accept their respective responsibilities. 7. The *rite of baptism* in the incorporation of the child into the body of Christ through water and Spirit with baptism by sprinkling, pouring, or immersion, which is increasingly recommended. 8. *Confirmation* by the laying on of hands by pastor, sponsor, family members and anointing with oil and signing of the cross, followed by first communion with the child receiving the elements mixed together and given by touching the lips of the child with a silver spoon containing the bread and wine. This is followed by robing the child in white, the giving of a baptismal candle and a baptismal book and other gifts. 9. The *rite of baptismal remembrance at church* where the child's baptismal anniversary is remembered and celebrated. 10. And *baptismal remembrance at home* where the child's baptismal date is marked with prayer and celebration, recalling images of the baptism, the water and its meaning, the anointing, the love of sponsor and family, the commitments of parents, other children and families, the church family, the lighting of the baptismal candle, the celebration of the child's entrance into the community of faith and the identification of blessings which continue to flow from this life in Christ.[11]

This catechumenal approach may well be too extensive for many congregations or families. However, variations of this approach are being considered by many congregations as a way to enhance the support and nurture of families as they prepare for and celebrate the birth of a child and the incorporation of the child into a community of blessing. The position we take concerning confirmation emphasizes the need for ongoing nurture and for lifting up and celebrating God's empowerment and identity for the person at the different stages in life's pilgrimage. These additional affirmations of one's baptism can be seen as occasions for expressions of self-understanding and clarification of one's identity as a person and as a member of the universal priesthood of all believers. These additional affirmations are genuinely sacramental and can become powerful blessings in the life of the person as well as the community of faith. At each stage differing needs become known and can be the organizing principle for a fresh in-depth study of the Christian faith and an honest and clear response of redefinition and commitment. Such occasions can take place with integrity at anytime the person is moved by the Spirit to seek redefinition of identity and sense of direction in mutual ministry or at expected times in the normal stages of faith development: adolescence, young adulthood, mid-life, retirement or at the times of personal crisis or normal reevaluation. Certainly, one of these periods will need to be adolescence—probably middle to late adolescence—where the celebration of confirmation is increasingly occurring. As we have discovered in our survey of major denominational practices, many are moving to middle to late adolescence rather than late childhood or early adolescence. As far as it goes, this movement is healthy because it corresponds more fully with the search for an authentic faith which is distinct from the faith of the parents and the congregations. Young people need and want to own their faith. This process should follow engaging opportunities to explore the meaning of their commitments in an honest, open, and dialogical way. Youth need to find the gifts with which they have been blessed and discover creative ways to share those gifts in significant ministries within and beyond the faith community, to be responsive to God's leading through the Spirit, to make fresh contributions to the thinking and actions of the congregation, to sort out their sexual identities and their roles as fathers and mothers of the future, to find healthy and wholesome models of marriage and family life to which they can be committed.

As Søren Kierkegaard said so well, youth need to be weaned from the faith of their parents and come to a first-hand faith. This is a faith which faces the fact that Christianity is an affront to many in our world, and that following the contemporaneous Christ is not an easy road. Youth must discover for themselves the truth of Christ's way of love, trust, and justice by experiencing what it means to give oneself away in order to find oneself![12] Those who take into themselves the "solid food" of the mature faith can be strengthened to venture forth as disciples and ministers of Christ in this complex world of sexual disorientation and threat, marriage and family disintegration, struggle for social and political equity and justice, civil unrest, ecological imbalance, international tension, the fear of war, and religious and philosophical diversity. If these explorations can lead to affirmations of their original blessing through baptism into the community called to become a blessing to our world, the confirmation commitment can be genuinely liberating and empowering.

Having underscored adolescence as a lively time for such a reaffirmation we must hasten to add that studies in faith development by James Fowler and others have made it clear that other stages of faith follow quickly. This is especially true in young adulthood where individuative-reflective thinking is most likely to take place, where the experiences of the individual have been wide and deep enough to critique the Christian faith "as a system" of belief and where the struggle to define oneself in terms of vocation, marriage and family or singleness, etc., become central. It is our opinion that this period is one largely overlooked by the church as a time for education and celebration of one's decisions to be in ministry through occupation or voluntary service. Often this is the time for focus on the Christian vocation of laity and the confirmation of such decisions publicly before the congregation. Such a view of confirmation as a repeatable sacrament can celebrate baptismal renewal as persons seek God's blessing and empowerment to serve through the priesthood of parenthood, through teaching, health care, business, industry, science, government service, the helping professions of law, medicine, social work, nursing, counseling, etc. Each of these occupations along with special task forces on justice, peace, ecology, race, sexuality, etc., can become the avenues where individuals can "bless the families" of our earth through their ministries. Likewise, some may have the gifts and graces necessary to prepare for ordained or consecrated ministries through the church. Such a focus can include many beyond young adulthood, but this age group will undoubtedly provide the primary candidates. Fresh educational programs and authentic new liturgical celebrations are needed for this emphasis to bear fruit. In Part III of this book we will give concrete examples of confirmation as repeatable blessing at various stages of life.

We will also discuss how confirmation as affirmation of baptism or baptismal renewal can and should take place in response to the awareness of God's Spirit at any time in life's pilgrimage. Robert Kinast captures this idea well when he states that confirmation is "a celebration and intensification of what already is given: it does not supply what is lacking." However, it is very important because "it personalizes this gift of the Spirit . . . Confirmation is the Church realizing concretely the presence of the Spirit."[13] Kinast's view of pastoral care and the movement of the Spirit is holistic. In helping a lay eucharistic minister, Ruth, to minister to an aged man, Mr. Reynolds, who is depressed at being alone, Kinast helps Ruth see that she is a channel of God's Spirit to Mr. Reynolds. Her presence to him is a real presence; her response to him is a real communion. As she shares the eucharist with him she is giving him herself in love and faith just as Christ gave himself for us and continues to be a *real* presence in the eucharist and in the eucharistic community which is continuing his ministry.[14]

Confirmation as a repeatable sacramental experience is celebrated by the faith community in response to the awareness of God's grace and love, in response to the presence of the Spirit in the lives of persons at whatever age or stage in life. It is this Spirit-filled community of faithful people who in fact bless the child, the youth, the adult, or the aged through relationships of love, acceptance, trust, forgiveness, and renewal. Such relationships, such "laying on of hands" actually heal, actually make whole, actually bless. The sacramental act, the action parable of confirmation (the laying on of hands, the anointing with oil and the signing with the cross on the forehead) is a powerful symbol of the actual presence of the Spirit of God within the community of faith and above and beyond the community calling it to faithful incarnations of that life-giving presence of God in all aspects of life.

Of course, we have to be open to the movement of God's Spirit in those who respond. This loving spirit can be seen in the imaginative caring of baptized, confirmed, and communicant children, in the adventuresome and vital contribution of confirmed youth whose responses to God's Spirit may challenge established leaders and "the way we have always done it," in young adults whose commitments to be in ministry through their vocations as well as through the governance of the church may be the source both of threat and renewal for the church, in the awareness of persons in mid-life that renewal of their baptismal covenant can provide empowerment and a second or third chance to fulfill personal potential and corporate solidarity, in the distillation of the unique qualities of aging but vital and wiser members of the body of Christ who make fresh commitments to be in new forms of ministry in their "mature years." In all of these ways God is blessing us and we are being empowered to become blessings to others.

NOTES

1. Aidan Kavanagh, *Confirmation: Origins and Reform* (New York: Pueblo, 1988), p. 93. Also, see Paul Turner, "The Origins of Confirmation: An Analysis of Aidan Kavanagh's Hypothesis," in Worship 65:4 (July, 1991), pp. 320-338.
2. Ibid. p. 116.
3. Claus Westermann, *Blessing in the Bible and the Life of the Church* (Philadelphia: Fortress, 1988) p. 18.
4. Ibid., p. 117.
5. Ibid., p.118.

6. Thomas G. Simons, *Blessings: A Reappraisal of Their Nature, Purpose and Celebration* (Saratoga, Cal.: Resources Publications, 1981), p. 50.

7. Ibid., p. 53.

8. Ibid., p. 62.

9. Myron C. Madden, *Blessing: Giving the Gift of Power* (Nashville: Broadman, 1988), pp. 30-32.

10. Ibid., p. 49.

11. See Gail Ramshaw-Schmidt, "Celebrating Baptism in Stages," in *Baptism and Confirmation: Alternative Futures for Worship*, ed. Mark Searle (Collegeville, Minn.: Liturgical Press, 1985) p. 135f.

12. Søren Kierkegaard, *Fear and Trembling*, trans. by Walter Lowrie (Princeton, N.J.: Princeton University Press, 1941), pp. 12-15.

13. Robert L. Kinast, *Sacramental Pastoral Care* (New York: Pueblo, 1988), p. 145.

14. Ibid., p. 173.

PART II

WHAT IS HAPPENING IN THE CHURCHES

Chapter V

FINDINGS FROM A STUDY
OF SEVEN DENOMINATIONS

In our concern about confirmation as teachers in a theological school we have endeavored to stay in touch with attitudes and practices in the local church. We prepared an inventory to help us with this task. The inventory was sent to an ecumenical spectrum of churches where confirmation is a common practice (Roman Catholic, Presbyterian, United Methodist, United Church of Christ, Evangelical Lutheran Church of America, Episcopal, and the United Church of Canada). In addition, we surveyed the various study documents and projected new curricular designs of the various denominations. We interviewed various leaders and participated in many dialogues with pastors and laity in workshops and seminars. No attempt was made to make a "scientific" study. However, we did seek balance in our samples from rural, small town, urban and suburban settings as well as racial, ethnic, and gender balance. We found our representative churches by asking denominational leaders to give us the names of churches and pastors who "take confirmation education and celebration seriously." Since our sample is not comprehensive what follows is a snapshot of an ongoing process. Most of the denominations are involved in significant rethinking of confirmation or baptismal affirmation. Because of this, we decided to report our findings on a denominational basis first and then present a summary of the major trends we discovered on an ecumenical basis. It is our hope that the denominational pictures will not only be helpful to those in each group but also to all who are on pilgrimages to a pattern of confirmation or baptismal affirmation which is theologically, educationally, and liturgically sound and creating authentic commitment.

Our survey questions can be found in the Appendix. In general we were very interested to discover to what degree confirmation was being seen as a part of the unified initiation, to what degree confirmation was being seen as baptismal renewal or as baptismal affirmation. We wanted to learn how confirmation was related to baptism and to eucharist in the varying denominations. We sought to discover whether or not confirmation was seen as a repeatable experience related to various stages in the life cycle. We probed local church patterns of confirmation education and celebration. At what ages, using what resources, with what leadership did confirmation programs get conducted? We were interested in seeing how confirmation was seen in relation to the identification of laity with the universal priesthood of all believers and the assuming of individual responsibility for the ministry and mission of the church in our world. These and other questions motivated us to get as close as we could to the real life of the parish. We discovered many strengths and also many frustrations. Below is a report of our findings:

Roman Catholic

Catholics see confirmation as a part of the unified initiation of baptism, confirmation, and eucharist. This unity is clear when it comes to adult catechumens. Such persons have responded to the invitation to explore the Catholic faith, have been enrolled as catechumens, and have participated in the intense program of catechesis which culminates in baptism by water, confirmation by the laying on of hands and anointing, and eucharist—usually at the Easter Vigil.

There are, however, many variations on the unified initiation and the Rite of Christian Initiation of Adults associated with it. While baptism, confirmation, and eucharist are seen as the sacraments of initiation the sequencing of the sacraments varies considerably. In our study of actual practice we found the following patterns:

(a) Infant baptism, followed by preparation for and celebration of first communion at about age seven. There is then a period of preparation and confirmation at Easter in the eighth grade. The age for confirmation can also be much earlier in this pattern.

(b) A delayed sequencing of the unified initiation which includes infant baptism, first communion at about age seven, followed by a strong educational and pastoral program for children and adolescents culminating in the celebration of the sacrament of confirmation in the junior or senior year of high school. This approach has gained much support in more recent years.[1]

(c) Infant baptism, followed by preparation for and celebration of confirmation and often the sacrament of reconciliation (penance) at age seven or so followed by first communion.

(d) The enrollment of infants as catechumens and the commitment of parents, sponsors, and the congregation to nurture the child in the faith community until the age of accountability at which time the child or youth is baptized, confirmed, and has first communion. Several churches have embraced the practice of bringing children who have not been baptized as infants into the body of Christ through such a catechumenal program and the celebration of the unified initiation.

One priest reported, "By Covenant Church discipline we must initiate this way (the unified initiation) for all people of catechetical age, but not for infants. I believe infants also should be initiated this way." Another priest agreed that unbaptized children of catechetical age should celebrate the three sacraments together. He states, "Beginning with children around nine years or ten—when anyone comes seeking baptism, they celebrate baptism, confirmation, and eucharist together— whether they are a child, adolescent, or adult. So far it has been very positive. Of course, we continue to celebrate confirmation with adolescents baptized as infants."

(e) For children baptized in another denomination or not baptized, there is a tendency to delay initiation until they join their peer group in confirmation. At this time they complete the steps not already taken in the unified initiation.

(f) For adolescents and adults seeking to enter the Catholic church without previously being baptized the rigorous and supportive preparation associated with the Rite of Christian Initiation of Adults is followed. This one– to three–year program of catechesis, liturgical participation, ethical reflection, and spiritual development culminates in the celebration of baptism, confirmation, and eucharist normally at the time of the Easter Vigil.

The confirming minister traditionally has been the bishop. This is still true in many dioceses. However, increasingly the minister leading the celebration of the sacrament is the local pastor. The leadership of the confirmation educational program is shared with Christian educators, lay catechists, parents, deacons, and sisters participating cooperatively, depending on the size of the parish.

The movement away from requiring the bishop to be ordinary minister of the sacrament of confirmation was the result of the studies initiated in Vatican II and is related not only to the difficult logistical problem of having the bishop present for such celebrations but to the changing theological views of Roman Catholic leaders. The theology is moving away from substantialistic views of the imparting of the Holy Spirit in confirmation to a relational view. One priest wrote: "Our understanding of confirmation is moving much more toward being a celebration of the Gift of the Holy Spirit within the community. The focus being on 'gift' and 'community' (rather than the individual)." Such a movement puts much higher value on the involvement of parents, the supportive community of believers, and the support and guidance of local catechists, Christian educators, and pastors.

One of the interesting emphases in Catholic responses to our study was the distinction between confirmation and baptismal renewal. Since confirmation is seen as a one-time sacramental celebration which not only seals baptism but imparts a distinctive character to the confirmed, it cannot be repeated. However, baptism can be renewed even before confirmation. This happens at least annually, usually, at Easter when the promises of baptism are renewed. While the unified initiation has confirmation as an integral part of the baptismal liturgy, in Catholic understanding, it cannot be renewed even though baptism can. Another priest responded, "Confirmation is an initiation rite and is (or should be) celebrated with baptism and first communion as sacramental entrance into the church. Baptismal renewal, on the other hand, is appropriate in connection with significant passages and transitions, as well as various liturgical celebrations through the year . . . e.g., Easter, Pentecost." Other respondents called for baptismal renewal at different stages of life: young adulthood, when becoming parents, mid-life, and retirement times.

Among the frustrations Roman Catholics are experiencing with confirmation education and celebration is the tendency for confirmation to become "graduation" from church. This seems to be true for Catholics who are confirmed both during junior high and senior high. The move to the senior year of high school for confirmation takes place in order to keep youth active and growing during the high school years rather than losing their participation after confirmation around the eighth grade. However, some who moved confirmation to the senior year report, "Once high school students receive the sacrament of confirmation, they graduate from high school and often stop attending church." Several Roman Catholics are urging the movement of confirmation to young adulthood, a time which correlates with serious life decisions. This is urged in the light of the high satisfaction participants seem to have as members of the RCIA program and the celebration of confirmation inside the unified initiation at the climax of the program with the mystagogic reflections between Easter and Pentecost. It is during this time that decisions are made concerning the unique ministries the newly initiated persons want to embrace for the sake of the continuation of Christ's ministry in the world.

One of the significant hopes for change concerning confirmation was the desire to see the unified initiation take place in infancy. One priest said, "I would like to see the Roman Catholic Church celebrate 'confirmation' with infant baptism. And then celebrate 'confirmation' throughout life (beginning in adolescence) as a renewal of baptism/celebration of the gift of the Spirit (the repeatable sacrament concept)." Another priest lamented, "Infants born to devout Christian parents are denied full initiation, according to our current church discipline." One can see that there is considerable thinking about the meaning of confirmation as a sacrament. If Roman Catholic thought moves toward the historic unity of initiation for adults and their children, including infants, or toward the Orthodox unified initiation for infants, there might be openness to the rethinking of the sacramental nature of confirmation, including the possibility that confirmation could take place in infancy and then be repeated at various times in the life cycle.

At the grassroots level Catholics are also becoming sensitive to the fact that the gift of the Holy Spirit is not necessarily tied to the meeting of various standards of knowledge or performance *or* tied to the laying on of hands of a bishop or presbyter. One respondent reflected, "We see the sacrament as being a celebration of the *free gift* of God's love. It is not something which is earned by passing an exam on knowledge, etc. This is a fine line to walk, but needs to be emphasized again and again."

The Episcopal Church

The Episcopal church has sponsored engaging and responsible studies of the nature of confirmation, primarily inside of the wider concern for the unified initiation. The Book of Common Prayer makes this quite clear. Infants are baptized with water, the baptism is sealed by the signing of the cross on the forehead in oil, followed by the eucharist. While all baptized persons are welcomed to the Table of the Lord few Episcopal churches actually give the elements to infants, as in the Orthodox tradition. Rather, it is quite common for children to wait until ages three and four before receiving the eucharist. This is very much a matter of the pattern followed by the rector and the parents in a given congregation. One rector said that water, oil, and food equal a motto for the nurturing community. Favoring the unified initiation, he saw the eucharist as little Easter and Pentecost experiences which extend and nourish the new life given in baptism. "Why give birth if you intend to starve the child?"

One of the major problems with the extension of the unified initiation in the Episcopal church is the practice of confirmation only by the bishop. While many Episcopal priests, educators, and laity favor the unified initiation in infancy they cannot call the rite of anointing a confirmation rite unless the bishop baptizes the infant. The same is true for youth or adults. There still exist the vestiges of substantialism. Only the bishop had the power to seal with the Holy Spirit. An authentic argument is made that the bishop represents the continuity of the faith community, without undue emphasis on the matter of power. One priest in our study identifies the dilemma. He says, "For us, baptism is full and complete initiation into the Body of Christ. The bishop must be present for confirmation. If he (she?) baptizes and anoints a child, confirmation is not necessary. However, he is rarely present for baptisms." Another respondent agreed with the unified initiation approach but recognized that "confirmation is reserved for bishops and is then a separate rite." Another said that he was strongly for the unified initiation "tho' I'm not sure all in the Episcopal Church understand that's what the Book of Common Prayer is doing."

Another fascinating dimension of this issue is to be found in the high affirmation of the pattern of baptismal renewal. Most Episcopal churches celebrate baptismal renewals at the times (often five) of baptism in the regular services of worship each year: at the feast of Jesus' baptism (January), at the Easter Vigil, and at Trinity Sunday (the Sunday after Pentecost) and at the time of confirmation when the bishop visits. Often adults elect to prepare themselves for a renewal of their baptismal covenant by participating in a 10 to 16 week study of the essentials of their faith as they anticipate their public declaration of faith and the laying on of hands by the bishop during the service of confirmation. In a sense this practice is in line with the view that confirmation should take place in infant baptism, and, being a repeatable rite, can take place in adolescence, young adulthood, adulthood, at retirement, or at any time a person wishes to make a public renewal of commitment to Christ and to ministry as a member of the body of Christ. There appears to be some inner tension present between the general belief in the value of the unified initiation and the one–time confirmation only to be done by the bishop. This internal conflict is further illustrated by the growing pattern of baptismal renewal and the implied "reconfirmation" by the bishop of those seeking renewal of their commitments.

The confirmation education programs are aimed at middle to late adolescence, primarily those less than fifteen years of age with many favoring eleventh or twelfth grades. The programs are from thirteen weeks to two years in length for adolescents and are led by priests, Christian educators, some laity, with parental support for "homework." For young adults and adults the programs are usually for ten to fifteen weeks.

Such programs emphasize the clarification of personal faith, knowledge of Episcopal history, beliefs, and especially liturgical practices including the use of the lectionary and an understanding of scripture which undergirds its use in corporate worship and private prayer. The emphasis upon confirmation as a commitment to a unique form of ministry was present to some degree in Episcopal patterns, especially for young adults and adults. Youth often have a requirement to be involved in some form of service, but this does not appear to be related very clearly to decisions about their vocation and how they see themselves as ministers within the ministering body of Christ. Such an understanding is more likely to be focused on young adult confirmation preparation. One respondent said that "with young adults hours of service (ministry) outside the family and congregation are required. Don't do that with adults, but should." Another states, "Each person identifies an area of ministry (in consultation with a sponsor) and works in that area for six months or more." Another indicates that "training is given in lay ministry opportunities in the work-place, home, etc., as well as at the church."

While confirmation is celebrated, using the liturgy in the Book of Common Prayer, with rather high expectations and the drama that accompanies the bishop's visit, there is concern about those who "drop out" soon after the service of commitment. In order to counter the problem of nominalism many Episcopal leaders are calling for deeper and more personal spiritual development, moving the time of confirmation to adulthood, a pattern advocated by John Westerhoff and William Willimon.[2] One priest reflects such a stance as he says, "Perhaps if people participated in it as adults it would take on more meaning and could be linked to people's growing understanding of themselves as ministers in the world." Another called for the strengthening of the unified initiation in infancy and of periodic opportunities for deeper education leading to public baptismal renewal, perhaps every ten years. He concludes "In 35 years of parish ministry I've seen the need for these kinds of changes and haven't had the courage to do them alone."

In a major fresh study the Episcopal church is revealing a genuine sense of renewal concerning many of the issues associated with the sacraments of initiation.[3] A new program, *The Catechumenal Process*, has been inaugurated which emphasizes the education of adults who are unbaptized, along with older youth and adults who have been baptized and/or confirmed but want to make a fresh commitment and reaffirm their faith publicly at the time of the bishop's visit for confirmation.[4]

Evangelical Lutheran Church of America

The Evangelical Lutheran Church of America, a relatively new denomination which brought together various previous groups, continues the Lutheran tradition of strong emphasis on confirmation. Even though this is true, a new study commission has projected a fresh approach to confirmation.

One of the issues important for the ELCA leaders is the matter of grace. Too often confirmation in the Lutheran tradition has been the result of "good works," meeting the requirements involved in a two, three or even five year program of instruction and testing. For instance, in our survey of ELCA beliefs and practices we found a high set of expectations and standards which were enforced prior to confirmation along with considerable demurring about the legalism and the perfunctory nature of much of confirmation education and liturgy. Requirements typically included attendance at all classes and worship services, note taking on sermons, tests on material with an 80 percent accuracy rate in order to pass, completion of assigned work, memorization of biblical passages and creeds, a certain number of hours of service, a written statement of beliefs to be shared with church officials and the congregation, acolyting during and after the confirmation program, participation in the youth group, etc. The high standards have brought a certain respect for the seriousness of confirmation but also a certain ethos of resistance if not resentment. One pastor reports that while many parents affirm the high expectations many youth "have objected to making such a commitment. They feel caught between the 'must/should' of our church and their parents. For almost 40 years confirmation preparation was a 'necessary evil' endured to obtain one's 'right' to confirmation. The last of these groups are the parents of our present confirmation classes." Other pastors report a similar situation but are pleased with the movement in recent years away from an atmosphere of law toward an attitude more consistent with the traditional Lutheran emphases on "justification by faith" and a life blessed by God's grace.

The latter emphasis can be seen in the more recent language being used. The new position is "Confirmation ministry is an opportunity for congregations to renew the vision of living by grace, grounded in Baptism. This vision is especially important for ministry with young Christians, but it also has lifelong implications."[5] Not only is the language changing but also the quality of the education and liturgical celebration. There is much more emphasis on the inclusion of all baptized Christians in the total life of the faith community. Historically, communion was reserved only for confirmed persons. More recently a focus on baptism has created an atmosphere of grace in which children may come to the Lord's Table at various ages in different congregations. The Confirmation Ministry Task Force Report affirms this trend. The decision concerning when the child comes to the Table is being seen as the shared responsibility of the pastor, parents, the child, family sponsors, and the congregation.

Also, more recently, confirmation programs have placed a higher value on relationships, support, and modeling. There has been more use of adult mentors and sponsors, and more parental participation along with the presence of leaders of youth who have been confirmed a year or so before. Such an approach has recognized that the experience of affirmation of one's baptism is a process that should continue all through life and is, therefore, not only repeatable from a theological perspective but also and crucially from the point of view of the personal pilgrimage which life is for each individual. Approximately 1500 ELCA congregations have mentoring programs in which adults are selected and trained to build relationships with youth "in which the sharing of faith can occur."[6] New understandings of faith development and spiritual formation have greatly influenced Lutheran views and can be seen in the early drafts of the new theological statements and educational/liturgical recommendations coming from the current study commission.

The Confirmation Ministry Task Force Report takes a strong position on baptism as the entrance into the family of Christ. It states that confirmation does not make one a member of the church; rather baptism does. Furthermore, it asserts, "Confirmation ministry does not complete baptism, for baptism is already complete through God's work of joining us to Christ and his Body, the Church. In him is salvation. Moreover, confirmation ministry does not *compete* with Baptism."[7]

The new position also sees affirmation of baptism as continuing throughout life, stating that: "While Baptism happens only once, affirmation of Baptism . . . can happen many times. . . . A rite that is truly an affirmation of Baptism can be of great benefit . . . as the community of faith seeks to minister to members experiencing life's transitions. The church discerns and proclaims God's movement in people's lives as they experience endings and beginnings, connecting these significant transitions with the baptismal understanding of our dying and rising with Christ."[8]

While the strong focus on baptism and baptismal affirmation in adolescence or young adulthood, and baptismal renewal as a lifelong process, is consistent with the unified initiation there is not much evidence in our survey of such a theology being put into practice. Many pastors favor it theologically but find old practices hard to change. One respondent said that she favored the unified initiation *but* "the congregation is light years behind the pastor in theology. Rather they rely on tradition which is non-unified theology. I feel confessionally we are held to a unified position and have expressed that. The Council has suggested it, but parents still will not participate. Education takes a long time. . . . Theology and practice should be held together. Otherwise we send mixed messages. I practice early communion at parents' discretion. I break with the practice of the church as do many pastors." Some reported that there is a very small number of churches where infants are participants in the eucharist. If this is true, the unified approach may be gaining adherents.

The baptismal liturgy in the new Lutheran Book of Worship does include the laying on of hands and the signing of the cross on the forehead of each of the baptized, with or without oil. There is, however, no celebration of the eucharist. Rather, there is the giving of a lighted candle to each person or to the sponsor of a child and the exchange of the peace with the baptized, the parents, sponsor, and the congregation.

The study commission has developed several models of confirmation ministry. These include the following:

(1) *The Longer and Later Programs.* This approach integrates confirmation ministry with early childhood and grade school education
in an attempt to create a family support for confirmation. The program features in-home visitation, modeling by pastors, prebaptismal preparation of parents and congregation, early elementary
cooperative learning experiences and parental covenanting—all
done to strengthen the fabric of the family and to undergird the
young person's movement into catechetics in the upper grades and
into lifelong ministry.

(2) *Meeting of Young People.* This approach emphasizes knowing
and affirming each young person. The emphasis is upon genuine
meeting of minds and hearts instead of "classes." Experiential
learning, conversation, and peer interaction are emphasized but in
relation to the great biblical themes and the central beliefs of the
Christian faith.

(3) *The Confirming Community.* Here older youth are related to
younger persons as tutors or peer counselors. For instance, Junior
High Youth studying the sacraments help fifth graders who are
preparing for first communion. High School Youth work with
Junior High Youth and both serve as counselors in the Vacation
Bible School. Community building is crucial. Meals are shared
as well as dialogue and service.

(4) *The Catechumenal Parish.* This approach follows the classical
catechumenate model which is marked by rituals of enrollment, the
preparation time, the baptismal service in which the person is
received fully into the body of Christ with baptism by water, the laying on of hands or anointing, and eucharist; and the mystagogic
period when the person probes the faith even more deeply with
attention to finding specific forms of ministry.[9]

It seems clear that the ELCA can indeed build on a rich tradition, moving in fresh directions, toward more grace oriented goals, resources, and
methodologies.

The United Methodist Church

Confirmation in the United Methodist Church does not have a long history. John Wesley did not recommend it to his pastors nor to the new
church in America. While pastors did have membership classes they did
not recognize confirmation as a liturgical celebration until the official

service was published in the Methodist Hymnal (1964 edition). The current study document on baptism, *By Water and the Spirit: A Study of Baptism For United Methodists*, prefers to replace the term "confirmation" with "public profession of baptismal faith." If this recommendation is accepted at the 1996 General Conference the use of the term confirmation may slowly atrophy. If it is retained it will be seen as the first of several public affirmations of one's baptism.

The problems associated with the earlier pattern of confirmation were widely identified in our study of United Methodist Church understandings and practices. Several respondents decried the earlier understanding of confirmation as a completion of baptism and "joining the church." Children baptized as infants were seen as "preparatory members" until they completed confirmation classes and publicly affirmed the faith, after which they were counted as full members. Such a view was a misunderstanding of baptism, according to the position being articulated in the new study document. Baptism is the engrafting of the child or adult into the body of Christ, into the ministering community. Confirmation does not complete baptism or make persons members of the church.

The new document states, "Because it gives a misleading view of baptism the continued use of the term 'confirmation' in the United Methodist Church is incompatible with our understanding of baptism and membership in the Church. . . . Persons baptized in infancy are, under the guidance of the Holy Spirit and the nurture, grace, and love one has received from God through the community of faith, expected to make a public profession of faith in Jesus Christ and commit themselves to responsible discipleship. This moment now called confirmation is more aptly titled Profession of The Faith Into Which We Were Baptized. This profession is not concerned with Church membership as such, but is the first significant affirmation of one's baptism and owning of one's faith."[10]

This first affirmation is a time when the person responds to God's Holy Spirit and call to be in ministries of love and justice by consciously "embracing Christian vocation; the priesthood of all believers, in which she or he was included in baptism." This experience may be and should be repeated throughout life as new self-understandings and deeper understandings of faith take place. Such occasions are to be seen as "reaffirmation of baptismal faith" or baptismal renewal.

If this new direction is affirmed officially the concept of "preparatory members" will be dropped and baptism will be the entrance into the body of Christ and membership. The new United Methodist Hymnal presents an inclusive liturgy of baptism with laying on of hands integrated into the service, with a recommendation that the initiation culminate in the celebration of the eucharist.[11] The term, confirmation, is used in this unified initiation for adults along with the rubric, "As the pastor, and others if desired, place hands on the head of each person who has been baptized, or is being confirmed, or is reaffirming faith, the pastor says to each: *"Name*, the Lord defend you with his heavenly grace and by his spirit confirm you in the faith and fellowship of all true disciples of Jesus Christ."[12]

The responses to the attempt to unify initiation vary but are promising. Several pastors indicated their own affirmation of the practice and are taking the initiative to introduce the elements of laying on of hands and the eucharist. One said, "I anoint babies and confirmands and lay hands on them. The adults in general shy away. We will get there in time. I use this with new members." Another pastor said, "This congregation experienced for the first time the laying on of hands at baptism of infants/children (did not use oil). I think in time they will be comfortable with the new liturgies. This unification may come slowly. They are open to new liturgies. Openness is half the battle."

While few pastors have been brave enough to include communion for infants several wish to do so. While the liturgy recommends eucharist after baptism and confirmation there is no suggestion concerning *how* this can be done with infants.

The United Methodists have affirmed the open table, often without a well formed theological rationale. This stance is reflected in the new study document. The latter links communion with baptism but does not exclude any person from the table. "When Christians gather to celebrate the Eucharist, we remember the grace given to us in our baptism and partake of the spiritual food necessary for sustaining and fulfilling the promises of salvation. The Lord's table should be open to all who respond to Christ's love and acceptance, regardless of age. Persons receiving communion who are not baptized should be counseled and nurtured toward baptism at an early time."[13] Such an open stance makes it possible for United Methodists to look beneath the rituals to the essential meanings being symbolized. Such an atmosphere augers well for the reception of fresh understandings and practices.

Current practices concerning confirmation move in the direction of seven to thirteen weeks of confirmation education led by pastors or Christian educators, with lay teams often, climaxing at Pentecost in the service of confirmation. The most common time is seventh or eighth grade with sixth grade and ninth grade also urged. Some churches have year long confirmation education and a few have two–year programs. One church, the Centenary United Methodist in Winston–Salem, North Carolina, has a three–stage confirmation program for seventh, ninth and twelfth graders built on a program inaugurated at North Broadway United Methodist Church in Columbus, Ohio. This program was developed with the understanding that confirmation should be a repeatable experience which correlates with growing self–understanding and deeper commitment of Christian faith and discipleship.

Several churches are integrating Christian education for children with preparation for confirmation. One pastor wants intentional preparation to start in the fifth grade and the decision making to be invited during the eighth grade. Some churches are consciously working with children on their understanding of baptism, eucharist, and their upcoming confirmation not only in church school but in the corporate worship. The latter takes place especially at the times of the infant baptism, children's sermons, and "children in worship at the celebration of the Baptism of our Lord." One pastor said, "I make a point of bringing children forward in church and explaining to them, and the adults present, what is going to happen, every time we have a baptism."

At the time of our study most United Methodists seemed to be employing denominational resources for confirmation education. Several churches have confirmation programs for senior high or adults who have missed the earlier period of preparation. Some of these programs are shorter in duration, but others are up to thirteen weeks in length. A few pastors would prefer confirmation education to be for older youth or young adults. One pastor chose age twenty as the optimum time for confirmation in terms of independent thinking and action as well as appropriateness for vocational and personal commitment.

One area where United Methodists are moving out adventurously is in baptismal affirmation or renewal. Many local churches as well as district and annual conferences are experimenting with services of reaffirmation. Using water, either in the sprinkling of the congregation or in signing of the cross on the forehead, pastors are calling the faithful to remember their baptisms and to recommit themselves to extend Christ's ministry into the world.

Over 90 percent of the respondents from the United Methodist Church are already celebrating baptismal renewal services either regularly or upon the occasion of the baptism of others, the commissioning of persons to serve, at the Easter Vigil, Epiphany, Pentecost, even Christmas morning ("a person asked to make a renewal commitment. We used the baptismal renewal service."). The high percentage employing reaffirmation is probably due to the publishing of alternate services on an experimental basis, prior to official acceptance. This fact has made United Methodists more open to seeing confirmation, or public profession of faith, as a repeatable experience clearly related to baptism.

Such renewal experiences must not be interpreted as rebaptism and the use of water in the liturgies is to be made in a way that clearly makes a distinction between baptism and reaffirmation or renewal of one's baptism.

United Methodists commissioned the development of new confirmation resources in advance of the decision of the General Conference of the church to approve the recommendations found in the study document on baptism. The resources are in harmony with the new liturgies concerning baptism and confirmation in the new United Methodist Hymnal and the new United Methodist Book of Worship. The new resources are also in line with the general direction of the study document's recommendations: namely, that baptism engrafts the person into the body of Christ and into full membership, that confirmation through the laying on of hands is an integral part of the baptismal initiation along with the celebration of the eucharist, that confirmation be seen as a repeatable experience during life's pilgrimage, appropriate when the individual affirms publicly his or her baptismal covenant and is strengthened for unique ministry.

The new confirmation series is entitled *Follow Me* (Nashville: Cokesbury, 1993). The student's book is written by a team of authors. The new materials explicitly indicate that there will be various times in life when the baptized will become aware of the need for baptismal affirmation experiences both as individuals and as members of the community of faith. Each church will periodically need to reassess its faithfulness and its ministry focus. A *Handbook For Pastors, Parents, Congregations* has a section on the theology of confirmation and five study sessions concerning baptism and confirmation for use with the education work area, the council on ministries, and congregational groupings. There is a section concerning various specific ways parents may take an active role in the process, including the invitation for them to consider the reaffirmation of their own baptismal covenant. There is also a Leader's Kit with detailed basic and supplementary lesson plans, plus audio and video tapes.

The new resources are organized around thirteen core modules in which an action/reflection approach is taken. Starting with a weekend spiritual retreat, the young adolescent participants seek to create a community of trust, care and renewal over a period of time selected by a team of pastor, lay leaders, parents, and participants. Time options are of thirteen weeks, twenty-six weeks, one or two full years. Other options are possible. Supplemental resources are included, making possible not only an expanded program but also a second confirmation experience for the participants when they become juniors or seniors in high school. Such an inclusion of supplemental materials and designs "put teeth" in the concept of confirmation as a repeatable strengthening of the spirit within the individuals involved as well as within the congregation.

Those wishing a deeper study of Methodist theology and practice concerning baptism and confirmation will be greatly enriched by reading Gayle Felton's *This Gift of Water: The Practice and Theology of Baptism Among Methodists in America* (Nashville: Abingdon, 1992).

Confirmation/Commissioning in the Presbyterian Church U.S.A.

In our study of Presbyterian practice, conducted just prior to the publication of their new curriculum resources, we found almost no use of the unified initiation for infants or adults. However, Presbyterian studies affirm baptism as the engrafting of the child into the body of Christ. The Table of the Lord is, therefore, open to children after baptism rather than after confirmation. Children from age three, in some parishes, are prepared to receive the eucharist through the regular church school curriculum and in special six–week sessions on communion in the second grade. Another clear trend is the practice of baptismal reaffirmation or baptismal renewal. Such a trend was greatly stimulated by the publication of liturgical resources for use in renewal services (1985). As previously noted, the new book of worship also has several baptismal or renewal services addressing special situations in the life of faith.[14]

While most confirmation classes are geared for seventh to ninth graders with patterns from six weeks plus a retreat to two full years, some churches are emphasizing baptismal classes for new and expectant parents, reconfirmation classes for young adults and older adults, and reconfirmation sessions and celebrations for the parents of adolescent confirmands. The latter is being done as one pastor said, "because I'm tired of 'giving kids faith' while families sit on their . . ."

Presbyterians generally have placed a high value on theological education for both clergy and laity. Such an emphasis can be seen in many of their confirmation education programs. In addition to regular attendance at sessions, young people are expected to complete home work, participate in service projects, write a personal statement of faith "reflecting trinitarian faith in their own language," pass a written examination and give an oral presentation before the church session. Even though these academic standards are often met, there has been considerable expression of frustration with past confirmation understandings and practices. Along with the usual complaints—low participant motivation, lack of parental support, confirmation prior to appropriate mental, emotional, and spiritual maturity, the problem of dropping out of church life immediately—after confirmation, leaders expressed unhappiness especially about previous confirmation curriculum resources. It is hoped that the call for "a decent confirmation curriculum from our national church" has been met with the publication of the new confirmation resources. Our study found early attention to the concept of confirmation/commissioning and the employing of the marks of membership found in the constitution of the *Book of Order*. This foundation became the organizing principle of the new confirmation resources published in 1990. The new approach is flexible, intentionally relational, and personal in tone. It leads to the affirmation of one's baptism and the commissioning of the person to move out in ministry within and beyond the church.

The new approach is called *Journey of Faith: Confirming and Commissioning Young Members of the Church.* (Louisville: Presbyterian Publishing House, 1990). The resources were written by members of a team who studied confirmation theologically, historically, educationally, and liturgically until agreement was reached on the theology of confirmation and a design for confirmation/commissioning education. The new approach presents several formats from six weeks to thirty weeks with sessions from one to two hours each, depending upon the possibilities and goals of local leaders, sponsors, parents, and participants. A flexible Guide Book with session plans and resources in looseleaf form is rich in concrete possible session outlines and suggestions. Local leadership teams of pastors, educators, and lay leaders are invited to start with a "Faith Review" where seekers are invited to explore the possibility of beginning a faith journey which can culminate in confirmation/commissioning before the congregation. The Faith Review is to be a relaxed, personal time of getting acquainted at a level of depth which will set a very personal tone to the total confirmation/commissioning journey.

This initial event can be a two or three day retreat, an overnight and a day, an all-day meeting including breakfast, lunch, and supper, two or three weekly meetings of two hours each, or an intensive four–hour meeting with a meal. The focus is on sharing each person's faith story, creating a community of trust, and exploring the meaning and power of the confirmation/commissioning journey.

Confirmation is related clearly to baptism. Confirmation preparation is to make possible a response of faith in the form of a "public profession of personal faith in Jesus Christ as Lord and Savior." It is an occasion for youth to clarify what they have learned and experienced within the faith community in its worship, education, and caring, and to "decide for themselves to publicly affirm the vows taken on their behalf in baptism, if they were baptized as infants, or to profess their faith in Jesus Christ and be baptized."[15]

Recognizing that confirmation as an anointing or sealing in the Spirit was originally a part of a unified initiation which became split during the growth of the church, the Presbyterian approach still emphasizes that "the intimate relationship of confirmation/commissioning to baptism points to the gift of the Holy Spirit. . . . Confirmation/commissioning is an opportunity to recognize the presence and power of the Spirit in maturing lives. The entire process presumes and should acknowledge the presence and activity of the Spirit" (p. 6). This emphasis on the Spirit is not dogmatic, however. There is no direction about who is empowered to seal with the Spirit and how the Spirit moves to the recipient. "The service of confirmation/commissioning can be a celebration of the mystery, joy, and support of the Spirit. Faith discoveries go beyond understanding, love that comes from growing relationships, and belief even in things unexplained—all point toward the presence of the Holy Companion."[16]

Emphasis on honest questing, exploring of doubts and questions as well as affirmations, is clear. Young adolescents and older adolescents will find sessions especially designed for their unique questions and life concerns. The workbook identifies specific concerns and asks the local team to decide which to use for what purposes. The matter of the proper age for confirmation/commissioning is left with the congregation in relation to the knowledge of the stages of growth normal for adolescents in general and of individual youth. "The question of the proper age for confirmation/commissioning can be answered with no more certainty than can the question of when and where the Spirit will move! However, after analyzing factors of faith development, the period of middle adolescence is recommended (ninth and tenth grades). This is true because in middle adolescence youth are not only able to think concretely but can also deal with abstract ideas and hypothetical situations. They can imagine possibilities. Such thinking makes 'theologizing' possible. Ability to think abstractly is necessary for one to think about the meaning of the resurrection, of Jesus' presence today, or of his being the Word from the beginning of time." Middle adolescents "have a greater degree of independence and personal freedom in decision making than do younger adolescents."[17] Moreover, they are better candidates for commissioning to take up the mission of the church in concrete ways—not only personally but corporately. Young people are confirmed and commissioned to become involved in the full life and governance of the church, through intercessory prayer for members of their family, the church, and the world, through service and outreach projects such as food distribution, through peace making and ecology programs, through efforts to bring social justice.

The examination of the pilgrim's faith has been retained but moved away from a test of how well youth have learned matters of belief and practice and toward a relational session between youth and elders. The session includes an evening meal, dialogue between one elder and one young person about faith and mission, opportunity for drawing symbols or making banners (by both youth and elders) concerning their perception of the church's nature and mission, a time for youth to ask questions of elders and vice versa, and a time for sponsors to share what they have experienced as fellow pilgrims with their young people.

At the confirmation/commissioning service youth accept Christ's call to be involved responsibly in the ministry of the church and to affirm the "marks of membership." These include: proclaiming the good news, taking part in the common life and worship, praying and studying scripture and the faith of the church, supporting the work of the church through the giving of money, time, and talents, participating in the governing responsibilities of the church, demonstrating a new quality of life, responding through service to others, living responsibly in personal, family, vocational, political, cultural, and social relationships, and working for peace, justice, freedom, and human fulfillment.

Leadership teams of pastors, educators, parents, sponsors, elders, and the youth themselves are invited to do a lot of planning and caring along the way so that each congregation will develop a unique way of meeting real needs.

United Church of Christ

There is clearly a movement in the United Church of Christ to relate confirmation to baptism and to emphasize confirmation as the public affirmation of one's baptism. There is some yearning for the more inclusive stance of the unified initiation (baptism, confirmation, and eucharist) in infancy or whenever baptism takes place, but this is not happening very often. Baptismal renewal experiences are celebrated in the new liturgy for new members who have transferred into the community of faith, at the times of infant baptism, confirmation, and at certain festivals of the church year, especially Easter. Some churches have baptismal renewal annually. One pastor said, "I ask the entire congregation to respond to their baptismal promises, and invite them to come forward to receive a watermark cross on their forehead, saying 'Remember your baptism'."

One of the difficulties being reported by U.C.C. pastors and educators is the strong Reformation tradition of associating communion with confirmation rather than baptism. Many churches still insist on eucharist being received only after confirmation. The church's official position has changed to emphasize baptism as the engrafting of the person fully into the body of Christ which includes invitation to an open table for all baptized persons. The struggle between those who approve of the change and those who are committed to the reformed tradition is sometimes resolved by compromise. One pastor writes that the congregation studied the theology of baptism, eucharist, and confirmation and "decided to adhere formally to the Reformed tradition in which communion is post-confirmation. Families who bring other practices are welcome to participate in the sacrament, however, according to their perspective. The pastor/teacher is responsible for communication with these persons to assure them of the 'open' posture of the church according to 'conscience'." Another pastor, recognizing this resistance to change said "I think denominations need to emphasize the openness of the Lord's Table to all, and educate these churches."

It can be said that the United Church of Christ has made a serious effort to educate congregations about the new understandings, especially parents and congregational leaders, concerning baptism and the openness of communion to baptized children.

Confirmation still tends to take place after one to two year programs of confirmation education, following the official curriculum, *Confirming Our Faith* and the new *Book of Worship*. Confirmation camp experiences have been especially successful and are required in several churches.

One confirmation camp has a fifteen–year history in Ohio and is firmly established as a rich resource which moves the confirmation program to levels of depth, personally and corporately, which are less possible in class formats so common in local churches.

While many leaders in the U.C.C. would like to see confirmation as a repeatable experience throughout the life span there is limited emphasis on young adult confirmation related to a sense of vocation or to commitment to embrace a particular occupation or voluntary service as a form of ministry.

The unified initiation is discussed and understood, but it is not often practiced. Several respondents, however, indicate a desire for the church to move in that direction.

While lay teachers and counselors, along with church leaders and parents, are involved in confirmation education, pastors seem clearly to be the primary teachers. In several situations religious educators take a major role, however. In other cases, lay mentors are recruited, often from the consistory, to relate to confirmands personally.

As with other denominations, United Church of Christ respondents lamented confirmation being seen as "joining the church" rather than baptism being perceived as initiation into the body of Christ. This issue, of course, is related to the difficulty of nurturing congregations to open the eucharist to children before confirmation. Several leaders are calling for a more personal approach to confirmation education with an emphases on spiritual formation, meditation and prayer. One United Church pastor reports that he believed in the latter so much that he designed his own confirmation program based on creation-centered spirituality. "What I wanted to do was to give the participants an experience of the affirmation of their personhood and their divinity through an intentionally whole-brain educational approach."[18] Emphasizing a positive picture concerning the potential of every confirmand as one possessing a divine spark within, called to be a co-creator with God in a world which is a global village, interdependent and interconnected, the program seeks to enable each person to see himself or herself as a gifted steward in God's world. It also seeks to help youth to affirm belief in Jesus Christ and the continuing ministry of the body of Christ as transforming forces in our world. Using silence, journaling, imaging, and story telling, patterns of meditation are developed in dialogue with biblical and theological stimulus. "These meditative, creative, silent times were far and away the most popular part of the class. In the middle of all the busyness of our world and of being an adolescent, this gave them a chance to be quiet and centered. It is very powerful. Spiritual breakthroughs occur on a regular basis."[19]

The relating of confirmation to a sense of vocation and a commitment to a particular form of ministry in the world is not too clearly seen. Several leaders have made service projects a part of confirmation preparation, however. Some focus on the importance of helping youth discover their gifts and offer them. One leader stated, "Gifts for ministry are emphasized. . . . The sharing of gifts is affirmed and celebrated . . . in order to bless our world."

Another woman pastor was especially hungry for an approach to confirmation, with supporting resources, which would encourage faith development and spiritual formation. She described a condition often identified with confirmation education where "'wise' pastors and lay persons pour information into the heads of the confirmands. This does not lead to faith development but rather to bored, resentful young people." For this reason she has found the camp setting to be conducive to the creation of a personal, supportive environment for opening up and pursuing the issues of spiritual and faith development. "Our congregation requires that our youth attend Confirmation Camp, paying 2/3 of the cost."[20]

United Church of Canada

The view of confirmation is firmly anchored in baptism. "At baptism, all join the church. As youth or adults, they renew their baptismal faith that others had affirmed earlier on their behalf. At this time, these youth or adults may go through a lengthy process of spiritual reflection and self-examination before making public affirmation. People may also renew their faith when they transfer their membership to another congregation, or at an important stage in their life journey."[21]

A strong emphasis is placed on the meaning of baptism as the engrafting of the child into the ministering community. In order to bring such a stance to fruition a program of parent preparation has been inaugurated. While not as lengthy as similar programs by Lutheran churches, for instance, the approach is theologically sound and inclusive of the whole family as well as sponsors and representatives of the congregation. The four hour- two session program is well constructed and includes the use of a video, *Baptism: Beginning and Belonging: A Congregation's Celebration*. The resource also includes materials for use directly with children (four years and older) who are to be baptized. These sessions help the children to understand that their parents are taking baptismal vows on their behalf.

The focus on baptism as "the visible sign of incorporation into Christ and of membership in the Christian Church" has made for clarity concerning confirmation. The baptismal liturgy is built around the unified initiation. Members of the faith community are given the opportunity to reaffirm their baptismal faith during the baptismal celebration but also at other times during the church year, especially at Easter. Confirmation, thus, can be repeated when persons who were baptized as children come to new understandings of the claims of the Christian gospel.

Parts II and III of the series prepare young people and adults respectively for public profession of their baptismal faith. The curriculum for youth has fifteen sessions which are geared to the needs and perceptions of young people in interaction with the life of faith as seen in the new creed of the United Church of Canada. The first ten sessions explore the nature of faith implied in the creed and the last five sessions focus on the nature of confirmation as a public declaration of one's baptismal faith and the vows which occur in the actual service. The adult curriculum, leading to adult baptism or baptismal renewal, is built on the essentials reflected in the journey of faith taken from Advent to Christmas, Lent and Easter, and the celebration of baptismal faith implied. These resources are relational in tone, creative in methodologies, and flexible in style.

In our study of actual practice in the United Church of Canada, we discovered that the new stance reflected in *Baptism and Renewal of Baptismal Faith* (for optional use in The United Church of Canada) is indeed an optional pattern.[22] While several churches are using the new approach including the curricular resources for parents of infants and the confirmation material for youth and adults, many other churches are employing other denominational resources or have developed their own designs and resources. The optional resources do seem to have made an impact in that the theological perspective of the new resources comes through often even in churches where other resources are still in use.

There is a solid trend toward the preparation of parents for infant baptism. Numerous churches are using the unified initiation with infants and children, and also with adolescents and adults. Several churches not reporting such practice say that they are "moving in that direction." One pastor said, "No, but I favor it." Another said that it was not the practice but he is moving in that direction "but doing so deliberately and slowly so that it is especially understood and appreciated for its full significance." Still another stated that the unified initiation was being used "because otherwise baptism is an incomplete sacrament." Several are including the confirmation rite of laying on of hands but not celebrating the eucharist with children or youth during the liturgy. Congregation response in those churches which have moved in the direction of the unified initiation and the reaffirmation of baptism (at different stages of life) has been positive. Comments included: "Great. It is a bonding," "Quite positive and members are appreciative of seeing the unity of the three," "Good, taken for granted now," "Some questions, but a growing sense that 'adult' profession of faith is not the gate to the table," "Baptism (unified) is the rite of initiation at whatever age or stage. The congregation appreciates the variety and flexibility."

The United Church of Canada does have a history of serving the eucharist only to those confirmed. More recent theological thinking has highlighted the full inclusion of children at the Table after baptism. One respondent says, "We stress when a child is baptized they become a full member and as soon as they wish (we suggest four years and up) they are encouraged to be part of the eucharist celebration." Other pastors report that the Table is open to all whether baptized or not. One church invites "all who hunger and thirst after righteousness." One pastor says that she believes that you "don't have to have been confirmed or even baptized to come to the Table—although that is the norm. Exclusiveness was not our Lord's Way." Some report tension on this point between "the new and the old guard." Several are including education concerning baptism and communion with children and their parents in order to help understanding grow along with the joy of full participation in the liturgy.

Few United Church programs have agreed upon standards for confirmation beyond attendance and participation. A few have included the requirement of service and the importance of a sponsor or the assigning of an elder for the purpose of the exploration of the adolescents' beliefs and intended roles as a part of Christ's ministering body in the world.

Few churches are linking decisions concerning specific forms of ministry to education and liturgical celebrations for young adults or adults. Several responded, "No, but a good idea, however." One church reported that "each person is asked to list their special gifts and invited to present the Card (on which their gifts are listed) to the Chair of the congregation in the ceremony." Another church has selected a volunteer coordinator. "Young people are invited to make a commitment to a spe-

cific volunteer position. This is lots of work but it works out well."
Another states, "No, but a good idea. It calls us back to Elizabeth
O'Connor's *Insearch/Outreach* ideas. Thanks!."

The prevailing pattern in the United Church of Canada still appears to
be some prebaptismal education or counseling with parents prior to infant
baptism; an open table for children after baptism; adolescent confirmation programs for seventh, eighth, or ninth graders (of six to fifteen
weeks), and membership programs for young adults and adults of from
two to fifteen weeks. Some of the latter programs include adults who
have been confirmed and wish to reaffirm their baptismal covenant.
Several pastors wish to see confirmation as a repeatable experience at
"all ages and stages" of life when the individual wishes to make a public
commitment and "to deepen and refocus faith."

The leadership of baptismal or confirmation education is still heavily in the hands of pastors but with increasing involvement of laity,
parents, sponsors, and church elders. Several teams have been formed
of lay leaders, pastors, and Christian educators along with parental participation at times. Such teams appear to be highly productive and
affirmed by the participants and the congregations involved.

United Church of Canada pastors and leaders are feeling quite positive
about more recent moves to make baptism the entry fully into the body of
Christ and to adopt unified initiation and the possibility of multiple opportunities for deepening and reaffirming faith throughout life. Frustrations are
still present. The "joining the church" mentality at confirmation is also
present. The idea that those confirmed as adolescents have "graduated"
from the church is very much alive. The recognition that older youth, young
adults, and adults can and need to participate in education that is linked to
some form of concrete decision to be in ministry is growing. There is
increasing awareness of the potential of the renewal of one's baptismal
covenant before the congregation and the focusing of this commitment
toward the use of specific gifts for ministry through occupation or volunteer patterns. Much remains to be done, nevertheless, to transform this
growing awareness into engaging educational and liturgical expressions.

An Inventory of Attitudes and Practices
A Summary of Major Trends

1. *The so-called "unified initiation," i.e., initiation as baptism/hand lay-*
   ing/anointing/eucharist is a feature of tradition and current discus-

sion which is widely understood if not practiced. This awareness showed up in several forms, but especially in a conviction that confirmation is something rooted in baptism. There is a strong will to pull them together. As one pastor affirmed, "If you wash and cleanse, you must give new life."

There are many kinds of problems in achieving a unified initiation. Episcopal traditions calling for the presence of the bishop at confirmation were seen as frustrating to some. Other respondents reported relaxation of "Episcopal necessity," in some dioceses. The relation of eucharist to initiation is also a difficulty for many. Some pastors wish to celebrate initiation with the Supper, but think this an "innovation" people would neither understand nor appreciate. Some see the failure to include the eucharist as a serious problem in the basic understanding of initiation. Numerous questions arose concerning the unified initiation as sequential initiation. Is laying on of hands and/or anointing a rite which should be repeated? If so, at what times, or stages, relative to what relationships to the community of faith or faith's evolution? What is the shape of this pilgrimage process? What are the possibilities for engaging education and liturgical experiences throughout life?

2. *We found a high level of awareness of the Catholic program called The Rite of Christian Initiation of Adults.* Many Protestants are unaware of this program, but across a broad ecumenical spectrum it is having a significant influence on the conception of initiation, the scope of catechesis which initiation into Christ's fellowship requires, and the liturgical life helpful to a catechumenate pilgrimage.

3. *Renewal of baptism, confirmation or baptismal affirmation as repeatable experiences are becoming more common as liturgical/spiritual actions in the churches.* This is not universally so. It was commonly reported by United Methodists, Episcopalians, United Church of Canada, the Presbyterians, the United Church of Christ but less so by Lutherans or Roman Catholics. In the developing understanding of many Lutherans, confirmation is a lifelong process. This has not been worked out systemically in life and liturgy, however. Roman Catholics differentiate between baptismal renewal, which many affirm, and confirmation, which is a one–time sacrament. Some Roman Catholics are beginning to question the adequacy of their theological view of confirmation and are exploring a stage theory of confirmation. There is general resistance to any movement away from "confirmation" as con-

fession of faith in adolescence. Issues of *what* should be done *when* remain much discussed, but elimination of adolescent commitment seems little sought. Indeed in some respects, and perhaps surprising to some Protestants, the direction of Catholic "reform" of confirmation appears generally toward its celebration in "late adolescence" rather than at or about seven years of age. There is considerable sentiment for the unified initiation in infancy while still retaining the liturgy of commitment in adolescence. One priest responded, "I would like to see the Roman Catholic church celebrate confirmation with infant baptism, and then celebrate confirmation throughout life (beginning in adolescence) as a renewal of baptism's celebration of the gift of the Spirit."

4. *There is widespread general agreement that affirmation of baptism or confirmation should take place in late adolescence or even early adulthood rather than in early adolescence.* This "movement" is advancing and where it is not it is a yearning in the minds of many responsible for confirmation programs. There is, of course, major frustration with confirmation as "graduation from church," and one can see that some of the appeal of a later confirmation is simply to postpone graduation as a way of "holding on to the kids." More generally the desire to confirm older adolescents or young adults is a concern to correlate the availability of the commitment liturgy and the personal/cultural process of fundamental life-choices. As one Episcopalian reported, "Perhaps if people participated in it as adults it would take on more meaning and could be linked to people's growing understanding of themselves as ministers in the world."

5. *Substantialistic and individualistic understandings of confirmation and the renewal of baptism are being replaced by phenomenological/relational and communal ones.* A pastor wrote, "Our understanding of confirmation is moving much more toward being a celebration of the gift of the Holy Spirit within the community. The focus being on *gift* and *community* rather than individual." Complaints typically refer to pastoral concerns: "We are not succeeding in relating sacrament to general ministry." One reads in the responses more about life in community and mission in the world than about individual salvation and personal destiny. Concern for the "personal" commitment is certainly expressed with effort obviously given to help youth explore personal/spiritual dimensions of the life of faith. One can read in our survey responses that a balance of communal and individual expressions of

Christian commitment is seriously attempted. What is especially apparent though is the emphasis on building the faith community. This includes the use of retreats, field trips, and a variety of service oriented group activities.

There is much more about grace than works. "We see the sacrament as being a celebration of the free gift of God's love. It is not something which is earned by passing an exam of knowledge." Relating human/Spirit gifts and graces to vocations in the world emerges as the primary theme. This theme, while dominant, is accompanied on the part of some by a strong sense of frustration and failure.

6. *Service has become one of the strong ways of presenting the theme of mission.* Reading, studying, lecture, and discussion are being augmented in many situations by a significant element of active, personally involving service in church and community. One suspects, and can read between the lines to notice, that service is sometimes little more than another requirement to be met for graduation. In many situations though great integrity and ingenuity is obviously involved to develop projects of service which can involve youth significantly and confront them with the realities of the need and the potent grace in faith's mission.

7. *There is growing conviction in the ecumenical church that baptism, not confirmation, is the engrafting of persons into the family of Christ.* There is ferment at present about initiation, and it takes quite different shapes in the different communions. Matters are by no means settled, but reactions in our inventory show a clear conviction among many that baptism is *belonging* in the church. This is an important shift for denominations where baptism has been traditionally understood as significant but preparatory to belonging. While the conviction about baptism's meaning is apparently clarifying for many, questions of how to *do* what baptism is persist as a difficulty.

We may know that Christians are made not born, but we are unsure about the means. What is encouraging in the inventory is the clarity on some issues, like baptism as belonging, and the persistence of the search for a way.

8. *The conviction that eucharist should be withheld until confirmation is apparently a failed idea.* Few are withholding communion until confirmation. Postponing admission to the Table until confirmation was usual among Lutherans but our responses indicate that some Lutherans are admitting children to the sacrament at early ages. Some in the

United Church of Christ tradition find themselves conflicted on this issue. There is in the Reformed churches a tradition that connects confirmation with communion more than with baptism. Even so, there is increasing understanding in the United Church of Christ that baptism is belonging, with the Table communion open to all baptized, including children. This view is challenged by many for whom confirmation is still basically a matter of "joining the church." A compromise is emerging as typical where individual families may decide this matter for themselves with children permitted by their parents to participate in the eucharist either after baptism or after confirmation. While confirmation is a major liturgical celebration of membership in the Episcopal church, many parishes open the Table to children after baptism, again, in communication with parents.

9. *There is a general appeal for a richer bank of curriculum resources and educational designs.* There is a great deal of borrowing going on. People are finding resources that make sense to them wherever they can. Denominational loyalties are bent. Many create much of their own material. The situation has improved with several denominations producing new material, but probably the resources will continue to be shared.

10. *While pastors are still the central teachers many confirmation teaching teams are emerging.* There was some complaint in our responses about the burden of confirmation ministry and the "pastor does it all" expectation. There was also considerable evidence of *team* approaches to this ministry. Church staff and lay people in many churches are collaborating to share ideas, resources, and tasks in the effort to challenge young people to Christian commitment.

11. *The use of adult mentors is increasingly evident.* Individual young people are linked to specific adult mentors who help to engage the youth in "life involvement" discipleship patterns. These typically replace "right learning" patterns. The use of mentors is spoken of very positively in our inventory.

12. *Conviction was expressed that the confirmation education ought not to be a rehash of all that should have been learned in church programs of Christian education and in the family up to the time of confirmation.* Confirmation should be about faith commitment in actual life. While this was stated the complaint was sometimes made that the enculturation in the faith was often very shallow. "Students seem to have so little foundation to build on that they are confirmed with an

almost superficial understanding of the Christian tradition and what it means to be a member of the body of Christ." Getting into confirmation presupposes what? This question troubles.

13. *Questions about sacramentality, about the meaning of sacrament itself sometimes emerged.* Answers have been clear, even *pat* for most Christians for a long time. Ongoing ecumenical discussions have complicated the issues for some, particularly as they may find ideas beyond their own tradition inviting. Tucked into issues about sacramentality is the question of what to call this "sacrament," if it is a sacrament: confirmation, profession of baptismal covenant, baptismal renewal, etc. These alternatives to "confirmation" are titles whose intent is to connect the rite to baptism.

14. *There is a significant emphasis on infant baptism and strong programs of preparation for parents and the congregation.* Excellent resources for parent education and congregational participation are emerging from the United Church of Christ, the United Church of Canada, the ELCA, the Episcopalians, the Roman Catholics. It is clear in the response to our inventory, however, that infant baptism continues to raise questions for many in denominations which have traditionally followed the practice. More often it is the complaint that we need to be doing a much better job of baptizing infants. In part the difficulty is seen as indiscriminate practice, something out of hand as a problem too big to handle. This is viewed as a difficulty especially in large churches. Some see the problem mainly as a matter of deficient parent involvement, education, and commitment. In situations where pastors affirm the practice of baptizing infants they sometimes feel that the culture of the church does not support the practice in terms of follow-up and genuine engagement with the baptized child. At the same time, it is clear that the so-called "norm" of adult baptism is not operationally threatening the practice of infant baptism. While the impulse for reforms seems strong, especially for Roman Catholics, there seems little impulse for revolt. Many respondents commented upon *parent involvement* in confirmation. We noted more complaints about the lukewarm support of parents than one would expect. Busy at school and in extra-curricular activities many young people see the confirmation program of the church as much too demanding and time-consuming. Apparently some parents, in large measure, agree.

Obviously many more things could be said concerning responses to the sort of index of attitudes and practices we compiled. These highlights seemed to us to be particularly worth noting.

NOTES

1. The Archdiocese of Milwaukee, following the decision of the Episcopal Conference of the U.S.A. that the age for confirmation be determined by the individual bishop, announced that the minimum age for Confirmation is sixteen years of age. A recent survey of diocesan policies, done by the Diocese of Youngstown, found that 51 percent of the dioceses that responded have followed the Milwaukee pattern, celebrating confirmation during high school, grades nine to twelve. One hundred thirty-one dioceses (79 percent) responded to the survey.
Archbishop Rembert S. Weakland stated in his introduction to the new policy, that the pastoral concern for a new vitality in the faith responses of youth in our troubled and confusing time, led him to make the change to late adolescent confirmation (from confirmation at age seven or much later in adulthood with the unified initiation). Such a change, he mentioned, was in response to the guidance of the Holy Spirit. "If one believes that the Spirit animates the Church and these many movements within it, then one can see the emphasis on confirmation today and the struggles within the Church to articulate its theological and pastoral impact as truly a gift of the Spirit to our times." *Confirmation Guidelines*. Archbishop of Milwaukee, 345 North 95th Street, P.O. Box 2018 Milwaukee, Wisconsin 1981. Page 1.
2. See John Westerhoff and William Willimon, *Liturgy and Learning Through the Life Cycle* (New York: Seabury, 1980).
3. See Daniel Stevick, *Baptismal Moments: Baptismal Meanings* (Church Hymnal Press, 1987).
4. Also see, *The Catechumenal Process: Adult Initiation and Formation for Christian Life and Ministry* (New York: Church Hymnal Corp., 1990).
5. *The Confirmation Ministry Task Force Report* (The Evangelical Lutheran Church of America, 1993), p. 6.
6. Larry J. Smith, *Shared Journeys: Mentoring Guide* (Evangelical Lutheran Church of America, 1993), p. 2.
7. *The Confirmation Ministry Task Force Report*, p. 4.
8. Ibid., p. 9.
9. See these and other models in *Six Models of Confirmation Ministry*, by Ken Smith (Division for Congregational Life - ELCA, 8765 West Higgins Road, Chicago, Illinois 60631, 1992).
10. *By Water and the Spirit: A Study of Baptism for United Methodists* (Nashville: General Board of Discipleship, 1993), p. 44.
11. *The United Methodist Hymnal: Book of United Methodist Worship* (Nashville: The United Methodist Publishing House, 1989), p. 49.
12. Ibid., p. 13.
13. *By Water and the Spirit : A United Methodist Understanding of Baptism*, p. 48.
14. See *Holy Baptism and Services for the Renewal of Baptism: Supplemental Liturgical Resources* (Philadelphia: Westminster, 1985).
15. *Journeys of Faith: Confirming and Commissioning Young Members of the Church*, p. 3.
16. Ibid., p. 61.
17. Ibid, p. 19.

18. Bruce M. Morrison, "Confirmation: A New Vision," in *New Forms Exchange*, United Church Board for Homeland Ministries, 132 West 31st Street, New York, New York.

19. Ibid., p. 3.

20. Letter from the Rev. Ann Kear, Pastor of the Trinity United Church of Christ, McCutchenville, Ohio.

21. *Preparation for Baptism and Renewal of Baptismal Faith*, Part I. Preparing Parents for Baptism of their children by Margaret Spencer (The United Church of Canada, 1988), p. 5.

22. *Baptism and Renewal of Baptism* (Division of Missions in Canada. The Task Group on Christian Initiation, Toronto, 1986).

PART III

CONFIRMATION/AFFIRMATION OF BAPTISM AS REPEATABLE: EDUCATIONAL ISSUES AND DESIGNS

INTRODUCTION

Sacramental theology has undergone what Joseph Martos referred to as "massive shifts" in the last four or five decades.[1] Under the influence of convincing theological leadership scholars like Edward Schillebeeckx and Karl Rahner and the authority of Vatican Council II, the Catholic community has generally moved away from scholastic theories of sacrament which stressed ecclesial authority, institution by Christ, and substantialist causality of grace. The direction of theology has been toward more existentialist and phenomenological understandings which rely heavily on scriptural language for interpretation and authority, upon conceptions of symbol, and upon human experience in sacramental liturgy and life. All of this, as we have pointed out elsewhere, has been revolutionary, and has spawned an abundance of theological work concerning sacrament and a rich liturgical labor which has affected almost every community of Christians. The various theological and ecclesial families—within the denominations and across denominations—have contributed special perspectives. They tend to have some elements in common. We summarize these as seeing: (1) life itself as sacramental; (2) sacraments as symbols of the world as God's gift to humanity; (3) God's grace made visible in Jesus Christ; 4) the church as the sacrament of Christ; (5) sacramental event as a presence of Christ in the church and the world; (6) sacraments as power now, Spirit energy evoking commitment and action; (7) sacraments as kingdom events and signs of the future; (8) sacraments as human events, natural in the life cycle and nurturing of evolving faith.[2]

In the exploration of these images we fail to find new definitions of sacrament. What emerge are new visions or models of sacrament. The model we have presented in *The Sacraments in Religious Education and*

111

Liturgy[3] affirms the root of sacrament in God's Word in scripture and acknowledges the logic and validity of the evolution of sacramental life in the dynamic tradition of Christian people.

The term "sacrament" finds its way into Christian usage as a translation of the New Testament word "mystery." Both of these terms are determinative in our understanding of sacrament. As *mystery*, sacrament eludes any final definition and is of the divine and is personal and dynamic. God's ineffable mystery, even the revelation of God in Christ, never ceases to be mystery. Its celebration, articulation, and realization in the life of the church, however, become occasions of affirmation and experience. The undefinable, even if undefinable, must become real in our human experience. This is the logic of the translation of *mystery* into *sacrament*. A living faith will express itself in reality in gestures of commitment. The translation which the early Latin theologians accomplished to express *mysterion* as *sacramentum* made, and still does make theological and pastoral sense.

In the Gospel of Mark a simple model of *mysterion* is pictured in the word of Jesus to the apostles about parables: "Unto you is given the *mysterion* of the Kingdom of God" (Mark 4:11). God's mystery is Christ as God's kingdom sign and Christ with his people. God's mystery is a revealing that is both personal and relational. In St. Paul's use of the term *mysterion* there is an extended social and evangelical perspective: "This is how one should regard us, as servants of Christ and stewards of the mysteries of God" (I Corinthians 4:1). In St. Paul's vision God's mystery alive in the world is a universal activity redeeming the world. Christians are not the exclusive possessors of this mystery. They are its servants and stewards. Sacrament as mystery is an idea and/or action which is rooted in these biblical images.

As *sacramentum*, sacrament is commitment in certain sign acts which function in the church as symbols of the *mysterion*. The sign-actions are as different as water or bread or touching or forgiveness. They are commonly agreed upon gestures of commitment where the signs of God's mystery touch us as moments of choice when we decide for Christ, for one another, and for the world.

This image of sacrament as *mysterion/sacramentum* is not a definition. It is a picture that is scriptural and liturgical. Christians managed for a long time without a real definition of sacramentality. We do need an image, and one that encompasses both theology and tradition.

Within such an image of sacramentality, new possibilities emerge for our understanding and practice of individual sacraments. The rite of baptism, which eventually fell apart in the Western church into separate sacraments of water bath and laying on of hands, is being reunited. This reunion makes theological and pastoral sense to many, but for those who practice the baptism of infants and for all who see baptism as encompassing all of life, the movement of the rite to infancy can pose a problem. Public commitment and acknowledgement of faith is given no room for mature expression. So it is not surprising that the reform which has recovered the "unified" initiation has not motivated many to seek to abolish a separate and, in the case of infant initiation, "later" event of confirmation or affirmation of baptism. In the minds of many it is logical that such an affirmation should be a repeatable sacrament or sacramental occasion which we might celebrate at any time when the renewal of baptismal understanding and commitment would be appropriate. We attempt to specify some of the occasions when such a sacrament might be logical. These are educational and liturgical opportunities which we suggest as occurring at natural stages of life and faith evolution.

There are times in an individual's life story when changes in life, awareness of particular movements of God's Spirit in a person's life, or special relations or responsibilities in the family of faith prompt renewal of the primary commitments of baptism. Several Protestant denominations, as we have seen, have moved to or toward such a conclusion about the repeatable nature of what we have in the past called confirmation. The call for this development is also common in Catholicism. We noticed it in our survey. The conclusion of Craig Cox is representative: "I propose that we rethink the tradition of having only one celebration of confirmation in life. Would it not be more appropriate to celebrate the ongoing sacramental reality of 'confirming faith' in several stages at critical junctions in life, with a catechesis and rituals appropriate to the needs of people in those periods?"[4] Cox then proposes that the "present anointing with chrism at the baptism of infants be expanded into the first stage of confirmation. . . . This would enable the church to reunite the ancient ritual of initiation, for, as in the Eastern tradition, first eucharist should be celebrated here as well . . . The ritual of the unified celebration would also strongly emphasize the fact that it begins a process in which other stages follow, that the gift of God bestowed in baptism and confirmed for the life-stage of infancy (or at whatever life stage the newly baptized is experiencing) will require further growth and ongoing confirmation."[5]

Cox develops his scheme by projecting a second stage at the time of first communion and penance, a third stage in adolescence at the time of a rite of passage, a fourth stage at the young adult period where a "mature profession of faith" should occur, a fifth stage during the challenges of the so-called mid-life crisis where a deeper incorporation into Christ is needed, a sixth stage in older years where again new realities call for fresh recommitment. Cox continues to maintain a theologically "correct" view that confirmation is one sacrament. He does this using the analogy of holy orders, pointing to the revision of the Rite of Ordination (1968) wherein ordination is celebrated in three stages or grades but seen as a single sacrament which, along with baptism and confirmation, imprints a character on the soul, "that is, a kind of indelible spiritual sign whereby these sacraments cannot be repeated." Cox concludes that confirmation "is one sacrament, but I believe its very nature demands that it be celebrated in stages which lead to greater and greater fullness of initiation, just as the stages of holy orders lead to the fullness of priesthood. Thus, the sacramental character of confirmation and the definition of Florence and Trent are not insurmountable obstacles should the church judge that the Spirit is leading us to accept the proposed new practice of confirmation."[6]

We also have proposed that confirmation be a repeatable sacrament, but not necessarily a single sacrament. We see it as a sacrament similar to eucharist that can and should be repeated in response to evolutions in self-understanding and changes in personal response to God's living Spirit throughout life.

NOTES

1. Joseph Martos, *Doors to the Sacred* (New York: Doubleday, 1981), pp. 3-8.
2. Robert L. Browning and Roy A. Reed, *The Sacraments in Religious Education and Liturgy* (Birmingham, Ala.: Religious Education Press, 1985), pp.119-135.
3. Ibid.
4. Craig Cox, "Rethinking Confirmation: Possible Ways Found" in *Confirming the Faith of Adolescents*, ed. Arthur J. Kubik (New York: Paulist, 1991), p. 170.
5. Ibid., p. 171.
6. Ibid., p. 174.
7. Ibid., p. 175.

Chapter VI

INITIATION OF INFANTS
AND CHILDREN

Infancy—Confirmation As a Part of the Unified Initiation

The crucial nature of the first year of life to the subsequent development of a positive self-image and sense of well-being is exceedingly well documented. The profound importance of loving, trusting, dependable relationships between parents and the infant cannot be overstated. It is well established that children who have not developed a sense of trust in their environment, in those giving primary care, tend not to trust themselves, are plagued with what Karen Horney called basic anxiety, and develop circles under their eyes which reveal their loss of hope. Infants who have been deprived of these essentials of love and affirmation or who are physically or psychologically abused often do not survive the first year of life. They apparently give up. This phenomenon has been observed especially in infants abandoned during the Viet Nam war.

Erik Erikson's seminal work on the stages of ritualization and the stages of psycho-social development is unique in that he helps us see how love, trust, and care are communicated between mother and father and the infant in the most common, ordinary experiences of life. These experiences are so common that they take on the qualities of ritual. Love, acceptance, sensitivity to need, trust, and a life-giving spirit are communicated to the child through the very familiar rituals of nursing, elimination, dressing, undressing, greeting the child, naming, cleaning, lifting up and putting down. When a mother greets the child with a lilt in her voice, hugging and kissing the child, smiling instead of frowning, humming instead of complaining, the infant is receiving profound life-affirming messages which go deep into the slowly emerging sense of self.

Erikson found that it is through such everyday rituals of life that the infant can develop a sense of the numinous, an indwelling force or quality which animates or guides, evoking awe or reverence. Erikson saw this numinous sense as the very ground for higher forms of religious faith to be developed later. The importance of these family rituals again cannot be overstated. The rituals can communicate both positive and negative images of life and positive and negative images of self. These family–based rituals can and should be correlated closely with the great rituals of the faith community. The sacrament of baptism is a public celebration of God's unconditional love of the child and an engrafting of the infant into the family of Christ, making the child a full member of Christ's body, the church. Here we see a quality of eternal love, trust, acceptance, and righteousness which can empower both parents and the child.

Parents who are seeking to become priests to their own children have their own needs which the church vows to help them meet in baptism. These include support and inspiration, forgiveness for understandable times of frustration, feelings of inadequacy or resentment which tend to accompany the long period of special care-giving required for the nurture of a new offspring. Parents need to know that they are surrounded by members of the faith community who are with them on this important pilgrimage. They need to be strengthened themselves by a growing and lively faith in God's numinous presence in their lives. They are in a situation where it makes a huge difference if they see themselves as channels of God's blessing to the child or as persons who are essentially alone and limited by the finiteness of their own personal resources.

Erikson highlights the power of the sense of the numinous by comparing the higher religious rituals in which, as human beings, we feel the presence of God and "see" the meaning of life in the "face" of God with the everyday rituals in which the child sees the light of the parents' love and affirmation in the luminous eyes and face of the parent. Erikson believes that the way we relate to infants creates the very seedbed for religious faith. Through what he calls the "rituals of mutual recognition" between child and parents there develops a numinous quality which assures both a separateness transcended and a distinctiveness confirmed.

Here is a precondition for a sense of "I" as well as a sense of God's presence as the great "I am."[1]

James Fowler, following Jean Piaget, Erikson, Kohlberg, Selman, and others, agrees that these early rituals of life are very important and become the seedbed for the maturing forms of faith which can and should develop throughout life. He also agrees that sacramental life can be very important to the child and the parents as well as to the faith community seeking to support both. Fowler sees the first year of life as the time when the "seeds of trust, courage, hope, and love are fused in a undifferentiated way."[2] Fowler alerts us to the significance of the positive aspects of such beginning steps in the development of faith but also reminds us that the danger of this period is an excessive narcissism which can also develop within the child who has been "central" for a long period and must slowly discover that he or she is not the center of the universe.

In the unified rite of initiation we have an opportunity to help the child and the parents move out beyond themselves, to experience a sense of God's transcendence through the loving presence of the living Christ in the baptism by water, confirmation in the Spirit through the laying on of hands, anointing with oil or marking with the sign of the cross, and the celebration of the eucharist, where both child and parents join the whole body of Christ at the holy meal.

It is our thesis that the church's ministries before, during, and after infant baptism have the potential for engendering the central virtue of hope which must be the result of the first year of life, as Erik Erikson has so clearly pointed out. If the child and the parents have hope that they have meaning and a positive destiny, faithfulness is established and on its way, however unconscious their awareness is.

The key is the development of hope, as Robert Kegan says so well, "not the hopes they have or the hoping they do, but the hopes and hoping they are."[3]

Infant Baptism: Educational and Liturgical Experiences for Parents, Sponsors, the Congregation, and the Child.

Increasing numbers of pastors, educators, and laity are realizing the importance for ministry with the whole congregation that is resident within infant baptism. Robert Chiles, pastor of Worthington United Methodist Church in Worthington, Ohio, reported that one of his greatest frustrations has been the lack of a clear local church policy concerning infant baptism. He was continually receiving telephone calls from couples or individuals wishing to have their child baptized within two or three weeks because the grandparents were going to be visiting, or for some other reason. Often one or both parents were not members of the congregation and in several cases one or both parents themselves had not been baptized and were unfamiliar with the deeper meaning of baptism and the commitment implied. Without a clear set of guidelines having been worked through by the worship commission of the church this pastor was left with a very unsatisfactory situation. He found himself pressured to perform baptisms where parents had not been well prepared, where no sponsor had been selected to support and follow through with the child and the parents, where members of the congregation were ill-informed about the sacrament as well as their responsibility to nurture and strengthen those baptized to take up their own unique ministries.

In a ministry with an expectation of sixty to sixty-five infant baptisms each year, Chiles shared his frustration and anxiety with the worship commission. Together with study of the theological insights which are now available concerning the genesis of infant baptism and optional models of baptismal education and liturgical celebration, he and the commission established a new ministry around infant baptism. This ministry included a statement of the local church's understanding of baptism and its relation to confirmation and eucharist, a set of normal procedures for persons to follow in communicating with parents and the congregation concerning the purpose of infant baptism, and the expectations for counseling, education, and liturgical celebrations. Specific dates for infant baptisms in the total congregation were established, following the liturgical calendar (Advent, the First Sunday after Epiphany [the baptism of Jesus], Easter Vigil, Pentecost, etc.). Specific dates were established for educational and support sessions for the parents, sponsors, and other members of the congregation or family (older siblings, grandparents, god-parents or sponsors) in advance of the celebration of the sacrament. A subgroup of the worship commission was organized to administer and carry out the goals of this new ministry. These persons worked with the pastor, the worship commission, other pastors and the Christian educator in discussing: (1) the baptismal educational sessions; (2) a home visitation program to expectant parents or interested parents; (3) an "in-take" program in cooperation with the church secretary who was responsible for interpreting the new ministry to inquiring par-

ents and other persons; (4) the liturgies to be used in the actual celebration and how these were to be coordinated with the wider educational and music ministries of the church; (5) the recruiting of sponsors
who were to surround the parents and child with love and ongoing care;
(6) orientation and training of sponsors concerning the opportunities
for significant relationships as well as personal enrichment which can be
a by-product of sponsorship, including identification of ways to follow
through on commitment to the child and the parents within the life of the
family and the congregation; (7) ways to evaluate the new ministry and
to build in responsive and self-corrective patterns so that all participants
can grow in faith and be strengthened in spirit.

Attempts were made to recognize the exceptions to the normal expectations and to leave the final decision concerning such exceptions to the
pastors and the subgroup. These included emergencies the group considered related to the health of the child or the parents' situations where
only one parent will agree to the responsibilities inherent in the "priesthood of parenthood" implied in the vows at infant baptism, how miscarriage and still-birth situations should be handled, and the situation of
single or unmarried parents. The worship committee also considered
specific educational or liturgical resources to be employed from session to session in relation to the potential of each period of the church
year, including new materials, audio and video tapes, and books and
guides for parents and sponsors. Criteria were established concerning the
interplay between the lay visits, parental visits and counseling educational
sessions for parents, and the roles of sponsors and others and the preparation of the participants and the whole congregation for the liturgical celebration. Many of these issues were dealt with creatively in the written
guidelines which the commission on worship approved, published, and
distributed. Many of the issues called for some flexibility to be undertaken
without undermining the integrity and direction of the new ministry.
The worship commission members made their recommendations to the
Council on Ministries and the Administrative Board of the church for
thorough discussion and approval. A policy concerning baptism of youth
and adults will follow along with a position concerning the integration
of baptism, confirmation, and eucharist whenever initiation into the
faith community takes place.

The pastor and the worship commission members became excited and
inspired concerning the possible strengthening not only of the ministry
with parents but with the entire congregation. They also celebrated the fact

that the United Methodist Church has a commission studying the biblical, theological, liturgical, and educational issues related to baptism, that several other denominations are making similar studies, and that several new educational and liturgical resources have already been generated and published either as official materials or as alternate resources. They were pleased to be a part of a movement much broader than they originally suspected. They were surprised to learn that new liturgical materials concerning baptism were already published in the new United Methodist Hymnal and that these four services (Baptismal Covenant I, II, III, and IV) were much more extensive and theologically and liturgically richer than previous official services. Also, they were surprised to discover that the infant baptism covenant liturgies were in the direction of the historic unified initiation (baptism by water, the laying on of hands by the pastor and others such as parents, sponsors, god-parents) which could be followed by Holy Communion in "which the union of the new members with the body of Christ is most fully expressed."[4] The worship commission was pleased to learn that the Orthodox Church has always practiced the unified initiation, that the Roman Catholic Rite of Christian Initiation of Adults emphasizes the unified initiation, and that other denominations are moving in this direction in their study committees and new books of worship. While many differences of interpretation are still present, the engagement of hearts and minds implied by this movement inspired the group to move ahead, knowing that they were a part of a wider community of reform. The response of parents, sponsors, and the congregation has been very positive.

Various versions of the above story are forthcoming from many denominations.

Educational Designs Which Have Potential For Blessing

As we think about approaches to religious education we are helped if we remember for whom we are designing. First, the child who is to be baptized is the central person. This seems self-evident. Nevertheless, often the child is largely overlooked in the educational design and sometimes in the liturgical celebration. We all know how powerful it is to have not only the pastor hold and touch the child but also the parents and sponsors as they present and receive the child and as they place their loving hands on the child in "the laying on of hands." Also, this Spirit power is evident when the pastor takes the newly baptized child in his or her arms and goes up and down the aisle introducing the child by name to the congregation, welcoming the child as a full member of the body of Christ, a member who is already making a difference, is already evoking responses of love and hope from the other members of the body. When the sacrament is celebrated in a deeply personal and warm way the child is being educated profoundly at the existence level concerning the nature of God's love, and the nature of faith within the community, the nature of joy and the celebration of life itself, the nature of life in a community which promises to extend that love, truth, and hope into the child's future. These promises can be empty or they can be full of integrity as sponsors, parents, teachers, and family members commit themselves in advance to concrete ways to fulfill the promises. *When these elements are present the child's life is truly blessed.* The child is largely overlooked as a person when baptism is the result of little or no preparation of the parents and the congregation, where no counseling and educational experience preceded the ceremony, when no sponsors are selected, when little or no community of trust and love has been created in advance, where the baptismal liturgy is hurriedly and perfunctorily conducted between two hymns.

The blessing of the unified initiation through baptism, confirmation, and eucharist can be a continuing blessing as baptism is remembered and celebrated annually. This blessing extends when confirmation is repeated at moments of special meaning throughout the child's life and as the eucharist is celebrated with the child included from the beginning at the experience level and with increasing understanding as the eucharist is interpreted by parents, sponsor, pastor, educators, teachers, and others in creative ways in childhood, adolescence, and adulthood. The memory of the baptismal event can be shared with the child as the baptismal candle is lighted each anniversary of baptism, as pictures or videos are shared, as baptismal gifts are identified and celebrated, as relationships with sponsors are deepened and reinforced, as baptismal clothing is treasured and interpreted anew, as the deeper meaning of baptism is explored around the family table in terms of the unique gifts the child is discovering and is perceiving to be the core of his or her opportunity to give imaginative forms of ministry within and beyond the body of Christ. When these experiences are celebrated in thoughtful but natural and spontaneous ways, God's living presence—always alive and moving—can be recognized, celebrated, and extended to all the areas of the child's life.

Parents

Many significant baptismal ministries to and with parents are being explored and experienced in ways that engender more adventuresome and positive attitudes on the part of denominational leaders, pastors, educators, and the parents themselves. Many of these programs start when the mother and father announce the pregnancy and the anticipated date of birth of the new offspring. A series of congregationally sponsored pastoral and lay ministries are commenced at this time in several of these programs. The highly developed series of steps associated with the adaptation of the R.C.I.A. to infant baptism has already been discussed in chapter IV as a illustration of how parents can be in fact blessed and strengthened in preparation for the birth and baptism of the child.[5]

Another approach is found in the Episcopal adaptation of the catechumenal process. In this approach there are three stages and three rites.

Stage One follows the announcement of the pregnancy as the pastor rejoices with the parents to be and looks ahead to the birth and baptism of the anticipated child. Godparents may be chosen. They must be baptized persons and at least one of them a member of the congregation. A schedule of meetings throughout the months prior to the birth is planned. This leads to the first rite: the blessing of parents at the beginning of pregnancy. The *Book of Common Prayer* already has a blessing for a pregnant woman. This particular liturgy is altered to include the father if he is present and involved in the process. The rite is to be held during the Sunday eucharist after the Prayer of the People, followed by the Peace.

Stage Two consists of ministries during several meetings prior to the birth, with the parents, their other children, if any, and the godparents or sponsors. These meetings are with one or more persons (catechists) to probe the parents' own baptismal commitments and how these are being expressed within "their vocation of marriage, family, and child-bearing." They also reflect upon their own formation in relation to "salvation history, prayer, worship, and social ministry." They, along with other parents who are expecting, strengthen one another as they explore how their family life can be an extension of the body of Christ to the children being baptized. This stage culminates with the second rite: Thanksgiving for the Birth or Adoption of a Child. Again in corporate worship the celebrant signs the infant with the cross and announces the date of the baptism. Thereafter, the child is to be prayed for by name during the Prayers of the People until the baptismal day.

Stage Three: The parents, godparents, sponsors, and others continue to meet with the catechist(s). Couples who have raised children and others with rich experience may be brought in as resource persons. This is a time to explore the deeper meaning of baptism and the responsibilities of parents, god-parents, and others in the congregation. Also, models of ministry and prayer are discussed along with ways to introduce the child to the great faith stories of the gospel and to include the child in the eucharist and its meaning. This stage climaxes in the celebration of Holy Baptism, following the liturgy in the *Book of Common Prayer*. The celebration includes the parents, godparents, other laity and clergy representing the congregation. Children in the congregation are invited to come close to the font to observe the baptism and to participate more fully in the celebration. The liturgy includes the baptism by water, the laying on of hands and anointing with chrism if desired and the recommendation that the child may receive Holy Communion (with the receiving of a few drops of wine if the child is not yet weaned). Here we see a clear affirmation of the unified initiation. Other symbols of the celebration could be included if desired.

Various adaptations are possible including combining stages one and two for those who do not start the process at the beginning of pregnancy and deferring baptism until the child is old enough to participate in the catechumenate. In the latter case the parents participate in stages one and two but instead of infant baptism they enroll the child in the catechumenate process and publicly celebrate that enrollment.[6]

We are attracted to several other educational and liturgical approaches to baptismal ministry, some of which are more informal and/or intimate in pattern. One of these is an intergenerational small group practice first developed by the American Lutheran Church. It includes the normal pastoral communications with the parents prior to the birth of the child but emphasizes the formation of a group which will meet in homes of the participants for six sessions prior to the birth and subsequent baptism. The sessions are led by a pastor and/or lay catechist who has been trained to lead the group which consists of two more mature members of the congregation, two peers of the parents, two teenagers, and the parents. These persons seek to create a caring, supportive faith community as together they share their own baptismal stories, recall their own faith journeys, discover ways to nurture the expected one, study the theology and meaning of baptism, explore and plan the baptismal service, decide on ways to receive and celebrate the new life, write down specific hopes for the child which are turned into prayers for the awaited child.[7]

Another theologically and educationally sound program is one created for optional use in the United Church of Canada. This program again is very supportive of the parents and is clearly committed to the unified rite of initiation. The program is grounded in the basic theological assumption that "baptism, whatever the age of the candidate is the sole rite of initiation into communicant membership in the Christian Community, the body of Christ. The service celebrates the graceful initiative of God in calling and claiming us and the faith response of the people, both as individuals and as a community."[8] This optional pattern includes guides to help a local team of clergy and laity start the process, carry it through as an experimental program and evaluate it. As a follow–up to the optional liturgy (the unified initiation) many additional resources were prepared for parents seeking baptism for their child and for young people and others moving toward confirmation. Delineating clear roles for the church secretary and lay visitors to assist the pastors in making agreements with parents concerning the baptism of a child, the program suggests ways to include and prepare sponsors, ways to nurture the total family, the parents, grandparents, other children in the family, in preparation for the celebration of infant baptism. A two–session/four–part educational design has been published and enhanced by a filmstrip and a video on baptism as well as booklets and books especially prepared for parents. The program is easily adapted to the dynamics which flow out of other traditions. The visitation, pastoral counseling, lay sponsorship, and more focused educational experience provide a less complicated format for churches seeking to "start from scratch," so to speak.[9]

The unified rite of initiation of the United Church includes the baptism of children and adults as well as the renewal of baptismal faith by individuals seeking confirmation or reaffirmation of their baptismal faith. In this approach the confirmation rite of laying on of hands takes place in infant or adult baptism, but it can be repeated when persons want to make their first public declaration of their faith. This confirmation celebration for adolescents or others is made after study of new resources and the decision to affirm. Commitment to their baptismal covenant can be renewed later in relation to varying life experiences.[10]

The United Methodist Church is involved, as we have already noted, in a major study of baptism including infant and adult baptism and their relation to confirmation and eucharist. New confirmation resources and new resources for the education and support of parents around infant baptism and eucharist for children are being developed or are already available.[11] The same is true for the United Church of Christ,[12] the Evangelical Lutheran Church of America, the Presbyterian Church, U.S.A.,[13] and the Roman Catholic Church.[14] All of these programs aim at making the process of infant baptism a genuine engagement of parents with the deeper meaning and experience of baptismal covenant with God, with others in the faith community, and with one's own self-understanding. It is our hope that local teams of pastors, Christian educators, parents, sponsors, and congregational leaders will employ available rich resources in ways that will, in fact, bless the parents who are seeking to be blessings to their children.

Sponsors

It is significant that in most of the programs listed above there is a strong recommendation that sponsors be selected and be involved not only in the early stages of visitations and communications but also in the education sessions in homes or church, take an active role in the liturgical celebration itself, and follow-up with support. Such support can include loving acts over the years in the remembrance and celebration of the child's baptismal anniversary, and in general a relation at a personal level with the child as he or she grows into mature Christian commitment and living. Being a sponsor is no small task. But what a blessing such commitment could be not only for the child and the parents, but also for the sponsor.

It is important, therefore, to have clear understanding concerning the purpose, roles, and functions of sponsors whether these are called god-parents as in some traditions, or sponsors or companions, as in others.

The term "sponsor" is used in varying ways in different baptismal programs. In some cases the parents select the sponsors in consultation with the pastor or the lay visitors. In other situations the sponsors are selected by an official body of the church. In other cases one or two sponsors are termed "congregational sponsors" and are responsible to support all parents and children coming before the congregation. In some churches there are sponsors selected for each couple or individual where only one parent is presenting the child for baptism. The sponsor concept was greatly enhanced by the return of the Roman Catholic Church to the historic catechumenate. In this early approach candidates for baptism were assigned sponsors who worked with them in each of the four basic stages of the catechumenate which lasted from one to three years. Today, there has been a reemphasis upon the catechumenal process whether in Catholic or Protestant settings. Along with this rediscovery has come a rebirth of concern for the meaning of our baptismal covenant on the part of the entire congregation. The power of sponsorship has thus been reclaimed and is seen as an extension of the congregation.

Both the emphasis on sponsors and many of the resources written for the training of sponsors have come from the Roman Catholic Church. Many of the specific purposes, roles, and functions mentioned in such resources have meaning for sponsors in most denominations, however. Some guidelines are applicable mostly in Roman Catholic programs. For instance, *Guide for Sponsors* by Ron Lewinski helps sponsors see their great responsibility for sharing their faith and helping others discover their own needs and showing how the Christian faith meets those needs at a profound level. He states quite accurately, "As a sponsor you will be asked to extend in a personal way the community's welcome and support. Through your companionship with the one you sponsor you will informally pass on the spirit of the community. You will experience first hand the challenge new members face. As you share with them some of your own life and faith as an active member of the church, you will probably uncover for yourself new dimensions of being a . . . Christian. You may also gain a new friend for life's journey."[15]

Lewinski goes on to describe in more detail what it means to be a sponsor ("representative," "witness," "companion," " model") and what traits sponsors need ("to listen," "respect the uniqueness of the person who is being sponsored," "serve as a bridge between the person and others who can help," "give freedom to the persons involved") and what are the major questions people tend to ask. Many of the suggestions could be helpful to any sponsor, but the type of questions raised have mostly to do with the Roman Catholic tradition and would be helpful especially to sponsors in that tradition. Another resource in the same series is *Finding and Forming Sponsors and Godparents*. Again, there is considerable help for all local teams even though the resource is especially focused on the Roman Catholic tradition.

The Congregation

It should be made clear that it is the assembled congregation which is celebrating the sacraments of initiation. It is the people of God who visit and encourage the parents. It is the people of the congregation who form and sustain the baptismal ministry in all of its dimensions—pastoral, educational, liturgical. It is the congregation which selects, prepares, and commissions the sponsors.and catechists. It is the members of the congregation—sponsors, friends, teachers, peers of the child, other parents in all their different roles—who will be the incarnation of love and grace for the child as he or she grows in the knowledge and love of God through Christ. It is, therefore, very important that the baptismal celebration in its three parts be celebrated within the assembled congregation at the Sunday corporate worship service if possible or at some other gathering of the community of faith. It is the congregation which gives assent to the baptism, and it is the congregation which must be educated and inspired through teaching, preaching, and pastoral ministries to support the continuation of the baptismal ministry in all of its phases. There are many subtle baptismal issues that emerge which can be the occasions of joy and solidarity or the occasions for misunderstanding and bitterness. The norms for the baptismal ministry with parents and grandparents need to be agreed upon and carefully and prayerfully interpreted within the congregation. For instance, if preparation sessions are normative, if pastoral and lay visitation and counseling are expected, if it is agreed that baptisms of infants will not be done at the last minute when the grandparents are to be visiting in two weeks, then all of these agreements must be well understood, publicized, and sustained by the entire congregation. All exceptions regarding these guidelines should be well known and the rationale for the exceptions well understood and sustained. There should be room for flexibility and a clear understanding that certain conditions could arise where ministry to persons as sacred children of God may call for a unique path to be followed. Again, such a nonlegalistic approach must be well supported while at the same time sustaining the basic set of agreements concerning the ministry of infant baptism preparation, celebration, and follow-up. By bringing the congregation into this total baptismal ministry, not only of infants but of children, youth, or adults, as well as baptismal affirmations or baptismal renewals, it becomes clear that baptism is not a private matter but is "the common treasure of the whole Church of Christ."[16]

Affirmation of the Baptismal Covenant by Children

In our studying of varying denominational understandings and practices we found several creative ministries with children which involved early professions of faith or confirmation of their baptismal covenants. Many Roman Catholic churches emphasize both preparation for and celebration of the child's first communion and confirmation, often preceded by the sacrament of reconciliation. Several Lutheran churches have a curriculum concerning communion for children which is part of a four or five year educational program culminating in confirmation in early or middle adolescence. The United Methodist Church, The United Church of Christ, The Presbyterian Church U.S.A., and The Episcopal Church are bringing the study of baptism and Holy Communion into the curriculum of children in authentic and natural ways. These fresh emphases are an outgrowth of the renewed interest in the power of the sacramental ministry and the whole worship life of the total parish in forming the child's self-understanding and spiritual development.

There has also been more concern to meet the need for affiliation on the part of children. John Westerhoff and William Willimon have made this point in their schema.[17] Middle to late childhood is a time when boys and girls need to belong, to have a group identity, to know that they are Christians or Jews, United Methodists, Presbyterians, or Baptists. They respond very well to stories about their roots, the sources of their beliefs, the great figures in their past who have led the way to the present and may be guides for the future. James Fowler calls this period the Mythic-literal stage of faith. It is a period when children tend to take everything at face value or literally. It is a sensitive time when they are sharpening their awareness of themselves as adequate or inadequate, competent or incompetent. It is a time when they perceive their peers and their teachers, parents, and others evaluating them. It is a time when they need to be brought more deeply into the stories, beliefs, and observances of the faith community and to be surrounded by a supportive and affirming climate of acceptance. In such a climate they can test out their strengths and weaknesses and find a sense of direction. We now know that these school–age years are very important for the whole development of children. We have long since given up the idea that these are the "latency years." This psycho-sexual view implied less of a struggle for the person in middle or late childhood than is experienced in early childhood or adolescence.

We know that children are being introduced through television and computers into experiences which push them to grow up much faster than they needed to only scant years ago, and to deal with materials which their grandparents experienced at a much later stage of development. We are learning that children have intuitive insights concerning the nature and meaning of life which are often very engaging if not amazing, even if there are genuine limitations in their ability to think abstractly and critically. Robert Coles' study of the spirituality of children from many different religious and cultural backgrounds is full of illustrations of the perceptivity and insight which children can and do bring to our common lives. We need to do a lot of listening to children as well as sharing adult views. Child psychiatrist Coles was often put "on the spot" by children whose views of God, themselves, and good and evil were indicative of insights or questions to which he as a Harvard professor could not intelligently and honestly respond.[18]

Coles found children with visions of a spiritual future for themselves and others which were "an amalgam of lessons told by elders and a child's embellishment of them." These visions have stayed with him and propelled him, his wife and their grown children to probe deeply into the spirituality they have found in the lives of children. They have found that children from Christian, Jewish, Moslem, secular, or a nature religion all see themselves on pilgrimages. They are seeking to understand the nature of reality, of life and its meaning and purpose, of death and our common final destiny. Coles found himself connecting not only with the lives of the children he studied but their parents and grandparents. He probed the cultural and religious assumptions revealed in everyday responses to life. He marveled at how young the spiritual pilgrimage started, as children wonder about it all. He found children hungry for spiritual direction and meaning. There were typical patterns expressed by children in relation to their up-bringing in a particular religion or culture. Jewish children were questing about righteousness. Islamic children voiced a need to surrender to Allah's will in all of life. Christian children were concerned about salvation, what it is and how to attain it. Children from secular families were no less concerned about what is life's ultimate destiny and its best way to be lived. One of Coles' most commanding images came from Natalie, an eight–year–old Hopi Indian girl. Coles interviewed her, walking with her dog, Blackie, as they looked in the direction of the mesa in the big sky country of New Mexico. Natalie had been taught to love nature. The wind, the rain, the stars were her spiritual friends. She had been taught that she had a spirit and that she should love and respect her ancestors who were spiritually still present. She had been given an image of life's ultimate meaning which she embellished in her own way. Here is her word picture:

I was walking with Blackie, and I saw some smoke in the sky, a trail of smoke. I realized it was a plane. I wondered who was in the plane. I've never been to an airport. They showed us pictures of one at school. I pictured Blackie and me in that plane; we'd point it toward the sun, and keep going! I know the plane would melt; they told us in school everything would melt if it came near the sun. But the sun doesn't melt your spirit! We'd wave to the sun and the stars! They send us light, and it is a gift to us, and they sent it a long time ago, and now we have it.

I'm just [day] dreaming, I know! I dream of meeting our Hopi ancestors, and we sit together and talk about the time that will come—the time when all of us are together, and the waters of the river are full, and the sun has warmed the cold part of the world, and it has given the really hot part a break, and all people are sitting in a huge circle, and they are brothers and sisters, *everyone*! That's when the spirits will dance and dance, and the birds will swoop down and they'll dance, and all the people, everywhere, will stand up and dance, and then they'll sit down again in a big circle, so huge you can't see where it goes, how far, if you're standing on the mesa and looking into the horizon, and everyone is happy. No more fights. Fights are a sign that we have gotten lost, and forgotten our ancestors, and are in the worst trouble. When the day comes that we're all holding hands in the big circle—no, not just us Hopi's, everyone—then that's what the word "good" means. The teacher asked us to say what is good, give an example. Blackie is good; she is never going to hurt anyone; the whole world will be good when we're all in our big, big circle. We're going around and around until we all get to be there.[19]

Such a vision of our human pilgrimage is indeed powerful. It is similar to what other children have voiced in other research.[20] Such intuitive and acculturated mixes which are voiced by children do not really counter in a fundamental way research which identifies the limitations of children to think abstractly or to critique their thinking logically, or to get beyond the mythic or conventional thought into which they have been introduced in their families or culture. James Fowler's work on the stages of faith development still provides helpful guidelines for how we may enable children to grow spiritually from stage to stage.[21] Fowler is sensitive to the power of faith stories and to the intuitive grasp of the meaning of a God of love and the life of trust seen by children even though they have limitations concerning their ability to get beyond the symbols or critique their beliefs and compare them with alternate beliefs. What is being seen by Coles and by religious educators such as Gabriel Moran[22] and Maria Harris[23] is that we should recognize both the spiritual hunger and the spiritual depth that children bring to our interactions. Moran also urges us to expose children to the stories and beliefs of other world religions than their own so that a genuine religious education can take place—an education which will encourage the clear commitment to Christ, for instance, but in a way which is in dialogue with other visions and in a way which engenders respect and the hope that one day we will all be able to be in a huge circle together hand in hand in harmony with one another and God's whole creation.[24]

We have emphasized the positive aspects of the pilgrimage of children because we believe we have had expectations which are too low for children as persons of insight, as persons who are already and can be even more in imaginative and sensitive ministries with one another, within their families, within the faith community, and in their wider walks of life.

We must find creative ways to stimulate children to hear the Christian story and to appreciate the Christian beliefs concerning God's revelation in Christ and God's continuing presence through the Holy Spirit but we must also find ways to hear their stories, their questions, their hopes, their sharing of their spiritual pilgrimages. This can be done in a way that celebrates the freshness of their visions in dialogue with the more experienced testimonies of parents, teachers, grandparents, and mentors in the faith.

James Fowler's research emphasizes the importance of sharing the great faith stories and the essential beliefs and practices in increasingly ordered ways. We are agreeing but emphasizing even more the ability of children to make connections with their understanding of their baptism. They are full members of the body of Christ who have been in ministry as they have already shared their love and their spontaneous truthfulness and imagination with others, as they have participated in service to others along the way. Moreover, they need to be able to express their *awareness* of their unique calls to fulfill their baptismal covenant, so that they can affirm the fact that they *have been* and *will be* in mutual ministry with other members of Christ's body. Confirmation experiences do start and should take place in childhood in relation to where children are honestly in their pilgrimages.

Several churches have recognized the importance of such affirmation or confirmation experiences by scheduling their confirmation education during the fifth and sixth grades with confirmation taking place around Pentecost in the seventh grade. Some start the more focused educational experience in the sixth grade with a climax in the seventh grade. These approaches can be rich in meaning for children and should be extended. The affirmation and spiritual strengthening that takes place *should not be the first and last such experience*, however. Several affirmations can take place authentically as the pilgrimages of the individuals involved continue through the normal stages of growth in faith and ministry. One of the people articulating such a position has been Richard Osmer in his recent study of the power of the teaching office of the church. He reflects on the loss of thoughtful catechetical initiation in most mainline denominations. He sees this omission as a loss because the catechism was one of the central ways of initiating all members into the Christian story. The problem was not that it was done but *how* it was done and to what end.

He says, "While much of the content of classical catechism was far too difficult for children . . . to understand (requiring abstract reasoning not yet achieved) there was real genius in the basic intent of teaching a common catechism. It served as a way of mediating normative beliefs to every church member, beliefs that possess the authority of representative bodies and not merely that of individual minister, church educator. . . . Mainline Protestant churches would do well to reestablish the functional equivalent of catechetical instruction during this stage of faith."[25]

"This stage" is the Mythic–literal stage identified by James Fowler as the stage most children go through in which they need to learn the great faith stories and beliefs of the church with their mythic power without being caught in literalistic patterns they will have to unlearn in adolescence and adulthood. Osmer thinks this can be done by using story and narratives for the content of such instruction while challenging children to grow with a question and answer format.

Osmer believes elementary children can profit from a confirmation-like structure which will not only introduce them to these central stories and beliefs but also enable them to make faithful responses. These affirmations of their respective baptisms, however, should be but one important step in the ongoing need to grow in faith and to affirm their baptism at different times in life's pilgrimage.

Following Fowler's stages of faith development Osmer implies that important education and celebration of commitment should take place at the Synthetic–conventional stage. Most adolescents in mainline Protestant churches and in a large number of Roman Catholic churches experience confirmation at this stage. Commitment should also be celebrated at the Individuative-reflective stage where persons critique their faith "as a system." This happens often as young adults work out an "owned faith" which is adequate to give guidance to their decisions in all facets of their lives: personal, sexual, social, and ideological. Osmer's approach recognizes that what happens in many of our confirmation programs for adolescents, while very important in terms of identity as Christians, really does not enable the youth to critique his or her faith as a system of belief and practices but usually ends up being an affirmation of the beliefs and values of the church family. This a conforming pattern rather than a critiquing or "owning of one's own faith."

Such thinking moves the idea of a common catechism *away from* correct answers and public examination, often identified with confirmation preparation, toward catechetical approaches for children and youth which encourage honest dialogue between the self and the faith community's beliefs and commitments at each of the stages of faith and in response to the individual's experiences of God's presence in life. Such a position provides a basis for confirmation or affirmation of baptismal faith at various times in life's pilgrimage. Certainly, one or more of those times should be during the wonderful and growing childhood years.

We have established already that a primary concern for children of ten to twelve years is the need to identify themselves as belonging to the community of trust and love which is the church. The fact of their belonging can be celebrated in infancy in the unified initiation. It can then be reinforced in the feeling of being fully accepted and loved by God and the other members of the body of Christ, through the family and then in the church family. Faith can be nurtured and deepened through participation in the joyous and awe-inspiring eucharistic celebrations from baptism on. Through education and liturgy at these different levels children can gain strength by being given opportunities for expressing individual affirmations of all that they have already experienced as they are confirmed before the assembly of the faithful. The words of the presider in response to their affirmation of the baptismal covenants give public expression to the inner reality of the presence of God's loving spirit within the lives of parents, sponsors, and other members of the body of Christ who have been channels of grace to the children and expression also to the reality of the movement of God's spirit in the inner lives of those being confirmed. These words are spoken as the presider, parents, sponsors, and others place their hands on the head of each person being confirmed: "Remember your baptism and be thankful. *Name,* the Holy Spirit work within you, that having been born through water and the Spirit, you may live as a faithful disciple of Jesus Christ" (United Methodist liturgy).

An Optional Route

While we believe that infant baptism, which includes baptism by water, confirmation by the laying on of hands, and anointing and eucharist, can be the most meaningful and most nurturing way for persons to be brought into the family of Christ, we also recognize that people of good conscience and motivation can and do take another position. Some believe that infants are better served by the family of Christ, especially in a post-Christendom age, when they are enrolled as catechumens and are baptized, confirmed, and celebrate the eucharist when they are at an age of accountability or when they can make a conscious decision to center their lives in Christ and to be his disciples as ministering persons in our contemporary world. Some Roman Catholics who are enthusiastic about the Rite of Christian Initiation of Adults believe this approach will raise expectations and engender higher standards of church life and ministry, recapitulating a faith-culture similar to the early church when it was exceedingly demanding to say "yes" to Christ. In our contemporary world children and youth as well as adults can find many alternate religious communities and conflicting faith claims. We can no longer expect to find the Christian worldview reinforced in the rest of society. Solid Christian education within the church family is required along with participation in the worshiping and serving faith community after enrollment as catechumens. Some Protestant churches have had the pattern of infant dedication, followed by religious education in the family and in the church until an age of accountability at which time a special period of preparation culminates in a decision to be baptized and to be a responsible member of the body of Christ, after which the person is nurtured at the Table of the Lord. In Catholic churches the age of accountability has often been understood to be around seven. In Protestant churches it is more often in late childhood or early adolescence.

One problem which arises immediately in this option is the placing of first communion after confirmation. The problem is eliminated if the unified initiation takes place in infancy. Thereafter, children are invited to the Table as members of the family of Christ. In churches where infant baptism does not include the laying on of hands or anointing (confirmation) or eucharist, children are often asked to wait for a period of instruction prior to first communion or are asked to wait until confirmation before coming to the eucharistic celebration. Churches have sought to deal with this waiting period in a sensitive way. Often children come to the Table before confirmation or initiation and are blessed by the priest or minister. In other situations, children are asked not to come to the Table until after adolescent confirmation. The latter pattern has often been a negative experience of exclusion for children. From our theological perspective that the Table of the Lord should be an open Table, we can envision a pattern such as the following: the child is born and receives the careful ministries of the faith community including visits, naming ceremonies, education of parents concerning the joys and responsibilities of the catechumenal process into which the infant is to be enrolled; the enrollment celebration before the congregation; catechesis for both parents and child; celebration of the eucharist for parents with options for them to decide whether or not they wish their child to receive the elements or to be blessed at the Table; preparation for baptism, confirmation and eucharist to be celebrated at the age agreed upon by parents of the child and the faith community. These together constitute the unified initiation followed by the mystogogia or reflection on what it means to be a ministering member of Christ's body in the particular life of the baptized.

Julia Upton favors the unified initiation whenever it takes place, but calls for a "peaceful coexistence" of infant baptism and the enrollment of infants as catechumens. She states, "With the possibility of a catechumenate, the decision of whether or not to have the child baptized could more realistically be returned to the parents. Children in the catechumenate would be able to have a more personal understanding of how the faith is lived by contact with members of the catechumenal community. At the time of their baptism they would be able to make an unencumbered decision of their own in a ritual which will give dramatic testimony to their commitment."[26]

The issue of membership is refined in this approach. Upton agrees with Aidan Kavanagh that "the catechumen, therefore, is neither a non-member nor a non-Christian, but a Christian *in fieri* and a member of both the local community and the church universal."[27] In this sense the child is to feel included in the loving, trusting Christian community all along but decides to affirm such a feeling and commitment at a catechetical age, at which time the rite of initiation provided in the RCIA for children of catechetical age can be used. The rite, of course, is the unified initiation.

From the perspective of the child, real blessing occurs when the child is surrounded by authentic Christian values on the part of parents, family members, and the pastoral and lay ministries which accompany the catechumenal process in the worshiping, serving community. Love, trust, acceptance, and righteousness are the real nurturing food. The child, if so nurtured, will in fact feel included, will feel he or she is a member of the church family. From our perspective it is preferable for the child to be initiated fully as an infant and to be nourished regularly at the Table as lively expression of that membership in the body of Christ. However, if parents and others select enrollment in the catechumenate it makes sense for the child to be with them at the eucharist, actually receiving the elements or receiving the blessing as the parents elect.

In an imaginative program to keep the classic sequence of the unified initiation, the diocese of Spokane has inaugurated a pattern which makes confirmation prior to eucharist for seven year olds rather than the previous pattern of first communion, followed by confirmation at a later time. Because many children have already been initiated into eucharistic life but have not as yet been confirmed some leaders of the Spokane program found themselves recommending that the candidates for confirmation "be asked to refrain from eucharistic participation to deepen their hunger for the communion with the Lord in the fullness of the life of the Church."[28] While we understand the difficulties associated with the period of transition, we wonder about the proposed solution in respect to the message being sent to the children about their baptism and the meaning of their inclusion at the Table.

In the alternate approach there is an insistence that confirmation be integrated with baptism and eucharist and that confirmation be seen as a sign of the sealing of the Spirit which is no more related to maturity than baptism. Several churches which have moved to the unified initiation in infancy and early childhood have recognized the need for a ritual which celebrates mature, owned faith on the part of a middle to late adolescent. Such rituals of maturity are not called confirmation. The Diocese of Salford (England) has instituted such a ritual which coincides with leaving secondary school.[29] From our perspective the emergence of such rites illustrates and reinforces the inherent value in seeing confirmation or baptismal affirmation as a repeatable experience, first in infancy as a part of the unified initiation and then at other times in the life span when persons need and want to be strengthened and focused in a period of preparation and public affirmation.

Such a pattern would avoid the theological gymnastics we sometimes find ourselves recommending.

NOTES

1. Erik Erikson, *Toys and Reasons: Stages in the Ritualization of Experience* (New York: Norton, 1977), pp. 89-90. Also see Michael Warren, *Communications and Cultural Analyses: A Religious View* (Westport, Conn.: Bergin & Garvey, 1992), for a penetrating analysis of the values and rituals in society coming from mass media and their power to counter our best efforts to help youth embrace and express authentic Christian faith.
2. James W. Fowler, *Stages of Faith* (San Francisco: Harper & Row, 1981), p. 93.
3. Robert Kegan, *The Evolving Self* (Cambridge, Mass.: Harvard University Press, 1984), p. 45.
4. *The United Methodist Hymnal: Book of United Methodist Worship* (Nashville: The United Methodist Publishing House, 1989) p. 39.
5. See Gail Ramshaw-Schmidt, "Celebrating Baptism in Stages," in *Baptism and Confirmation: Alternative Futures for Worship*, p. 135f.
6. *The Catechumenal Process* (New York: The Church Hymnal Corporation, 1990), pp. 258-263.
7. Barbara J. Knutson, *Welcome to the Lord's Family* (Minneapolis: Augsburg, 1984).
8. *Baptism and Renewal of Baptismal Faith* (Division of Missions, The United Church of Canada, 1986), p. 4.
9. See Margaret Spencer, *Preparing Parents for Baptism of their Children* (Division of Mission in Canada: The United Church of Canada, 1981).
10. See *Preparing Young People for Profession of Faith: A Confirmation Resource* (Division of Mission in Canada: The United Church of Canada, 1990).
11. See Barbara Nan and Edward C. Peterson, *A Baby is for Loving*, rev. ed. (Nashville: Graded Press, 1985), and new confirmation resources.
12. United Church of Christ, *Birth, Baptism and Parenting* (New York: United Church Press, 1983); *A Day to Remember: My Baptismal Book* (New York: United Church Press, 1983).
13. Betty McLaney, *Beginning a Journey* (Philadelphia: Presbyterian Publishing House, 1988).
14. Roman Catholic Resources. See Gabe Huck, *Infant Baptism in the Parish: Understanding the Rite* (Chicago: Liturgy Training Publications, 1980).
15. Ron Lewinski, *Guide for Sponsors* (Chicago: Liturgy Training Publications, 1987), p. 1. Cf. Elaine Ramshaw, *The Godparent Book* (Chicago: Liturgy Training Publishing, 1993).
16. See Huck, *Infant Baptism in the Parish: Understanding the Rite*, p. 28.

17. See John H. Westerhoff and William Willimon, *The Sacraments and the Cycle of Life* (New York: Seabury, 1981).

18. See Robert Coles, *The Spiritual Life of Children* (Boston: Houghton Mifflin, 1990).

19. Ibid., pp. 54-55. Used by permission.

20. See Edward Robinson, *The Original Vision* (Oxford: Religious Experience Research Unit, 1977).

21. See Fowler, *Stages of Faith.*

22. See Gabriel Moran, *Religious Education Development* (Minneapolis: Winston, 1983).

23. Maria Harris, "The Original Vision: Children and Religious Experience," in *Family Ministry*, ed. Gloria Durka and Joanmarie Smith (Minneapolis: Winston, 1980), pp. 56-77.

24. See Gabriel Moran, *Religious Education as a Second Language* (Birmingham, Ala.: Religious Education Press, 1989).

25. Richard Robert Osmer, *The Teachable Spirit: Rediscovering the Teaching Office in the Church* (Louisville: Westminster/John Knox Press, 1990), pp. 234-235.

26. Julia Upton, *A Church For The Next Generation: Sacraments in Transition* (Collegeville, Minn.: Liturgical Press, 1990), p. 75.

27. Ibid., p. 76.

28. *Confirmation-First Communion* (Our Lady of Fatima Parish, St. Peter's Parish, Diocese of Spokane, 1984), p. 8.

29. Upton, *A Church for the Next Generation*, p. 85.

Chapter VII

ADOLESCENTS: FINDING AND AFFIRMING A GREAT FIDELITY

Erik Erikson's analysis of human development focused on the ongoing task of identity throughout life but emphasized the crucial nature of identity for adolescents. Erikson found that adolescents have a deep need to identify in a positive way who they are in relation to the qualities others perceive in them, and to discover a great fidelity, someone or something to which the young person can give himself or herself in order to give the self a sense of direction. In Erikson's classic study of the stages of ritualization in life he found that youth spontaneously define themselves in relation to values and commitments implied in and through *informal* rituals related to music, style of life of admired peers and celebrities, special "inside" language patterns, relations with the same sex and the opposite sex, learning to drive a car, dealing with biological changes in puberty, etc. Adolescents also define themselves through *formal* rituals such as confirmation or affirmation of one's baptism, induction ceremonies into various athletic or social groups, and graduation from high school. All of these rituals become important opportunities to declare to the self and to all the values, beliefs, and convictions the young person is embracing.[1]

Adolescents do indeed express such needs. However, they have countervailing forces working on them. They have the intellectual capacity, increasing progressively through the years from twelve to eighteen or nineteen, to examine their beliefs and the beliefs of others, seeking internal consistency, critiquing, comparing and testing the validity of faith statements. They have even greater needs: for acceptance from their friends; interpersonal relationships which test their ability to influence others; the development of wider and deeper associations; the discovery of their talents and abilities with feedback that tells them they are worth something, maybe even worth much to many and to God. It is for these reasons that formal rituals such as confirmation should have a strong, informal, relational dimension to them. Confirmation programs with high standards for learning basic beliefs, studying history and doctrine, memorizing creeds, and critiquing such beliefs and faith statements in order to come up with honest internalizations of these convictions, can be interpreted negatively unless they are done in a warm, supportive, grace-filled community which lives the life of love, trust, and justice to which the beliefs point.

Our study of denominational and local church practice revealed repeatedly that pastoral and lay teams are seeking to create Christian communities of care and creativity rather than legalistic programs through which young people are urged to march, with pressure from their parents and the congregation. Moreover, there is a growing recognition that confirmation or preparation for baptismal affirmation should be an interactive experience for youth, with the development of relationships and dialogue with a chosen or assigned mentor from the congregation, with engaging supportive and honest dialogue with parents and wider members of the congregation, with opportunities for imaginative forms of caring within and beyond the congregation. What is desired is the discovery of the validity and power of a Christian style of life which can interpenetrate the real life situations in which youth find themselves. This Christian style of life must deal with the issues of personal and social competence, sexual identity and decision making, the threat of AIDS, drug abuse, academic achievement, beginning discussions about vocation, marriage, family, community and church responsibilities. The emphases which are emerging for adolescent confirmation come to focus in education which helps youth identify with and affirm a life centered in Christ within a community which is seeking to be the body of Christ in the real world. What is being rejected is an abstract rite of passage from adolescent to adult status and assent to rigid doctrinal statements of faith which may have little transfer power in everyday life. The current tendency is to help youth work out their honest statements of faith in dialogue with historical and contemporary denominational statements. Such an honest internalization and affirmation of an authentic "first hand" faith is much more likely to occur in middle adolescence to young adulthood than it is in early adolescence.

Søren Kierkegaard, the Danish theologian of the nineteenth century, recognized the profound need of youth to be weaned psychologically from their parents and from their parents' presuppositions about faith in order that they develop their own firsthand existential faith around which they organize their lives and unify the self. Kierkegaard said that a happy upbringing is really a "presupposition" which comes from the parents. The child as a learner can easily be defrauded if he or she does not receive the treasure of the parent's loyalties, if he or she does not acquire the sacred heritage. But, eventually, the child will be defrauded even more if he or she is not helped by the parents to understand that what they have shared is not necessarily the absolute truth, but it is truth as they saw it in all honesty in their human finitude. Parents must face the hard fact that their children will have to come to their own firsthand faith, develop their own presuppositions about God, Christ, the church, and their eternal destiny.[2]

Kierkegaard was very critical of the confirmation practices in his day. He did not see any connection of confirmation with a clear firsthand faith in Christ as the center around which the young person unified the self and found a clear sense of direction. Confirmation in the state church (Lutheran) of his day was a "requirement" for social acceptability and a ticket to advanced education, job opportunities, and marriage. In other words, it was a very conventional thing to do. Once confirmed one could be as active or inactive in the church as desired. In our day when Christianity is not the religion assumed to be central in society's values and/or decisions, confirmation is seen largely as an activity with meaning within the faith community or within the individual. This is especially true in the United States. In Germany, for instance, confirmation at age fourteen still had a high social meaning until in East Germany the Marxist government ceased collecting church taxes and inaugurated its own secular "Youth Dedication" program and ceremony, *Jugendweihe*, to replace confirmation. In Germany's tradition the *Volkskirche* was a type of church quite unlike the church in the West. It was called the "church of the people" and stressed the church's responsibility for the nation and the community rather than an emphasis upon the local congregation. Christian education took place in the public school and attendance at worship was quite small. In East Germany, beginning in the fifties, the government pressed for the

Jugendweihe for all youth. This meant that most youth, except for a small resistance group, were lost to the church. The church did nothing until the seventies, when the decision was made to raise the confirmation age from sixteen to eighteen and to urge youth who had been given the privileges of the *Jugendweihe* (admittance to high school and university) to prepare for confirmation as well. Only an occasional youth, largely from the resistance group, was confirmed.[3]

What this vignette illustrates graphically is that youth need "coming of age" rituals in order to identify themselves as persons in or out of relation with dominant values of the culture. The Marxists quickly saw the social power of confirmation and replaced it with their own education and climaxing ceremony of commitment to the state. Again their type of confirmation became normative or conventional. Youth did not seek or write critical reflective comparisons or make free decisions to accept or reject. At what age and as a part of what dynamics can youth come to a freely chosen, firsthand faith in the Christian gospel of love and justice?

Adolescent Confirmation/Affirmation:
At What Age to be Authentic?

As we have discovered in our survey of confirmation understandings and practices, the most common age for confirmation/affirmation education and celebration is twelve or thirteen. Increasingly churches are moving to fourteen and fifteen (ninth or tenth grades) such as the Presbyterian Church's new program or to sixteen or seventeen (eleventh or twelfth grades) as in many Roman Catholic churches. A few Protestant churches have confirmation education and services of commitment in the fifth and sixth grades.

If we see confirmation as a part of the unified initiation in infancy and if we see membership in the body of Christ taking place through baptism and not tied to a later confirmation experience, then when confirmation/affirmation happens is less crucial for institutional health. Such a stance invited us to ask when young people are most in need of an education which genuinely engages them in honest inquiry concerning the power and truth of the Christian faith into which they have already been baptized and in which they have already been seen as members of the ministering community? Also, when can they make a free decision to affirm publicly their belief in the truth of that faith and their commitment to live a style of life, grounded in Christ and linked with others in and beyond the Church? The answer to the age question is changed if we agree that confirmation or baptismal affirmation is a repeatable experience which correlates with widening and deepening understanding of the Christian faith and with changing self-understanding related to the normal stages of human and faith development. Instead of one time, we may properly design a confirmation program with multiple experiences of strengthening in the Spirit, exploration of new understandings, and celebration of commitment.

The single confirmation celebration is open to several criticisms. One is that young adolescents are largely doing what their parents want them to do rather than responding with a genuine commitment on a firsthand basis after critiquing and reconstructing. Another is that middle adolescents are still too immature and too limited in their experiences to come to a firsthand faith but are doing what their peers are doing. Still another is that late adolescents and/or young adults are developmentally closer to a time when they have developed mentally, emotionally, and socially enough to be able to look more honestly at the essentials of the Christian faith, saying yes or no authentically, but that in too many cases the church has already lost communication with these persons. A persistent problem especially for young and middle adolescents is the feeling that confirmation is a graduation from the obligation of church life rather than the beginning of adult responsibility and full participation in the ministries of the church in the wider world. Older youth and young adult confirmation/affirmation preparation and celebration can be less plagued by the graduation mentality. However, "the graduation syndrome" is still an issue for high school juniors and seniors in Roman Catholic programs.

Sensitivity to Insights from Human and Faith Development Can Make Confirmation/Affirmation a Blessing

While it is increasingly evident that confirmation or affirmation of baptismal covenant need to be repeated in relation to the dynamic changes which take place within the self-understanding of the person from stage to stage, the adolescent period is one with high potential for the development of a vital faith. On the down side, James Fowler's research has revealed that decisions young or middle adolescents make are not as genuinely autonomous as those made by young adults or adults. However, Fowler agrees with Erik Erikson that adolescents have a deep need to find a great fidelity. Still he has found that adolescents have not moved out beyond the norms of their family and church to critique the "faith as a system." While adolescents want to rework and critique the values and commitments into which they have been introduced, they end up affirming the conventional beliefs of the community. As we have indicated, Fowler calls this period of development Stage III Synthetic-conventional faith. While more growth in faith is needed in older youth and young adulthood where Stage IV Individuative–reflective faith tends to take place, there are many factors which tend to inhibit such growth. Insensitivity to these dynamics of human and faith development can make confirmation/affirmation education and celebration somewhat formal and perfunctory. Sensitivity to these dynamics can make confirmation/affirmation a genuine spiritual blessing in the lives of the youth involved.

Fowler found that adolescents want to discuss their beliefs. Some even seek deeply felt and emotion–packed conversion experiences. However, their beliefs are tacit and largely unexamined at any level of depth. Authority for beliefs is still located mostly outside the self. In relation to the tasks of decoding the symbols of the faith community they do not really seek to get behind the symbols to deeper personal and social meanings. This is true even though middle to late adolescents want to question the assumptions they have been brought up to believe.

Programs aimed at young adolescents (seventh and eighth grades) where many confirmation/affirmation programs take place can be very positive but limited experiences for the youth involved. They can and do develop a clearer sense of identity, affirming themselves as valued members of the body of Christ into which they were baptized. They can feel a sense of belonging with their peers and the adults with whom they are related as mentors or elders in the faith community. They can be uplifted and inspired by the spirit of love, acceptance, and inclusion that is present in the public celebration of their affirmation. They can get a glimpse of how important their thinking and actions are in the governance of the church. However, at age twelve or thirteen they are still quite young to be accepted in the decision–making process in the church family. So, instead of being confirmed and strengthened by the Spirit for ministry within and beyond the body of Christ, they tend to feel they have graduated from ongoing education and worship. The drop-off of confirmed youth from patterns of regular attendance and participation is well known and often decried. If membership in the body of Christ is correlated with baptism and not confirmation, leaders can develop additional confirmation/affirmation programs that better correlate with middle to late adolescence where there is more evidence that youth will be more likely to grasp the meaning of the faith and identify gifts they can put into use in the governance of the church and in the outreach of the congregation within the wider world.

Being Blessed for Changing and Growing in Faith

Youth see themselves changing as selves as they grow from early to late adolescence. Dusek and Flaherty (1981) made a study of youth in grades nine, ten, and eleven dealing with changes in themselves. In their response to twenty-one adjectives dealing with questions such as anxiety, kindness, sociability, intellectual ability, dominance over others, etc., the youth felt subjectively that they had undergone a great deal of change. However, empirical data on similar groups of adolescents by Kagan and Moss suggest far less change in these qualities.

Jerome Kagan of Harvard has found that adolescents have the potential of changing their beliefs about themselves and the world (changing their frame) but that the structure of belief is very firm and resists change.

The frame determines the events that will be selected for accommodation and causes biases in the conclusions drawn from experience. In confirmation/affirmation programs with young adolescents it is very difficult to change the frame of youth from dependency and conformity to a frame in which the youth sees himself or herself as an independent yet collegial believer. Young adolescents are often not quite ready to make firm commitments to personal and corporate forms of ministry or to make a creative contribution which corresponds to appropriate qualities of youthful energy, imaginations, honesty, and drive. Kagan found that such a frame change can take place better as adolescents mature cognitively to the point of examining their beliefs and detecting inconsistencies. At this point change in their beliefs or their frame, their way of viewing reality, can more readily take place.[4]

Kagan found that it is difficult to generalize about such changes in adolescents. Each person is unique. He did find, however, that some twelve year olds may not have developed biologically and mentally to the point of being able to identify inconsistencies while many fourteen year olds have developed to the point of brooding about inconsistencies, for instance, in the following three propositions:

1. God loves humankind.
2. The world contains many unhappy people.

3. If God loves humankind God would not make so many people unhappy.

Kagan found that many fourteen year olds are troubled by the incompatibility that one immediately senses when these statements are examined together. Youth who note the contradictions have at least four choices. They can deny the second premise that people are ever unhappy. This is unlikely because the evidence of unhappiness is overwhelming. They can deny God loves humankind, but love of human beings is one of the qualities of God by definition. The adolescent can assume that the unhappiness serves some kind of ulterior purpose God has in mind for humans. Finally, youth can deny the hypothesis of God.

Kagan found that the last alternative, which has been chosen increasingly by many in Western society, has profound consequences. Youth who deny a belief which has been regarded as true for many years (a frame through which they have perceived their world) are tempted to conclude that if there is no God, all other equally strong beliefs previously held are in jeopardy. What an individual youth perceived to be permanently valid has become tentative. Kagan found fourteen and fifteen year olds especially vulnerable to doubt about the legitimacy of their beliefs. Some can find themselves "at sea" not knowing what they believe and feeling depressed or somewhat hopeless when they are faced with life's problems.[5]

What is needed is a community of acceptance and love in which middle to late adolescents can acknowledge their personal struggles and face their doubts. Many confirmation/affirmation programs are now focusing on middle to late adolescence. This is a time when honest feelings and beliefs may be explored, tested, refined, and reconstructed. Even though the outcome may be synthetic and somewhat conventional, it is the relational process itself which can be a blessing in the lives of the youth. Such a process, which involves adult mentors, older youth, parents, teachers and youth leaders, pastors, and church educators can be a spiritual experience of power. It can be an experience which encourages the young person to explore his or her self-understanding in relation to the understanding of the faith. This process is much more than an intellectual exercise. It is a relational experience of stimulus in an accepting, loving but honest and firm community. Such a process can indeed be strengthening as the Spirit of God moves through the lives of all to strengthen both the youth and those who are serving as co-creators with God of a viable and meaningful future. Changes in individual frames, or ways of viewing

self, others, God, and the world, can and should be identified and celebrated in liturgies before the congregation. Such rituals have power to
create a vision of the meaning of the new frame of reference for the individual as well as for the community of peers, mentors, and adults.

Being Blessed by a Confirmation/Affirmation Approach which Relates Youth in New Ways to Others and to God.

Adolescence is a period in life when self identity is particularly focused
on the issue of how well the youth is able to find a balance of independence and inclusion. While the need for independence is real the weight
comes down on the need for interpersonal relationships of meaning and
warmth. Robert Kegan in his classic study, *The Evolving Self*, presents a
developmental approach which highlights the central importance of
meaning-making and interpersonal balance, as the crucial concerns of
adolescents. The adolescent self is conversational. Other people, especially
peers, are essential for the self to feel secure. This quest for a shared
reality is somewhat compulsive. The self cannot consult itself about the
shared reality. It cannot because it is that shared reality.[6] The adolescent
self is almost devoured by the need for the affirmation and presence of the
other. The internal conflict within the self comes from wanting to be a part
of shared realities that are themselves conflicting in terms of time and persons. The interpersonal here is not intimate, Kegan believes, because
there is "no self to share with another; instead the other is required to
bring the self into being. Fusion is not intimacy."[7] Kegan found that the
quest for interpersonal balance is "holy ground," so much so that it is
hard for the youth to be angry. To be angry is to risk being a self separate
from the relationship. Adolescents are more concerned to keep their identity by keeping their relationships, which define the self, than they are to
define themselves via identity with various institutions. Kegan found
that institutional balance is the next stage, appropriate more for young
adulthood. The institutional balance involves the self in finding identity
by giving oneself to causes and purposes associated with organizational
commitments in a widening social setting. One such institutional identity, of course, is with the church as an institution with beliefs, practices,
values, loyalties with which the self can identify. Other institutional balance factors involve the person in work, social, political, and govern-
mental institutions.

Confirmation/affirmation education and celebration for middle to late adolescents has a greater chance than for early adolescents of correlating with the self's quest for institutional balance, but such timing is probably somewhat premature. Logistically and pastorally, on the one hand, and developmentally and educationally, on the other, it is positive to be one step ahead in terms of stages of faith and self-definition. By working with the dynamics of the interpersonal balance but challenging the self to grow by exposure to the questions and issues related to commitment to the church in a public affirmation of one's baptismal covenant, the self of the adolescent may be put into a state of disequilibrium enough that the young person will be stimulated to grow sufficiently to find a new equilibrium. In this process much new information and understanding may well take place as the person assimilates (fits one's experience to one's present means of organizing reality) and accommodates (reorganizes one's way of making meaning to take account of the new experiences associated with being called to affirm one's baptism and accept greater responsibility for the use of one's gifts for the extension of Christ's ministry through the church as an institution of meaning in society).[8]

Such a confirmation/affirmation experience in middle to late adolescence, again, can have real meaning if we see that it is not the end of baptismal affirmation but an important step along the way. Kegan reminds us that the balance achieved is often an evolutionary truce in which further assimilation and accommodation will necessarily have to go on.[9] It is for this reason that young adulthood has great potential for finding depth of commitment and for defining the young adult as a ministering person through a sense of vocation or call expressed concretely through one's occupation or voluntary service. (More about this later in the next chapter.)

The Blessing of Meaning-Making in a Self-Selected Group

Sharon Parks in *The Critical Years* helps us see the dynamics associated with adolescent commitment within the Christian community. It is characterized by a Stage III pattern in respect to what James Fowler calls "the bounds of social awareness." Adolescents tend to be committed not so much to the church as a total and universal community, but rather, more to primary face to face relations in a conventional group. The group is conventional because the relationships involved in the group "conform to class norms and interests and are 'ascriptive,' meaning that one belongs because one is located by birth or other circumstances in that assumed context. It is some combination of ethnic-familial ties, social class norms, regional perspectives and loyalties, religious system, techno-scientific ethos, peer values and pressures, and sex role stereotypes."[10]

Most adolescent confirmation groups are limited in the above ways. However, such confirmation/affirmation groups have the potential for being a very real blessing for the youth who finds acceptance, love, trust, and opportunity for honest reflection in a face to face community. It is very true that the values and norms coming from social class, family, region, etc., may compromise or distort the more authentic norms of the universal community which is the body of Christ. However, as a step in a process of growth in faith it is very important for youth to find relational validity in the Christian commitment to a life of love, trust, forgiveness, and justice.

The process of moving out to the wider community in late adolescence and young adulthood often means leaving these face to face groups that are local and conventional to find new relationships in new groups with new or different values and beliefs. This period involves a diffusion of community, says Parks, in the new setting of college, work, or travel. To move through this period of community diffusion to find new self-selected groups is not easy. It is especially difficult for that new community to be a genuinely free choice and also be grounded in the Christian faith, which may still symbolize the conventional somewhat "secondhand" faith which one affirmed in the past. It is during this transitional period that many young people become detached from a local church, even though saying that they "belong to the church and believe in God." Such persons do not leave the church so much because of changes in belief. They become detached because of a feeling of community diffusion. They have difficulty relating to their previous community of faith with its face to face strengths and limitations and have not as yet found a community of faith which they have self-selected.

Fresh patterns of confirmation/affirmation education and celebration need to be focused on young adulthood. If the climax of confirmation/affirmation is in adolescence, the journey is often seen to be completed instead of ongoing. If adolescent confirmation/affirmation is one important step in a lifelong process of discovering and affirming the meaning of one's baptism into the ministering community which is the body of Christ, such education and celebration can be a great blessing. Such a blessing can provide the spiritual strength to move out beyond the face to face community to find new more autonomously chosen communities.

Adolescents still have a dependency mentality even though they are seeking to be more independent in thinking and action. Erikson correctly said that a great fidelity cannot be found without exposure to a wide diversity of beliefs and behavior. For adolescents, their world of diversity is just beginning to expand. Young adults encounter much more diversity as they move out beyond the family and the local community. This diversity can easily result in a feeling that "all is relative." Such a result need not take place if young adults can find a network of communications, in which the church is a part which is accepting and supportive of their pilgrimage. In such a network they can move on to *counter dependence*, where the young person is freed from the authority of previous relationships and commitments to explore new ones but where the previous authority is still in control in the sense that the person is pushing out against it. The next step is for the young adult to develop an *inner-dependence* in which other authorities still hold credible power, but now one recognizes and values the authority of the self. The process should move on to a feeling of *interdependence,* usually in mid-life where the primary trust resides in "neither the assumed authority of another nor in the courageously claimed authority of the inner self. Rather, trust is now centered in the meeting of the self and other . . . the self-conscious expression of interdependence."[11]

At each of these stages we all need to be blessed by a community which holds on loosely but attentively. Such a community can celebrate growth in faith as it provides opportunities for meaning-making along with clear forms of creative ministry in the wider world with which to identify.

Confirmation/Affirmation Education in Middle to Late Adolescence

Let us recognize up front that middle to late adolescents need to be and are being educated by participating with integrity in the church as a worshiping, learning, ministering community. It is crucial for youth to be given high visibility in the total life of the church. Confirmation or affirmation education should not be an esoteric sideline. It should involve the whole church and be owned as an important ministry of the total congregation. The way confirmation/affirmation programs are designed, by whom they are designed, by whom they are led and who the members of the leadership team are—all educate the youth, parents, and the total congregation concerning the very nature of confirmation/affirmation. These factors imply what it means to be prepared to receive the strengthening of the Spirit and to affirm publicly one's baptismal covenant. It is very important for there to be agreement within the faith community concerning the purpose and desired outcome of the educational and liturgical experiences. These purposes and objectives need to be developed and owned locally even though denominational or ecumenical resources may be employed. Increasing numbers of churches are not only developing their own understanding of the purposes and design for confirmation/affirmation but are also developing their own interpretive materials and their own curriculum resources or adapting denominational resources such as the new Presbyterian resources or the new United Church of Canada approach. Most of these adaptations or unique designs are being developed by teams of pastors, educators, and lay teachers and mentors. One team has a seventeen–year history with new personnel being brought in from time to time.

Mentors. We highly recommend that an adult mentor be selected for each young person who is being nurtured toward confirmation/affirmation. Sometimes the mentors can be the sponsors who have been surrounding the person with love and support since infant baptism. Often, in our mobile society, such persons will need to be found. Mentors can participate in the educational or service setting on a one to one basis. Mentors can also help the youth see what the Christian faith means to them in their family, occupation, and community contacts. The education experiences can focus on dialogue between the youth and the mentor around basic beliefs and the power of the Christian faith to bless marriage or singleness, family or other relationships, a sense of call or vocation to find expression in one's occupation or voluntary associations. Mentors can invite youth to accompany them into their work settings in order to identify specific issues, problems, and opportunities for ministry they have.[12] Mentors can also help youth refine their beliefs and face their doubts and confusion. Of course, mentors will want to join the young persons in the liturgical celebration along with parents, other family members, pastors, and teachers in laying hands on the youth as they affirm the baptismal covenant first embraced by parents and the congregation. The relationship that can be created between individual youth and mentors can be a blessing for both participants as well as for the total congregation.

Possible Areas of Study and Action

A possible curriculum under the theme of Being Blessed and *Becoming a Blessing* could have the following components:

1. *Being blessed within the body of Christ*—from baptism on: Preparing for confirmation/affirmation of baptismal covenant so that the confirmands can see themselves as extensions of Christ's love and justice to others. Exploring what does it mean to orient oneself to Christ, to find the self unified and grounded in Christ? What does it mean to have a "firsthand faith" but also a faith that is in continuity, however uniquely, with the faith of parents, mentors, pastors, teachers, and people within the congregation? How can youth identify their unique gifts in order to become a blessing to others—not in a sentimental way but in a real way related to the tough issues in their lives and in the wider society?

2. *Seeing ourselves as ministering persons and members of the blessed community, the body of Christ.* Helping youth identify themselves as authentic participants in the universal priesthood of all believers. Inviting youth to decide to become blessings to others by using their gifts as fully functioning members of the general ministry of all Christians. While youth tend to focus on face to face groups, we can help them identify problems they are having in their daily lives that cannot be solved merely by being a Christian alone—problems and issues which invite youth to join with others to effect social change.

3. *Seeing and affirming the sacredness of all of life.* Here youth can be stimulated to find evidence of God's actions in the wider world. The sacramental nature of life can be studied in relation to the deeper meaning of the sacraments through which we come to know and experience God's acceptance, grace, and love. This focus can come alive by exploring some fresh understandings about the pervasive presence of God's grace in the very fabric of life and about Christ as the incarnation of that love, making visible the mystery of God's grace as the sacrament of God. This can then be followed by discussions of the church as the sacrament of Christ and the specific sacraments as experiences which make visible God's grace and strengthening spirit at the various stages of our lives from birth to death. The study will focus on baptism and eucharist as the central sacraments but also look at the other historic rites/sacraments such as confirmation, reconciliation,

marriage, ordination, unction, and footwashing. This unit is where the meaning of baptism as the initiation of the person into the body of Christ and the ministering community is explored as well as the importance of public affirmation of one's baptismal covenant. The nature of God's Holy Spirit is discussed and related to confirmation or baptismal affirmation or renewal. The possibility of repeating the public affirmation at different points in the pilgrimage of life can be highlighted or reinforced. The meaning of sacramental life for daily decisions and relationships can be pursued so that all persons of whatever race, creed or nationality can be seen as sacred members of the family of God, persons to whom we are called to become blessings.

4. *Becoming blessings to others in our world.* Here there is a genuine need for realism.

a) A place to start is to celebrate the priceless *gifts of our bodies as the temples in which God's grace, love, and trust can find a home and through which God's life-giving Spirit can flow to others.* This means that we face honestly ways to keep our bodies and spirits integrated and healthy. A positive approach should be taken to the importance of nutrition, exercise, and other habits of life (possible abuse of our bodies via smoking, alcohol, drugs) and the power of spiritual disciplines of meditation and prayer for healthful living.

There is a deep hunger on the part of youth for honest, non-moralistic discussion of these issues and for the discovery of older youth and adult models with whom to relate and from whom to find support for the affirmation of a lifestyle that produces and sustains a healthy body, mind, and spirit.

b) Here is the place for the study of *human sexuality as a gift and blessing from God.* There is a profound need for mentors who can help youth develop a positive and affirming attitude concerning their own sexuality and at the same time help them develop sexual ethics in harmony with God's call for a life of fidelity and trust. Dialogue concerning the crises involved with AIDS, venereal diseases, and teenage pregnancy should take place with the help of experts, pastors, parents, and peers. Focusing on the power of free choice and awareness the consequences of choices can enhance the discussion and help the persons to move beyond a mentality of legalism.

c) *Preparation for faithfulness in marriage* is increasingly being seen as an important arena for confirmation/affirmation education. It is in the marital state that many young Christians will seek to live out

their understanding of fidelity to God and the one chosen as a life part-
ner. The amazing lack of marriage preparation programs on the part
of the church must be corrected. While such preparation actually
takes place primarily in family life, and in social relationships from
infancy on, it needs to be more concentrated in late adolescence and
young adulthood. Contemporary marriage is being strained to the
breaking point with the pressure coming from a legitimate desire for
personal meaning for both husband and wife in independent voca-
tion/occupation. Some of this strain can be dealt with by the development of a new vision of a Christian marriage. This fresh vision
will bring a clarity of understanding concerning what it means to be
a man or a woman and what the male and female roles and functions can be in a marriage that is a blessing to both persons, any children born to this union, and others. Don and Carol Browning discuss the inadequacy of interpretations of the Second Commandment,
which emphasize self-sacrifice or self-fulfillment, and call for a third
model, a love ethic of equal regard. They say "loving your neighbor
or spouse as yourself means loving him or her exactly as much as you
love yourself. It means you must take the needs and claims of the
spouse as seriously as your own. But this love ethic also means that
you are obligated to take your own needs and claims seriously. It
includes values both from the independence and self–sacrificial models of love but avoids their excesses. The equal regard interpretation
of neighbor love fits the needs of the postmodern family faced with
a new range of issues around shared authority, more equal financial
power, and more nearly equal values in raising children and meeting
each other's needs in the midst of the 80-hours work week."[13]

The Brownings are embarked on a major Lilly Foundation sponsored study of the American family. At the very outset of the study
they are urging churches to educate young people concerning this
vision of Christian love and to find new initiation rites or rites of
passage by which to celebrate these new identities.

d) *Finding a more healthy and promising view of the blessings of
Christian Family Life.* Young people often yearn for a family of their
own but wonder if a healthy family life is possible in our fast moving
and disruptive world. Exposure to realistic but positive images and patterns of family life built on a love ethic of equal regard can take place
through distillation of the best thinking from research but also via
direct contact and sharing with families within the church who are

finding fresh forms of Christian family life. These couples and their children can be co-learners as well as mentors or models. Youth need to see the possibility of perceiving the family as a small church (*ecclesiola*) within the church (the *ecclesia*) where persons are in mutual ministries of listening, caring, confronting, forgiving, inspiring, long-suffering, loving, and recreating. The family so grounded in honesty and mutual regard can, in fact, become an environment where parents and children can bless one another. This image can guide one-parent families and surrogate families as well. It is important, especially in our day, to find ways to undergird the vision of a nuclear family without undercutting the integrity of many contemporary forms of family life. This can be done without implying that the only path to meaning and wholeness is marriage. Again, choosing one's future in the light of God's call to a sense of vocation is what is important. The family study must be very practical with attention to the trying yet fulfilling moments associated with child rearing. These moments can be experienced through drama, role plays, excerpts from videos or film. The goal is to help youth find hopeful visions of family rituals and experiences which engender the growth of parents and children as persons and also the family as a community of faith and joy. Ways to celebrate life within the family can be found and encouraged.

e) *Preparation for Christian Vocation* with attention to the discovery and refinement of talents that can be given to God and others through an occupation or voluntary association. Youth in the latter part of their high school experience are beginning to think more seriously about what they want to be in the world of work. While these explorations and decisions are better correlated with college or young adult years, it is important for the church to open up the doors of vocational identity in general, and in terms of the call of God to use one's talents to bring to fruition the kingdom of God in our time. Very few efforts to help middle to late adolescents to take these steps are to be found in our churches today. This was not always so. In the past the study of Christian vocation generally was emphasized, but also the many opportunities for service within the institutional church. This was done nationally in several denominations with resources and professional staff time dedicated to this purpose. Budget pressures and other factors have resulted in the omission of many of these efforts. The potential of a fresh emphasis on the relevance of vocational decisions to one's identity and meaning as a person and as a Christian can and should be recognized in confirmation/affirmation education and celebration. This important matter can be addressed through the study of recent creative efforts to reclaim this theme such as James Fowler's *Becoming Adult, Becoming Christian*, through relating to a mentor's work place and his or her perspective on opportunities for ministry in that context through vocational inventories, and through dialogue with resource persons from various fields who have identified the rich meaning found in work or voluntary service.[14]

Adolescents are not likely to make final decisions concerning occupational preference. They can, however, begin to sort out these matters. This should be done with attention to equity concerning male/female identification with various fields of endeavor and the issues of justice and openness. Also, issues of honesty, integrity, and social responsibility in youth's future work settings can and should be discussed. If confirmation/affirmation is seen as a repeatable celebration, one such occasion can be established sometime during young adulthood or later when the congregation will bless and support the individual in his or her decision to be consecrated for ministry in a particular occupation as a teacher, health worker, musician, computer programmer, attorney, actor, scientist, volunteer in some form of mission or ministry in the community, etc.

This blessing can be another reaffirmation of one's baptismal covenant with a strong emphasis upon Christian vocations and the celebration of the gifts and graces the person brings to a particular occupation or voluntary commitment. (More about this in Chapter VIII.)

5. *Education for Spiritual Growth.*

In our study of denominational and local church understandings and practices we found only two confirmation programs that emphasized spiritual growth for adolescents. One program by Bishop Joseph McKinney is based on the RCIA and is designed to help older youth or young adults prepare for their confirmation. While McKinney's particular interpretation of the central nature of confirmation as a gift of the Holy Spirit is not one with which we can totally agree, his emphasis upon the power of prayer and journaling is impressive. After a year of study of Catholic basics, candidates for confirmation are invited into a period of fifty days of spiritual preparation prior to their confirmation celebration at Pentecost. The pattern involves youth in daily meditation on a biblical passage having to do with the power of the Holy Spirit, God within us, to transform life. A student's book with pages for journaling on the biblical passage and six chapters on the life of the spirit is available along with a teacher's guide.[15] The other program was designed by one of the graduates of our theological school, Bruce Morrison. Emphasizing a positive creation–centered spirituality, Morrison used silent meditation, journaling, imaging, storytelling, and Bible study to give depth and life to youth in the confirmation program. The evaluation of the youth put these experiences at the top of the list of most significant and meaningful aspects of their life together. (See Chapter V for more detail.)

Too many youth grow up in churches where they have not learned creative approaches to personal prayer, meditation, and decision making. Many have seldom participated in corporate worship because they were attending church school as their parents were participating in worship. A telling sign of this tendency is a requirement that candidates attend corporate worship. Such a requirement assumes that they may not have been regular participants from their baptism on.

Several churches have included in their confirmation preparation a retreat during which corporate worship and opportunities for the development of personal spiritual discipline are rich experiences for youth.[16] Retreats have great potential for helping youth discover and practice patterns of prayer and meditation in an environment which engenders support and encouragement from mentors and peers. Such qualities can also be a part of weekly confirmation/affirmation sessions and are especially valuable if individual work has been done between sessions. An excellent guide for pastors and confirmation teachers is Joanmarie Smith's, "The Spiritual Education of God's People: Pastoral Burden or Opportunity."[17] She also has a comprehensive annotated bibliography at the end of the chapter. Many of these resources can be used in the enrichment of the spiritual growth of persons at each of the stages of life as well as for adolescents.

6. *Becoming Clearer About What I Believe and Why I Believe It: The Blessings of a Life of Faith.*

Most middle to late adolescents have already appropriated many of the basic beliefs as a by-product of participation in the many informal rituals, conversations and dialogues that have taken place in the family, within the life of the church at worship, study, and service. What is needed in confirmation/affirmation education is an opportunity to test the adequacy of these beliefs, to pursue deeper understanding that will correlate with life as they know it, and to be invited to put together these thoughts in a personal credo or statement of faith. Such expectations should start with the assessment of the central beliefs of the youth and the identification of difficulties they are experiencing concerning certain specific beliefs. These issues will no doubt include the central questions concerning belief in a good God in a world full of division and hurt, belief in Jesus Christ as the revealer of God's love, belief in the Holy Spirit, specific beliefs about the church as a community of caring, serving disciples when many appear to be concerned primarily about themselves, beliefs about sin, salvation, eternal life, ethical living, the importance of the sacraments and spiritual life, and so forth. While it is good to have resources which open up options and provide engaging methods for discussing these issues, it is important for the youth to have a genuine part in designing the course and in sharing leadership roles along with pastors, educators, laity, and parents. The study sessions should be collegial and take on the qualities of a close, face-to-face group which is seeking to be and become the body of Christ in actuality. The outcome of these explorations can be the writing of a credo in dialogue with the great historic and contemporary creeds. The United Church of Canada has approved a new creed and is using the new creedal statement as the organizing center for its confirmation education program.[18]

Of course, it is very helpful for youth to be able to have a personal conference with the pastor or educator in preparation for the decision to affirm publicly his or her baptismal covenant and to receive the laying on of hands or anointing as a living symbol of God's Spirit strengthening the person's faith and ministry within and beyond the local church.

The above elements are suggestions for the educational design for middle to late adolescent confirmation/affirmation. There is no attempt to be comprehensive but to stimulate fresh thinking and planning. As noted, many denominations are in the process of developing new curriculum pieces aimed at an adolescent audience and are building in considerable flexibility. Our study of local churches found most pastors, educators, and lay teams have used curriculum resources in ways unique to their own purposes and time factors. If the above avenues are integrated into adolescent confirmation designs it is likely that such learning experiences will take one to two years in a rhythm which is cognizant of other important elements in the life of the busy youth and in the total life of the parish.

The above suggestions have not discussed the approach to teaching-learning most needed. We believe it is possible to employ the above generative themes in a way which starts with the actual present behavior of youth, their stories and problem areas and then, moves on to a dialogue with the Christian story and vision with a view to increased critical consciousness and decision making which is honest and genuine: an action-reflection-action model. In addition, it is important to be clear about the specific understandings, attitudes and behaviors, which are the anticipated outcome for individual learners and for the learning group including the leadership team. The use of engaging and creative teaching methods and excellent resources cannot be overstated. All too often, youth especially are "turned off" during confirmation preparation due to the use of teaching methods and resources which are routine, repetitive and wooden. The development and nurture of the members of the teams of pastors and laity can turn out to be crucial.

NOTES

1. See Erik Erikson, *Toys and Reasons: Stages in the Ritualization of Experience* (New York: Norton, 1977). Also see Michael Warren, *Communications and Cultural Analyses: A Religious View* (Westport, Conn.: Bergin & Garvey, 1992), for a penetrating analysis of the values and rituals in society coming from mass media and their power to counter our best efforts to help youth embrace and express authentic Christian faith.
2 Søren Kierkegaard, *Thoughts on Crucial Situations in Human Life,* trans. by David Swenson (Minneapolis: Augsburg, 1948), p. 17.
3. See William E. Downey, "A 'People's Church' Out of Touch With the People," *The Christian Century* (April 24, 1991), p. 464.
4. Jerome Kagan, *The Nature of the Child* (New York: Basic Books, 1984), p. 9.
5. Ibid., p. 181.
6. Robert Kegan, *The Evolving Self* (Cambridge, Mass.: Harvard University Press, 1982), p. 96.
7. Ibid., p. 97.
8. See Robert Bellah, Richard Madson, William Sullivan, Ann Swidler, and Steven Tipton, *The Good Society* (New York: Knopf, 1991), for a penetrating discussion of the importance of commitment to healthy institutional life in a democracy.
9. Ibid., p. 44.
10. Sharon Parks, *The Critical Years: The Young Adult Search for a Faith to Live By* (San Francisco: Harper & Row, 1986), p. 64.
11. Ibid., p. 59.
12. We can find help from new mentoring programs such as one created by Lester Jipp, called *The Learning Juncture*, where high school youth are receiving course credit for experiences with mentors in various occupational settings with which they identify. Write for more information to: Dr. Lester Jipp, 135 Wilson Drive, Worthington, Ohio 43085.
13. Don S. Browning and Carol Browning, "The Church and the Family Crisis: A New Love Ethic," *The Christian Century* (August 7-14, 1991), p. 749.

14. See James W. Fowler, *Becoming Adult, Becoming Christian* (San Francisco: Harper & Row, 1984).

15. Joseph McKinney, *Perpetuation, Pentecost: Prayer Preparation for Confirmation and Pentecost* (Brown, 1991).

16. See Ailien A. Doyle, *Youth Retreats: Creating Sacred Space for Young People* (Winona, Minn.: St. Mary's College Press, 1986).

17. Joanmarie Smith, "The Spiritual Education of God's People," in *The Pastor As Religious Educator*, ed. Robert L. Browning (Birmingham, Ala.: Religious Education Press, 1989), pp. 107-125.

18. See *Baptism and Renewal of Baptism*, Division of Missions in Canada (The Task Group on Christian Initiation, Toronto, 1986).

Chapter VIII

YOUNG ADULTS: A TIME FOR BAPTISMAL AFFIRMATION FOCUSED ON VOCATION

Key issues for young adults have to do with institutional commitments, intimacy, and internal consistency between faith and life. It is somewhat amazing that the church has not placed a much higher value on ministry with young adults in order to deal with these issues. This is so because the evidence from studies of this period of life is overwhelming that this is the primary time for owning one's faith after genuine critique and review. Erik Erikson saw the primary task of young adulthood to be the finding of a deep intimacy with the opposite sex which would deal with the threat of isolation. He also saw this as the period when the self could be unified by moving the sense of fidelity, which was needed in adolescence, on to an ideology, to a total philosophy of life. The latter is needed by young adults in order to integrate their internal and external worlds and give them a clear sense of consistency and direction.[1] James Fowler identifies young adulthood as the time most likely for the development of an Individuative-reflective faith. Such a faith (Stage IV) is characterized by the quest to critique the faith into which the person has been nurtured not merely at the personal level but "as a system." Young adults who have moved into this stage of faith want to address questions of the truth of biblical and theological claims made by the institutional church and to get behind the symbols to understandings that make sense in relation to all of life. This is a great time for honest theological reflection and for relating fresh understandings to one's sense of vocation and one's decision con-

161

cerning occupational commitment. Also, the quest to resolve the need for love and intimacy can lead to a much deeper appropriation of the Christian understanding of marriage and family or of responsible and meaningful singleness. Young adults can look seriously at the concepts of the universal priesthood of all believers or the priesthood of parenthood and see the excitement and fulfillment possible in decisions to be in ministry in ways concretely related to work and family.[2]

Sharon Parks, as we have indicated, found young adulthood to be the time for the person to develop a "consciousness of the authority of the inner life of the self in the composing of truth and of choice." The young adult begins to trust and depend upon his or her own insides, his or her own awareness of consistencies or discrepancies "between the claims of the self and the capacity of the social structures of one's world to respond to those claims."[3] The central task is to develop a sense of innerdependence and a feeling that the inner self can be trusted.

In his study of the stages of the evolving self, Robert Kegan found young adulthood as the time when the individual begins to move beyond interpersonal balance (so important to adolescents) on to institutional balance. Young adults begin to define themselves by their institutional commitments and seek an ego balance in the construction of a legal and societal system which is normative. These commitments are "reflective of that deeper structure which constructs the self itself as a system and makes ultimate (as does every balance) the maintenance of its integrity."[4] By identifying with occupational, social, and religious institutions whose values and practices are embraced as being consistent with one's inner beliefs and values, the self is strengthened to express its authority. Of course, the young adult must find this internal consistency and authenticity in order to be able to make sense out of life and to make commitments. Young adulthood may be the prime time for honest affirmations of faith which are clearly tied to public commitments to be in ministry in and through the church as an institution. Such commitment will not take place unless the exploration of the church's claims and promises can be undertaken in an environment of openness and trust. No expression of doubt can be off-limits. No thoughts concerning new ways to be in ministry should be rejected without genuine consideration. The danger of this period is that the self can be too tied to institutional balance, once attained, and is not free to critique "the values which maintain the institution as an end in itself." Such a freedom within the self comes with growth toward an interindividual balance often found in mid-life. Young adults are on a pilgrimage to find institutional commitments and to find concrete expressions of those commitments in career, family, community, and world. Because of that, the self can be too caught up with the institutions that have brought balance. The next step is for the self to find enough transcendence over the values of the institution to be able to differentiate the self from "the duties, performances, work roles, career which institutionality gives rise to. One has a career; one no longer *is* a career."[5] More about this pilgrimage of the self in the next chapter.

Confirmation/affirmation in young adulthood is being recommended by increasing numbers of pastors and educators. The most concrete recommendations have come from John Westerhoff. In his several writings Westerhoff believes that there should be ritualized celebrations in late childhood and late adolescence as rites of passage between childhood and adolescence and between adolescence and adulthood, probably upon the occasion of the individual's birthday, but that confirmation education and celebration of baptismal covenant should take place "during early adulthood (in late twenties to early thirties) when persons can at least begin to assume mature responsibility for their faith and life. To expect an adolescent to make these responses without the necessary growth and learning is to expect too much."[6] We believe Westerhoff is right to emphasize confirmation in young adulthood but not as a one–time experience. There is no reason for the celebration in late childhood or late adolescence not to be public affirmation of baptismal covenant. If confirmation is a part of the unified initiation in infancy or early childhood it can be repeated with integrity when the self-understanding of the person changes in relation to his or her understanding and commitment to the Christian faith. It is such an understanding of confirmation or affirmation which is emerging in the ecumenical church, an understanding which needs only more specificity in terms of educational and liturgical designs for the various periods of growth in faith throughout life.

Educational Options

Young adults are particularly open to assessment of where they are in their basic self-understanding and their basic life-giving or life-denying beliefs and values. Very big decisions about sexuality, marriage, family, work, community involvement, politics, etc., are being made almost daily. As Kierkegaard said, adults learn backwards, back into their youth, back into their childhood in order to discover anew who they really are and what they want to do with their lives. This is a time for starting with these stories in an environment that is safe enough to risk telling the stories and putting those stories in dialogue with the many stories of faith which make up the Christian witness (biblical, historical, and present figures with whom to identify and refine faith). So often the church is not the community with which young adults are in communication. The central need is for church families to find creative ways to keep the dialogue and conversation going with young adults. Part of the task can be accomplished by offering creative and clear options to young adults along with challenges to them to take leadership in the church's ministry with those who are younger, those who are peers, and those who are older members of the body of Christ. Research has revealed that youth are most influenced by those one age level above them. Young adults are most influenced to remain in dialogue and conversation by their peers. And middle and older adults are greatly stimulated and enriched to be working with younger members of the faith community rather than separated as older adults. We must find creative roles for young adults to play in the life of the worshiping, learning, serving church. If young adults feel accepted, even in the midst of their need for more space (the psychosocial moratorium about which Erik Erikson speaks) they will be more inclined to decide to be a part of learning groups that are pursuing the core understanding of the Christian story in dialogue with their own stories, their own genuine questions, doubts, hopes, and visions of the future.

Young adults are not looking for predigested right answers. They are looking for acceptance and challenge to grow in faith but in community with others. As Thomas Groome says in his important study of Christian religious education "dialogue begins with one's self. At bedrock it is a conversation with one's own biographies, with one's own stories and visions. Of course, to be truly known by us, our self-dialogue must be externalized and shared with others, and they too, must be heard if we are to know more clearly our own stories and visions."[7] The next step is the sharing of the Christian story in dialogue with the real living issues that have become known in the sharing of each person's story. The church needs to train teachers and leaders who know the essentials of the Christian story and also are sure enough to be able to share that story in a dialogical manner. As Groome wisely believes the "dialogue requires that the story and vision be made available in a *disclosure* rather than a *closure* manner. This means that it cannot be imposed upon the participants monologically, but must be made available in a way that invites dialogue with the tradition from their own lived experience."[8] Both scripture and tradition can be used to probe the story but in relation to the (1) present actions of young adults and (2) their own stories. (3) Then probing the Christian story is a crucial third movement. (4) The next movement or step is to engage in a critical dialectic between the Christian story and the participants' present stories. This movement means that together we dialogue about "what does the community's story mean for (affirm, call in question, invite beyond) our stories, but how do our stories respond to (affirm, recognize limits of, push beyond) the community's story."[9] (5) Groome's final movement is to go back to the present action of the participants and look at the visions of the meaning of life implied and to critique those visions embodied in present actions in the light of the vision of God's Kingdom or realm implied in the Christian story—and then to decide on future action. As we have underscored in Chapter II, the process is an action–reflection–action model which is particularly appropriate for young adults but good for learning at any age.

Groome's approach has been highly affirmed but also critiqued appreciatively. Don Browning in his penetrating proposal for a fundamental practical theology refines and deepens the process. He agrees that we should start with present action but that we should persist with the actions of persons in more depth, to do descriptive theological thinking about our actions. We need to identify the questions that persons have about their actual practice in a *thick* rather than a *thin* way. As Browning asserts, "It is not the task of descriptive theology to discern a question in some simple, logical way. The task is to describe it in its thickness. The task of descriptive theology is to describe a question in all of its situated richness. This is basic for the later task of strategic practical theology."[10] Browning believes that we should use the best aids we can find from the social sciences to help us grasp these questions in their richness. He further emphasizes more than Groome the importance of approaches to ethical thinking and decision making. Young adults are often wrestling with ethical questions which result from conflict between their needs and how these needs can be met morally (e.g., my sexual needs in relation to sexual ethics before and during marriage). They are looking for ethical principles or guidelines concerning how honest to be with another concerning attitudes or feelings, how truthful to be concerning taxes or expense accounts, etc. They are concerned about how their behavior affects environmental and social issues. They are looking for clarity about ethical rules

and roles that will be consistent with the vision of the meaning and purpose of life which they can gain through their faith commitment.
Browning's emphasis on description does not focus on any attempt to
escape the religious or theoretical assumptions that are present in our
actions. Rather, he stresses the importance of admitting and decoding
these assumptions at the outset. Such an honest effort can be quite engaging if not exciting for young adults especially. The next step is to enter into
dialogue with the basic texts of the Christian faith, and "the non-christian texts to which Christianity has itself listened" to get in touch with
the narratives and metaphors of the faith (historical theology). Persons can
do biblical interpretation not only at the visional or moral obligatorial
levels but explore how the texts interpret human needs and tendencies or
the social or environmental issues of our time. This dialogue in the past
has been enriched by looking at the existential questions coming out of
practice in correlation with the great answers of the faith (Paul Tillich's
approach in his *Systematic Theology*). In this approach to the dialogue,
issues of personal anxiety, self–protective pride, the nature of sin, salvation, God, Christ, the Holy Spirit, grace, forgiveness, redemption,
incarnation, etc., were pursued.

Browning agrees with David Tracy that the dialogue should use a
revised critical correlation method. It is not only a listening to and identification of the real and existential questions persons are raising out of
their actions and the possible answers of the faith, it involves a level of honesty and dialogue beyond that. It becomes "a critical dialogue between the
implicit questions and the explicit answers of the Christian classics and
the explicit questions and implicit answers of contemporary cultural
experiences and practices."[11] The dialogue must not be hedged. It must
include conversation with all possible answers, from wherever they may
come. This dialogue is not an end in itself. It is undertaken in order to
explore practical ethical answers or strategies (strategic practical theology) which return the learner back to the real life actions which motivated
the exploration in the first place. Such a stance of honest sharing, probing the Christian answers in relation to concrete ethical discussion, but in
an atmosphere of genuine openness to all possible answers is one with
which young adults can identify. If Fowler's research is at all "on target" young adults are wanting a learning environment in which they can
come to an Individuative-reflective faith, one which is owned personally and yet finds support corporately. Education also needs liturgical
avenues to celebrate fresh interpretations and new discoveries of how

one can affirm one's baptismal covenant and be strengthened for ministries within and beyond the faith community. Confirmation/affirmation cele- brations are especially meaningful at this point in life. Such celebrations can be related not only to an owned faith but to decisions to embrace *some specific form* of ministry, some clear expression of the universal priesthood of believers.

Such an element should be an important exploration with young adults. What understanding of their sense of life's purpose and calling do they reveal in practice? What do their present actions imply in respect to ener- gies spent in work, in family, in leisure, in community outreach? What are the great understandings about life's purpose and call which come from the Christian story? What images of ministry are implied in their human stories and the Christian story, especially related to their baptism into the ministry of all members of Christ's body? And, on through the other steps to the exploration of possible decisions which can relate to daily actions within and beyond the church.

Clear options for education and celebration help persons see how they may be involved. Some of these options, not only for young adults but for middle and older adults are as follows:

A Core Curriculum for the Ministry of the Laity. John and Adrienne Carr have taken creative leadership in interpreting the need for such a cur- riculum and in designing and testing such an educational program. It is their belief and their experience that all young adults who have been a part of the baptized community are ripe for supportive educational experience in the core understanding of the Christian gospel of love and justice. This core experience should be much more than a course. It must include searching the scriptures, personal prayer and group litur- gical celebrations, and especially the development of an honest Christian community. The experience should start with a sharing of the stories of the persons in the group in dialogue with the Christian story. Finally, the core curriculum should include basic training for lay ministry. The latter includes four elements: a vision of what that ministry involves, along with a grasp of ways to make decisions about specific forms of min- istry, some fundamental ministry skills (listening, consulting, giving feedback, faith sharing, conflict resolution, strategizing for change in personal and corporate life), and a conviction that the learning process is ongoing.[12] The Carrs have written imaginative curriculum resources which can be used by pastoral and lay teaching teams to fulfill their vision.[13]

Denominational Programs for Lay Ministry

Several denominations have caught the vision of every person prepared and committed to live out his or her baptismal covenant to be in ministry. As the United Methodist program guide, *Vital Congregations–Faithful Disciples* says, "All the people of God, the whole laos, are called to ministry by virtue of being baptized. All baptized Christians are in full-time Christian service. All share the vocation of carrying on Christ's healing and reconciling ministry. And all have received by baptism the gifts they need to serve Christ in every walk of life, through school, work, civic activity, leisure, and home . . . No task in the church is more important than the equipping or fitting together of the gifts of the people for the work of ministry (Ephesians 4:12). Congregations need to devote much time to training lay persons so that their gifts can be utilized in the service of Christ."[14] The *Vital Congregations* document itself is intended to be used as a resource in such training.

The Episcopal Church in its general convention of 1976 resolved that each diocese should provide for the development of lay ministries through a program called *Total Ministry*. The program has been refined and strengthened over the years. The basic thesis is: clergy and laity are equally called to minister in the church and the world. Local congregations are asked to make a commitment to the program by having the local clergy and vestry members take the course first, followed by other interested persons. The program emphasizes two things: that the gifts and talents of both clergy and laity be recognized, and that concrete opportunities be provided for both to exercise these gifts in ministry. The *Total Ministry* curriculum includes a seven–segment introductory experience, followed by longer course patterns which go into much more depth. The introductory course includes community building, a theology of ministry, the enrichment for ministry, the baptismal covenant and ministry, spirituality and ministry, gifts and ministry, and next steps. Those who wish to go deeper in their preparation enroll in additional study of the above issues in an ongoing course pattern or in weekend or day-long retreats. Persons can conclude their preparation by committing themselves to particular ministries and by reaffirmation of their baptismal covenant upon the occasion of the bishop's visit for confirmation. A very comprehensive program, *Education for Ministry,* has been developed by the School of Theology, The University of the South. Over 30,000 lay persons have participated in this four–year series of studies. Laity not only from the United States but also from Germany, Great Britain, New Zealand, Australia, Canada, the Bahamas, Honduras, and Nicaragua have joined the program. The courses are now available in Spanish translations.[15]

Most denominational publishing houses have developed some resources particularly focused on the preparation of laity for their ministry.

Resources aimed at the preparation of lay persons for specific liturgical ministries have been designed by the Liturgical Conference. These resources can be used to prepare lay communion ministers, acolytes, ushers, musicians, liturgical dancers, and occasional ministers. *There Are Different Ministries* by Robert W. Hovda opens up the integrity of these lay ministries and identifies eight additional courses in the series.[16]

Resources that are oriented to the preparation of laity for the unique ministries in their work place and in the wider society are published by the Alban Institute[17] and the Cathedral College of the Laity.[18] A lay person who has taken his ministry seriously in the work place is William Diehl, former steel executive and President of Riverbend Resource Center in Allentown, Pennsylvania. He has modeled lay involvement and commitment through his workshops and his publications. His most recent book probes what it means to be Christian in the fields of law, education, medicine, public service, or homemaking. What is it to be faithful in these settings? Diehl interviewed seventy lay persons in depth about their view of the marks of a Christian in the workplace.

His book, *In Search of Faithfulness,* is a fine resource for the training of laity to see their daily occupation as an arena for ministry.[19]

Another ecumenical program which has trained lay persons for ministry across the world is the *Stephen Ministries* organization, founded by Kenneth Haugk, a pastor, clinical psychologist, and educator. Haugk's counseling skills and understanding make him particularly sensitive to the need of persons within and beyond the congregation for caring ministries. He developed a program to recruit, select, and train lay persons to minister with persons with special needs: the hospitalized, the terminally ill, those in job crises, those who are disabled and handicapped, the lonely or depressed, those affected by alcohol or chemical dependency, those in spiritual crises, and many others. Since 1975 the Stephen Series has been used to train Stephen Ministers in well over 2,000 churches. The training starts with a twelve day leader's course offered regionally. Then, the trained leaders (pastors, Christian educators, and lay persons) take the initiative at the local level, recruiting lay participants and providing a minimum of fifty hours of personalized preparation. Those who agree to become Stephen Ministers are then commissioned before the congregation and recognized as persons committed to the ministries of care within the church and community. It is then important to find creative ways to interpret the presence of Stephen Ministers and to link them with persons in need. The Stephen Ministry program has been affirmed widely as an authentic form of lay ministry. By limiting the focus to ministries of active listening and compassionate caring the training has been focused not only on the processes of caring but also on the specific arena of care from the ill to those who are bereaved, to chemical dependency, etc. Stephen Ministers are to serve in tandem with clergy, other professional care givers, and church and family members.

Efforts to move laity into the issues of our contemporary world have emerged ecumenically and denominationally. Solid theological and theoretical thinking has been done in both Catholic and Protestant communities. Those planning local church educational and liturgical designs will be assisted by doing additional reading in works by James and Evelyn Whitehead,[21] James W. Fowler,[22] and in our own earlier work.[23]

Again, it is important to employ well–trained leaders who are secure enough to invite honest questions and genuinely free dialogue. Such leaders should be able to personalize their approach for each member of the learning group. These approaches are especially important for young adults who are making their unique pilgrimages to mature Christian faith. Creativity in teaching methods and clarity about objectives and evaluation can greatly enhance the quality of the educational ministry with young adults and for persons at each of the stages of adult faith development.

NOTES

1. See Erik Erikson, *Identity: Youth and Crisis* (New York: Norton, 1968).
2. See James W. Fowler, *Stages of Faith* (San Francisco: Harper & Row, 1981), p. 180.
3. Sharon Parks, *The Critical Years: The Young Adult Search for a Faith to Live By* (San Francisco: Harper & Row, 1986), p. 58.
4. Robert Kegan, *The Evolving Self* (Cambridge, Mass.: Harvard University Press, 1982), p. 101.
5. Ibid., p. 105.
6. John H. Westerhoff III, "Confirmation: An Episcopal Church Perspective," in *Confirming the Faith of Adolescents*, ed. Arthur J. Kubick (New York: Paulist, 1991), p. 157.
7. Thomas H. Groome, *Christian Religious Education: Sharing Our Story and Vision* (San Francisco: Harper & Row, 1980), p. 189.
8. Ibid., p. 189.
9. Ibid., p. 217.
10. Don S. Browning, *A Fundamental Practical Theology: Descriptive and Strategic Proposals* (Minneapolis: Fortress, 1991), p. 94.

11. Ibid., p. 46.
12. See John Lynn Carr, "Needed: A Pastoral Curriculum for the Congregation," in *The Pastor As Religious Educator,* ed. Robert L. Browning (Birmingham, Ala.: Religious Education Press, 1989), pp. 41-44.
13. John Lynn Carr and Adrienne Carr, *The Experiment in Practical Christianity* (Nashville: Discipleship Resources, The United Methodist Publishing House, 1985), and *The Pilgrimage Project* (Nashville: The Upper Room, 1987). The latter helps people dialogue about their stories and the Christian story.
14. The United Methodist Council of Bishops, *Vital Congregations - Faithful Disciples: Vision for the Church* (Nashville: Graded Press, 1990), plus a leader's guide.
15. See *Welcome to Total Ministry: A Curriculum Model,* Episcopal Diocese of Southern Ohio, Mary Anne Wehnenl, Chair. Also, see *Education for Ministry Prospectus: A Program of Theological Education by Extension.* The School of Theology, The University of the South, Sewanee, Tennessee 37375-4010.
16. Robert W. Hovda, *There Are Different Ministries* (Washington, D.C.: The Liturgical Conference, 1978).
17. See resources such as Verna J. Dozier, *The Authority of the Laity* (Washington, D.C.: The Alban Institute, 1983).
18. See a wide range of resources on ministry in the workplace, business ethics, corporate leadership, moral character and development at work, etc. Write Cathedral College of the Laity, Washington Cathedral, Mount Saint Alban, Washington, D.C. 20016.
19. See William E. Diehl, *In Search of Faithfulness: Lessons from the Christian Community* (Philadelphia: Fortress, 1987) and an earlier book *Thank God, It's Monday* (Philadelphia: Fortress, 1982).
20. Kenneth C. Haugk, *Christian Caregiving: A Way of Life* (Minneapolis: Augsburg, 1984), or write Stephen Ministries, 8016 Dale Street, St. Louis, Missouri 63117-1449.
21. James D. Whitehead and Evelyn E. Whitehead, *The Emerging Laity: Returning Leadership to the Community of Faith* (Garden City, N.Y.: Doubleday, 1986).
22. James W. Fowler, *Becoming Adult, Becoming Christian* (San Francisco: Harper & Row, 1984).
23. Robert L. Browning and Roy A. Reed, "The Sacraments of Vocation: The Ordination of Clergy and the Consecration of the Laity for Ministry," in *The Sacraments in Religious Education and Liturgy* (Birmingham, Ala.: Religious Education Press, 1985).

Chapter IX

MIDDLE ADULTS: THE NEED FOR REASSESSMENT AND RECOMMITMENT

Middle adulthood is a time in life which is curiously the most counted on and the most overlooked in the church. If it were not for the contribution of middle adults to the ministry, the body of Christ would be much weaker than it is. And yet those who are in middle adulthood have unique needs which have not been well identified until more recent years.

Middle adults have lived long enough and have tried out their personal and vocational self-understandings to the point of considerable self-awareness. Many become increasingly aware of certain inner tensions. Erikson, for instance, sees the struggle of this period as the quest for generativity versus the threat of stagnation. After years of personal effort to succeed in work and family, men and women begin to take stock and to wonder if their early goals in life have been achieved, or if such hopes will ever be realized. Also, adults in the middle years are experiencing many biological as well as psychological changes. Women reach menopause during these years, and men often begin to question their sexual potency. In our contemporary society with the patterns of rapid socio–economic changes many find their occupational self-understanding being challenged. Whole corporations can be closed down with persons at all levels of endeavor losing their jobs and having to rethink who they are and what they can expect to do in the years ahead. They wonder if they can continue to do what they have done but in a new context or will be forced to do something quite different which probably will call for retraining in mid-life. Research has established that the needs of adults in middle life follow a rhythm of transition which oscillates between rapid change and relative stability. Daniel Levinson saw middle adulthood starting at around age forty and lasting until sixty. During these twenty years he found two transition periods: The first is a period of turmoil in the early forties, followed by a period of more stability. The second transition is around age fifty where there is new awareness of one's mortality and the difficulties ahead in the aging process. Aging parents may be needing more attention. The death of friends or parents can cause anxiety and disorientation unless spiritual resources have been developed. This second transition is followed by a period of relative calm in the mid– to late–fifties prior to another transitional stage into older adulthood.[1]

James Fowler's research concerning the stages of faith has identified the importance of growth in faith within an ongoing faith community for people in mid-life. His research found that persons in the middle years could be living with behaviors, beliefs, and values that reflect several stages of faith development. Some are still Stage II, Mythic-literal, in their faith. A sizable number of middle adults reflect Stage III, Synthetic-conventional values. While the Stage IV, Individuative-reflective, is most common for young adults, several middle adults do not have their more conventional belief system tested or challenged until the late thirties or early forties where a marital breakup, the death of a person who was important to one's self-understanding, or problems with children, etc., puts the person into disequilibrium enough to send him or her on a quest for an "owned faith." Fowler found a significant number of middle adults working on individuative-reflective tasks—critiquing their faith "as a system," seeking to get behind the symbols to the realities in life to which the symbols point. Fowler found few people moving into Stage V, Conjunctive Faith, before middle adulthood.

Persons in mid-life often go through periods of disequilibrium when they begin to question just how well they have worked out their beliefs and values or just how consistent they are in their actual behavior. Fowler found that persons begin to find a new equilibrium through a more dialogical way of knowing and seeing life. Increasingly mid-life adults see the paradoxical nature of life. Those things they thought they had put together may begin to fall apart or they begin to find as much evidence against as for their formulations of truth. The middle adult, working on a Stage V, Conjunctive faith, has become aware that he or she must be open to truths which come from others without imposing preconceived categories upon them. The Stage V pilgrimage cannot get underway until the person feels enough internal security to allow genuine diversity of belief and action to be internalized. Persons in Stage V begin to trust the authenticity, the perceptions and views of others. Middle adults in quest of a conjunctive faith use their critical skills but in a different mode. They are weary of critique for its own sake. They want to let the symbols of the faith speak with freshness and power to their inner spirits. They are capable of coming to a "second naivete," as Paul Ricoeur calls it, to an openness that lets religious symbols speak with new power. Such an approach "carries forward the critical capacities and methods of the previous stage, but it no longer trusts them except as tools to avoid self-deception and to order truths encountered in other ways."[2]

The demythologizing of the Christian story characteristic of Stage IV critical-reflection gives way to a desire to let the story speak with fresh power. This revitalization of the Christian Story can be appropriated and internalized in a way that does not close off the insight inherent in the stories of faith coming from persons of other persuasions. Stage V faith is one in which persons are willing to risk "going beyond the explicit ideological system and clear boundaries of identity that Stage IV worked so hard to construct and to adhere to. . . . Stage V accepts as axiomatic that truth is more multidimensional and organically interdependent than most theories or accounts of truth can grasp. Religiously it knows that the symbols, stories, doctrines, and liturgies offered by its own or other traditions are inevitably partial, limited to a particular people's experience of God and incomplete."[3] Conjunctive faith, therefore, is willing to move out, to have significant encounters with persons of other commitments without giving up the beliefs, traditions and practices around which the individual is organized and grounded. There is a certain respect for the unconscious and intuitive which comes back to give balance to the conscious decisions of the past.

It is for this reason that persons on mid-life pilgrimages are potentially much more open to the study of spiritual insights and methods of Christians from other traditions than their own and from other world religions and ideologies. Also, middle adults can learn through the music, art, prayer, and liturgies of others. Learning designs should go well beyond course offerings and include exposure to new insights via many media in individualized and group forms. Mid-life study groups can help persons integrate much that was suppressed or unrecognized before. This can be a very exciting mind and spirit expanding period, a time which pro-vides a new awareness of different balances in life. The mid-adult's quest for a renewable quality of life can be met with ministries within the church which balance mental, emotional, and physical dimensions in an interactive way. This approach should emphasize a spiritual develop-ment which includes these levels and is not detached from the issues of real life.

Learning Approaches for Middle Adults

As was stated above, middle adults can be in very different places in their faith development. What middle adults want is an environment where they can be honest about their actual strengths and struggles and their perceptions of their spiritual health. Such honest dialogue is enhanced greatly by a caring and safe environment where they can assess both their needs and the direction they want to go in their pursuit of fresh understandings of themselves and their faith. This means that the church should create options which respond to these genuine concerns. The struggles of life can cause a person with a mythic-literal faith to fall into disequilibrium, into a state of internal confusion about belief. We need to be sensitive to ways to help the person address these issues and work them through to the point of seeing the power of the stories of faith which transcend their literal interpretations. They can then discover that myth is a way to point to truths that are bigger than the understanding that often accompanies the literal story. Such a middle adult might come out with a stronger, tested, but still somewhat conventional Stage III faith. The process, however, may have brought a new equilibrium, a new sense of well-being and direction, and an attitude of openness to more growth as life unfolds.

Educational concerns of middle adults must be central in the options made available whether in individual or group learning settings. These con-cerns can include: matters of personal growth; changing relationships (marital, male-female roles and functions, teenage children, aging parents, friends, colleagues in the work place); career planning and reassessment in relation to a sense of Christian vocation; financial struggles in relation to an understanding of the stewardship of life; changes in self-under-standing in relation to changing beliefs; stress management, employing prayer and meditation; explorations of the beliefs and actions of others, including world religions or ideologies; mid-life crises, such as divorce,

alcoholism, or drug abuse; changing views of sexuality; fresh understandings of the church as a ministering community in a complex world;
new understandings of the sacramental nature of life itself and the power
of the sacraments throughout life; exposure to new understandings and
methods of spirituality; concern for social issues of racism, sexism, pover-
ty, ecology, health, peace, and justice. All of these are matters which
impinge on middle adults who are asked to assume a disproportionate
share of responsibility for their solution.

In other words it is important to remember that adults want to be self-
motivated learners. We need to start where they are and assist them to plan
to take responsibility for their own learnings. It is also important to recognize that middle adults have the experience and capacity to be interdependent. They can and want to work together to support one another,
to create networks of care, learning, and ministry.[4] Carol Gilligan found
this to be especially true in the experience and perception of women.
She found the human development of women to be different from men.
Women are not only interdependent they emphasize relationships and
interconnectedness more than men. Gilligan's observations are a helpful corrective to the thinking of Levinson who did his research entirely
on men. Gilligan correctly urges much more research on the unique
ways women describe their own developmental needs and issues.[5]
Certainly, Gilligan found quite different perceptions of women's rights
and responsibilities with quite different expectations concerning moral
development. She maintains that a change in the norms for maturity
changes the whole structure of moral development. When care itself is
the highest norm rather than fairness, as in Kohlberg's system, moral
development is defined in respect to responsibilities and relationships
rather than the understanding of right and rules.[6] Clearly much more
research is needed on these matters. Equally important is sensitivity to
such differences on the part of designers of educational approaches for
women and men in the middle years. There are many good guides for
educational ministry with middle adults.[7] These educational designs
will be greatly strengthened if they can be integrated with liturgical and
sacramental life.

The opportunity to celebrate new internal commitments in public can
have great spiritual power. Many middle adults who have experienced new
self-understandings in relation to deepened commitments to the Christian
faith hunger and thirst for visible ways to celebrate these new realities.

Affirmation of one's baptismal covenant or *confirmation as a repeat-*

able sacrament can be filled with meaning not only for the person making the fresh declaration of faith but for the whole community of faith. The several patterns of the adult catechumenate have much potential for adults at any stage but especially for middle adults who are seeking to deal with the realities of their lives and the need for spiritual depth and refocus. The liturgical celebrations which accompany and follow these catechumenal programs become significant moments of blessing and spiritual empowerment for both the new Christians involved and for those reaffirming their baptismal covenants and linking them to concrete forms of ministry in the body of Christ.

The Catechumenal Process as a Paradigm for Preparation for Confirmation in Mid-Life

The historic catechumenate with its four–stage process has not only been recaptured by the Roman Catholic Church in its Rite of Christian Initiation of Adults but also by other denominations, especially the Episcopal Church. The latter has experimented with various forms of catechumenal education and liturgy, including approaches that bring together both unbaptized and baptized: those who wish to affirm their baptismal covenant for the first time, usually youth, or reaffirm their baptism in a similar program of study. This includes sponsorship and preparation to be in some specific form of ministry. The baptized are not to be called catechumens. Rather, they are seen as assistants to the catechists who are themselves sharing their own faith-stories and identifying where they need or want to grow in faith. The Episcopal program is called *The Catechumenal Process: Adult Initiation and Formation for Christian Life and Ministry.* The process has been widened from the original focus on evangelization and the preparation of new Christians to include the following types of persons:

- persons baptized as infants who want to make mature public affirmation of their faith
- persons seeking out the church for marriage or for baptism of a child
- newcomers from other churches
- persons returning to the church from another church or denomination
- active members seeking to deepen their commitment
- nominal members seeking basic Christian formation
- lapsed members reconsidering their "Christian commitment"

This widened stance is based on the proposition that "persons reaffirming their commitment, renewing their vows, or seeking to deepen their understanding of faith need formation, just as do persons preparing for baptism."[8]

This approach has encouraged significant numbers of persons who have been baptized as infants and confirmed as youth to recognize their need for additional times in their life pilgrimages for reaffirmation and focus of their faith in concrete forms of ministry. Such a stance is a presupposition for the concept of confirmation or baptismal affirmation as a repeatable experience. The Episcopal program for both unbaptized and baptized culminates in the fourth stage of the catechumenal program, the Mystogogia period, a time after baptism or reaffirmation of one's baptismal covenant when the focus is on preparation for ministry, discovering the candidate's gifts for ministry, and making decisions concerning ways to share such gifts in the family, at work, in leisure, and in community and world.

The persons seeking reaffirmation of their baptismal vows participate freely with those who are catechumens preparing for baptism, confirmation, and eucharist (the unified initiation) which will take place at the Easter Vigil. Sometimes those seeking reaffirmation will not be blessed until Pentecost when the bishop most likely will be able to be present. Nevertheless, they will participate fully in the total process with appropriate variations which recognize their baptism and membership in the body of Christ. This means they will not participate in various rites of the catechumens such as the Rite of Admission to the catechumenate or the Rite of Enrollment as a candidate to be baptized. They will participate in the stage one *inquiry period* by sharing their own faith stories and explaining the issues of faith they wish to pursue in more depth. They will take part in the catechumenate period as the substance of the faith is explored in more depth, including the great Christian themes from scripture: creation, covenant, Christ, the church, consummation, and the personal beliefs and questions each brings. They will share in the enlightenment period where personal, spiritual, and ethical concerns are probed during Lent with a view to making fresh commitments at the Easter Vigil. During Holy Week or Maundy Thursday those making reaffirmation may participate in the footwashing service, having their feet washed by the pastor or catechetical leaders and then participating in the washing of the feet of members of the congregation who wish to come forward. They also take part in the other phases of preparation for the Easter Vigil celebration, especially those aspects which deepen prayer life and ministry. A special welcoming liturgy for baptized Christians seeking renewal is provided to be used at the principal Sunday Eucharist. This is followed by a liturgy to be used on Ash Wednesday, calling the baptized to continuing conversion. Those who have been participants in the program of spiritual growth are presented by the Senior Warden before the imposition of ashes. After they answer questions concerning their intent and their motivations, such as: "Have they joined us in our life of service to those who are poor, outcast, or powerless?" or, "Have they strived to recognize the gifts that God has given them and to discern how they are to be used in the building up of God's reign of peace and justice?" they receive ashes and participate in marking the members of the congregation with the ashes of repentance and conversion.[9]

A program such as *The Catechumenal Process* is planned to meet the needs of persons at various times in their life and does not highlight the unique concerns of young, middle, or older adults. Such a program, however, can have particular meaning for persons in mid-life who are reassessing their lifestyle and values, who are open to the reconstruction of their faith commitments. Such persons often are motivated internally to seek fresh meanings and directions for their lives. If a church offers some version of *The Catechumenal Process* many middle adults can find support for their honest pilgrimage in faith.

Snyder's Membranes of Meaning Approach to Planning the Second Half of Life

There are many other educational designs which have been generated by various denominations and agencies with potential for helping middle adults come to fresh self-understandings and renewal of faith and sense of vocation. One of the most promising we have found has been developed by Ross Snyder. In his retirement years he and his wife Martha have conducted extensive research on the most significant approaches to helping middle adults plan the second half of their lives. The Snyders have developed a framework and a process for helping persons in mid-life articulate to themselves and others their honest views about the meaning of their lives from birth to the mid-point and then, to project their visions of who and what they want to become during their years ahead. The Snyders have identified certain membranes of meaning from which each of us develops a sense of personal meaning and direction.

Their process is to invite individuals to meditate on and express these membranes of meaning. The first membrane is called *Lived Moments*. These are past moments in which events took place that became life shaping for them in a crucial way. The experience may not have been dramatic, but it was an event which became a model for the individual, giving the person an understanding of his or her essential nature and potential for living life fully.

The next membrane of meaning is the *Manifesto*. The participants are asked to write down and then state an experience in their lives when they as individuals stood up for something even when that stand meant some risk for them. Such a story of a manifesto reveals values held dearly, priorities which have been set, decisions believed to be important. The identification of their respective manifestos and the reflection on these moments can enable persons to start communicating at a much deeper level than is sometimes true in our church settings.

Another membrane of meaning or lens through which to understand our lives is the experience of sharing our *Psycho-histories*. Participants are invited to reflect upon the interrelationships between what has happened to them in their individual lives and the events which have taken place in their community, in nation, and world. Such a quest can open up to each person and to those in the group what they believe to be important personally in terms of ultimate commitments and beliefs and what they understand society's issues and problems are. This activity becomes an opportunity to look deeply at the goals individuals have had in relation to hopes and goals for their families, communities, and world.

Another membrane of meaning is the *Saga*. Individuals are invited to go beyond a description of lived moments, manifestos, and psycho-histories to seek the elements of connectedness between these episodes. After these connections have been made and shared, persons are asked to describe some major ongoing theme for their lives. One woman stated that the theme of her life saga was "Hospitality" because she could not remember when she was not accepting or hosting someone or some new ideas or projects. Snyder urges us to listen for the uniqueness of each life saga and not try to categorize persons.

After helping persons in mid-life to listen to their own stories, their own meanings, their own goals, the enabler of the process can then assist persons in planning ahead. In this process, the Christian understanding of vocation, of ongoing ministry can be explored in direct relation to the lived moments, manifestos, events in the various psycho-histories, and the pervasive life themes in each person's saga.[10] Such an approach is consistent with the praxis approach to Christian religious education, outlined in Chapter II, but it goes deeper into the individuals' life stories prior to exploring the story and vision of the Christian faith and the meaning of that story/vision for the life of the individual but also for the community of faith. William Phillips has developed an adaptation of the Snyders' approach for congregations. Phillips has assisted congregations to identify their lived moments, their manifestos, their psycho-histories, their sagas in order for congregations to know who they are, what their great values and loyalties have been. As congregational members come to see the uniqueness of their faith community they can begin to weave these membranes of meaning into a new and fresh tapestry for the future.[11]

It is our thesis that this process most powerfully can culminate in liturgical celebrations of new self-understandings and fresh commitments to be in concrete forms of ministry. Confirmation or baptismal affirmation in mid-life can be a way of recapturing a vision for individuals as well as for congregations in their middle age.

NOTES

1. See Daniel Levinson et al., *The Seasons of a Man's Life* (New York: Knopf, 1978). This study is helpful but limited because it was done only with men. It must be balanced with studies by Carol Gilligan and other women.
2. James W. Fowler, *Stages of Faith* (San Francisco: Harper & Row, 1981), p. 188.
3. Ibid., p. 186.
4. See Sharon Parks, *The Critical Years: The Young Adult Search for a Faith to Live By* (San Francisco: Harper & Row, 1986), p. 70.
5. Carol Gilligan, *In a Different Voice: Psychological Theory and Women's Development* (Cambridge, Mass.: Harvard University Press, 1982), p. 173.
6. Ibid., p. 19.
7. See Nancy T. Foltz, *Handbook of Adult Religious Education* (Birmingham, Ala.: Religious Education Press, 1986) and R. E. Y. Wickett, *Models of Adult Religious Education Practice* (Birmingham, Ala.: Religious Education Press, 1991).
8. This is an actual statement from St. Paul's Church in Indianapolis given as an example in *The Catechumenal Process* (New York: The Church Hymnal Corporation, 1990.), p. 234.
9. Ibid., pp. 255-257.
10. See Ross Snyder and Martha Snyder, *Theory and Documentation: How Meanings We Live Can Develop* (San Rafael, Cal.: Institute for Meaning Formations, 1986), a video series in which the Snyders model the sensitive process needed in helping persons share their stories.
11. William J. Phillips, "Getting a Perspective on Your Congregation's Identity," unpublished paper, 1985.

Chapter X

OLDER ADULTS: AFFIRMATION OF BAPTISMAL COVENANT TO BE A BLESSING

As persons approach older adulthood there is a resurgence of concern about vocation. Arthur Becker reminds us that there are three times in life when vocational concerns are uppermost: first, in late adolescence and young adulthood as we are seeking to make initial decisions about vocation and more specifically an occupation; second, during the middle years as we reassess what we have done with our lives and whether or not there is a good fit between our abilities and interests and how these are lived out in our work, family, and community; and third, as we enter into older adulthood. This third time begins to emerge with insistence during the transitional years between middle and older age, often late fifties and early sixties.[1]

Becker identifies the central issue for older adults as, "What will I do with the life that is left to me?" Usually this question is occasioned by impending thoughts of retirement or at least redefinition of how much time will be spent in work–related activities and how much time in leisure and learning activities. Many of us are torn by dated images of retirement years as primarily those to be dedicated to leisure. Yet, we know as Christians that God has called us to purposes well beyond such a destiny, as pleasant and rewarding as an increase of leisure legitimately should be. What is needed is an opportunity to explore the creative possibilities which can accompany a fresh understanding of our baptismal covenant to be in lifelong ministry as a member of Christ's body. Such an exploration can take place as we seek to break up preconceived notions of the stages of life (education for vocation in early life, work during adult years, in order to be rewarded with leisure in older years of retirement) and find a new vision of the older adult years. Such a vision seeks a balance between: (1) creative forms of vocation to be expressed in *work* as a volunteer or for remuneration depending upon need and desire, (2) new opportunities for *learning* related to needs central for older adults or interests which have potential for enriching life, and (3) fresh ways to experience the physical and spiritual renewal more leisure can bring.[2] Richard Bolles found in his study of these three arenas of our lives that a balance is needed at every period of life and especially in older adulthood. He found that when we move from one period of life to another, we go through a series of questions. They are: (1) What's happening? (2) How can I survive in this situation physically, emotionally, and spiritually? (3) After understanding what is happening and getting clues for survival the final question is, What am I going to do with myself or what is a mission for my life in the new situation that will bring meaning to me and others? These three questions are clearly present for persons moving into older adulthood. They are questions best explored in community with others on a similar pilgrimage. This should be done, however, in a way which encourages individual self-evaluation and firm planning for the future.

Such a period of reassessment and planning can be very helpful during the transition years or at any time older adults recognize their need for such reflection, support, and decision making. It is increasingly clear that corporate and public celebrations of decisions concerning vocation can have great spiritual power. Periods of preparation and reassessment can culminate in services of baptismal affirmation which are related to specific forms of ministry older adults envisage.

As Arthur Becker says, "The root and ground of our vocation is baptism. God's call to us to enter into his work of continuing creation in the world was issued to us in our Baptism and it is baptismal faith that generates and empowers us to respond to that call. . . . Like Baptism and its blessings this call remains with us throughout our lifetime; there is no retirement from Christian vocation."[3]

Becker is perceptive when he says that the real blessing of a sense of vocation for older adults is that it provides meaning and mission for the last third of life. We say "the last third" because it is now projected that the life span for women is soon to be ninety years of age with men somewhat less. It is also important to realize that the mature years have been extended so much that there are three distinct periods of older adulthood which must be taken into account in doing life planning or considering ministry with older adults.

The three periods of older adulthood have been given varying names. People are living so much longer that we can speak of young-old (60-75 years), middle-old (75-85 years) and old-old (85 to 100 plus). The maximum life span today is 114 years of age for humans,[4] with a few unsubstantiated illustration of persons living beyond that figure. A recent state of the art study of aging sponsored by the Carnegie Corporation of New York, The Aging Society Project, discovered three major models of aging. These models are supported by extensive research and yet are markedly different.

(1) The first and earliest is the *Cumulative-Decline Model.* Based on the research of Dr. Nathan Shock, one of the pioneers of aging research, this model maintains that humans develop a period of peak physical functioning during the twenties and early thirties, and then there follows a long gradual downhill slope. The research findings were published in the 1960s and were oriented toward different kinds of physical functioning: breathing, heart functions, kidney functions, etc., at difficult times in the life course. The model was very influential in medical school textbooks and teaching for many years.

The results have been questioned in more recent years because the study was made from stress tests, not of the ordinary functioning of older people; and older people studied in the 1950s and 1960s did not exercise regularly and watch their diets as many older people do now. In fact, today the same study made on exercising and vital older adults renders quite different results. Such new evidence is in harmony with the findings of Dr. Alvar Svanborg, a Swedish geriatrician who made a longitudinal study of twelve hundred seventy year olds in Gothenburg, Sweden. With two groups, starting in 1976-77 and 1981-82 respectively, he found that life-prolonging techniques such as antibiotics, pacemakers, beta blockers, and surgical procedures are having a positive impact on overall health and vitality of aging persons. Such techniques are helping older persons stay healthy longer and postponing the cumulative decline pattern of previous generations. Dr. Svanborg interviewed a third group which had made significant changes in lifestyle and routine. He found that most measurable factors of intelligence and memory remained virtually unchanged well into the seventies and eighties. This was true until the persons became physically ill or impaired.[5]

(2) The *Plateau of Vitality Model.* This model is also known as the Compression of Morbidity Model. Again, studies of older adults have found that for many there is a long period of sustained vitality—physically and mentally—until very late in life, into the nineties and beyond. For several, this long period is followed by a short period of illness prior to death, or for others no illness but a quiet death. In other words, the period of sickness or morbidity is greatly compressed and is very different from the cumulative decline model. Dr. James Birren of the Andrus Center on Aging found increasing numbers of persons who moved into a "plateau of healthy aging" at a point somewhere in their late sixties or early seventies and maintained this level until the very end of their lives— often for thirty years more. Birren found older adults still on the plateau of vitality well into their nineties and even past 100 years of age.[6] Clearly, a sense of vocation was one of the reasons for such a long period of vitality.

(3) The *Episodic Model of Aging.* This model is seemingly similar to the cumulative decline model. Some persons in their sixties become ill, often very seriously, but they have a total recovery from the illness and gain full physical and mental functioning for many years after the crisis. The health of the individual does not slowly decline or go downhill. Rather there is a zigzag pattern of good health, illness, complete recovery, illness, good health, illness/death. Norman Cousins is a famous example. He experienced two major illnesses, a degenerative disease called ankylosing spondylites and a heart attack. With a positive, holistic attitude about his life-threatening illnesses he recovered fully from each illness and continued his writing and research along with full physical activity. He died at age seventy five of cardiac arrest with no period of decline before the final moments.[7]

The Carnegie study concludes that there is no one model that fits all people or situations, because older people are quite diverse. Our objective should be to continue to research why these diverse patterns exist and, at the same time, recognize the large numbers of older persons who remain mentally, physically, and emotionally healthy. Moreover, it is the church's task to help them and discern how they can be affirmed in their effort to contribute significantly to society as they age.

Some studies do reveal that older persons tend to become more introverted and inward; but many who were extroverted earlier remain so. Factors which change personality patterns have much more to do with illness or health, family support or lack of it, financial security or lack of it, etc., than with age. One woman reported that her seventies were fairly serene but that her eighties, to her surprise "were passionate, intense, and bursting with 'hot conviction'."[9] We also know that many persons with basically good health and some with infirmities continue to be creative and mentally and emotionally vital into their nineties and even over 100 years of age. In fact, the increasing numbers of centenarians has sparked much more focused research with the age group, even to the point of some researchers stating that 100 years should be seen as a normal life span in the near future.[10]

A New Paradigm for Aging

A positive image of persons on a pilgrimage, in a continuing but changing ministry to fulfill God's call, is appropriate for older adults. The response in faith to God's continuing call provides a stimulus to the whole person. As the consciousness of God's presence and power is rekindled and an awareness of what one can do or be deepens, new energy can surge forth. The spirit moves within and motivates us to go forward. Lewis Sherrill in his classic study[11] depicts the stages through which the soul progresses. At each stage the question is whether or not the soul will go forward in faith or shrink back in fear. When we move forward in faith, the good news is there is a surge of energy present to help us move.

Perry Gresham, in his own mature years, discovered this truth. He describes three attitudes people in general have about aging. They have "the old car," "the old tree," or "the with wings as eagles" attitudes. The "old car" attitude assumes that the body and the mind gradually break down in all the parts until they are useless. The "old tree" image, widely held, is that human life is similar to vegetation that springs up (spring), matures (summer), grows old (autumn), and dies (winter) as the seasons turn. The "with wings as eagles" attitude correlates with the surge of energy mature eagles possess when flight is necessary. Gresham's study of older persons revealed that surges of energy are available to older persons if they have positive attitudes.[12] Sometimes adults in the old-old period do not have the physical strength to do what they once did to live out their baptismal covenant. However, if they move ahead in faith, they discover the truth of Paul's positive message: "So we do not lose heart. Even though our outer nature is wasting away, our inner nature is being renewed day by day." Paul ends his reflection with this victorious picture. "So if anyone is in Christ, there is a new creation: everything old has passed away; see, everything has become new! All this is from God, who reconciled us to himself through Christ, and has given us the ministry of reconciliation; that is, in Christ God was reconciling the world to himself, not counting their trespasses against them, and entrusting the message of reconciliation to us. So we are ambassadors for Christ" (II Corinthians 5:17-20a).

As we grow older with a faith that provides a positive attitude we can find surges of energy to reveal the new creation within us to others, whether in our actions or in our inner lives. We all know older, infirm people who radiate a positive spirit of love and hope to others. They are indeed ambassadors for Christ. They are clearly continuing a ministry of reconciliation. The key to a creative response to the aging process is the degree of passion for various aspects of living found in the person. There are general overriding passions, such as the extension of God's love and justice which motivate and energize older adults. They are basic. However, there are passions which are more like enthusiasms for things in life elders continue to love to do, whether reading novels, playing cello, or running marathons. "People who love what they do . . . are likely to pursue their passions as long as they are able. Thus, for some people, old age is a period of expansion."[13] Besides the many people we know personally who carry their passions for life with them into older adulthood we can point to many older adults who gained recognition for their creativity and wisdom such as Jean Piaget, Sigmund Freud, Picasso, Grandma Moses, Benjamin Franklin, Erik Erikson, John Dewey, and others.

The opportunities for creative ministries of reconciliation can increase in older adult years. Many have more time to give. Many are actively looking for ways to bring renewal and healing in the lives of others, their peers and persons at all of the stages of life. The most enriching are often intergenerational in nature or focused on children or younger families. The spontaneity and contrast are engaging and life-giving. Ministry with peers can also be very enriching spiritually. There are countless needs to meet: problems that emerge as older friends face separation from loved ones, illness, depression or stress, retirement anxieties or transitions, alcohol or drug abuse, concern about sexual adequacy or expressions. Many older adults who have become frail need simple help with the basics of living. Many church sponsored ministries with seniors start at that helping level but can move on to higher levels of spiritual renewal and growth.

Older Adulthood: A Time for the Development
of a Universalizing Faith

Erik Erikson saw the nature of the struggle for identity in the mature years to be the tension between the quest for a sense of *integrity* and the feeling of *despair* that can overwhelm the aging person. If the struggle can be resolved in a positive way the virtue that results is *wisdom.* Many associate wisdom with age, most people in fact, except the older persons themselves. They tend to identify wisdom with the qualities of empathy and understanding more than with age. Studies about wisdom do coincide to some degree with James Fowler's studies of the most mature form of faith, a Stage VI Universalizing Faith. Such an advanced form of faith does correspond well with formal operational thinking in which persons synthesize or bring together many previously conflicting ideas into new and more unifying or universal ideas. Fowler's depth study of 359 persons found only one person who was manifesting a Stage VI faith and that person was in older adulthood.

Other studies of wise persons indicate that they are able to get below the surface of problems and "go to the heart of things." They can recognize and deal constructively with uncertainties, ambiguities, and perplexities. They can also take into account the strengths and weaknesses of alternatives and sense the difference in the understandings and competencies of others. Wise people are also thought to have qualities such as perceptivity, open-mindedness, intuition, nonjudgmental attitudes, insight, foresight, and sensitivity about when to share ideas.[14]

Such qualities are not inconsistent with qualities Fowler found in those with a universalizing faith. He found in his theoretical studies and in his one living example the primary ability to spend the self on actions in behalf of a universal commonwealth of being. The ability to recognize paradoxical elements in life is important as persons grow in faith. Honest doubts and questions must be faced. However, the quest for a strong centering of the self in God finally transcends these conflicting ideas and feelings and finds a resolution. Such a resolution moves the person beyond the "second naivete" of Stage V Conjunctive faith to a firm, risk-taking stance in which the person is willing to incarnate the universal love of God for all creation and for all peoples.

Fowler states, "Stage 6 is exceedingly rare. The persons best described by it have generated faith compositions in which their felt sense of an ultimate environment is inclusive of all being. They have become incarnators and actualizers of the spirit of an inclusive and fulfilled human community."

"They are 'contagious' in the sense that they create zones of liberation from the social, political, economic, and ideological shackles we place and endure on human futurity. . . . The rare persons who may be described by this stage have a special grace that makes them more lucid, more simple, and yet somehow more fully human than the rest of us. . . . Life is both loved and held to loosely. Such persons are ready for fellowship with persons at any of the other stages and from any other faith tradition."[15]

Such persons often have developed the wisdom to see the wider and deeper truths, but they also are so centered in their belief in the universal love of God that they are passionate in their words and actions. Such a passion, however, is almost always expressed in nonviolent, caring, and healing ways.

They are able to articulate a vision of this universal community of love and justice. They can get inside of the shoes of their adversaries and questioners. They can reason about complex moral issues in a way that remains specific yet loyal to the sacredness of being present in all of life.

Fowler's example was an elderly member of a religious order. His life had been a source of liberating insight. He incarnated a certain courageous joy. In the depth interview he revealed a strong centering in "God, the giver." By this he meant that "God is the only person in this universe who is truly liberal: in the sense that he cannot receive anything, and he does not *want* to receive anything. God is the sheer giver and complete unselfishness. He is the God of love because he is the God of holiness. And, he cannot give unless we are willing to receive." He continued to explain that we look for meaning everywhere else, making idols and trying to conform everything to our selfish ideas rather than receiving from God what he wants to give. He believes that God wants to give us his love and wants us to become channels of love to others. He sees the aspiration for God in every heart as a gift from God.[16]

The life of this person was consistent with his beliefs. His life had been a source of liberation and love for many.

Fowler's gift to adults is to help them see that major periods for growth in faith and action are from young adulthood to older adulthood. The final three of his six stages of faith development take place in adulthood and the final stage of universalizing faith is probably most possible for older adults to embrace and live. Older adults can stimulate the thinking and nurture the positive attitudes associated with a universalizing faith as they work together with children, youth, parents, their friends, and with pastors, religious educators, and several helping professions increasingly dedicated to the well-being of the aging.

The Religious Education of Older Adults for the Realization of Their Ministry

Religious education can take place in many ways—informally, formally, in group settings, as a self-initiated and directed effort, in liturgical celebrations, in service settings, through meditation, prayer, reflection on scriptures, through sharing one's story with others in relation to the great faith stories, through self-analysis concerning the nature of one's faith and comparing authentic expressions of faith from various persons and faith perspectives, and so forth. Religious education for older adults is very important because it has to do with the refinement and commitment to values around which they organize life and out of which they live fully in the final stage of their earthly life.

Linda Vogel, building on the theoretical work of Thomas Groome,[17] outlines the nature of Christian religious education for older adults. She states that "Christian religious education takes place in the lives of older adults when their needs interact with the story and vision of the faith community so that growth in knowledge, understanding, and transformation can occur."[18] This growth in faith emerges as older adults share their past (their honest stories) and their hopes for the future (their visions). This process calls for much listening, dialogue, refining of ideas and feelings prior to sharing the Christian story and vision. This sharing is most powerful when it is in interaction with the concrete stories and visions of the older adults involved. Such sharing can be stimulated by identifying specific issues and needs, specific ethical concerns, specific spiritual struggles and hopes which can be the occasions for interaction between the stories and visions of individuals and the story and vision of the Christian faith. Vogel wisely states that "packaged answers and doctrinal affirmation will not do. What older adults need is a road map (e.g., scripture and tradition) and fellow-pilgrims (others in the faith community of all ages—young, old, peers, teachers, and pastors) who will join them on their journey."[19]

Those seeking to enable this process will be helped if they are sensitive to the possible pressing life issues. These issues may have to do with changes in self– understanding which follow retirement; or changes in self–concept which take place after not being able to find a job needed to supplement social security or retirement income; changes in personal relationships or family patterns; dealing with the sudden estate of widowhood; or the awareness of one's own impending death. On the upside the issues may be more positive: how to continue to make a contribution to society; how to continue to be creative and growing; how to work for social change, including changes which make aging more fulfilling for individuals and society; how to deepen one's relationships within the family and within the wider human family; how to grow spiritually through fresh forms of prayer, meditation, or physical exercises and deep breathing, etc.

The great developmental task for older adults is to take the time to review what has happened and is happening in one's life and to seek help from others on a similar pilgrimage in reconciling the normal struggle against death, and possible despair, with the sense that one's life is profoundly meaningful. Older adults, with realism but also as an extension of their faith in God's loving presence, can help one another anticipate their own death (the dying trajectory) and how they can die with grace and hope. Death education, which strangely started largely outside the church in our day, is being developed and sponsored within the Christian community now, not only for older adults but for persons of all ages.[20]

Christian religious education can be designed for older adults much better if it is recognized that learners are at very different levels of needs or well-being. Some older adults have great physical needs for food, shelter, finances, and may not have interest in issues of self-fulfillment or spiritual growth until the basic needs are met in a way that frees the person from survival anxieties. Other older adults have considerable personal resources (good health, adequate financial security, sound relationships, etc.) to bring to learning and growth in faith. Careful assessment of where individuals are is important. Several adult education programs have been developed which invite older adults to assess where they are. They are invited to share their perceptions of their needs, where they are in their stages of growth in faith, what their life stories are, what their visions and hopes are, and how these may interact with the Christian story and vision. This sharing is done with an eye to being aware of deeper needs and areas calling for decisions that are empowering and have the potential for ministries that bless others.[21]

Older Adults Taking Responsibility for Planning and Leading Their Own Ministries

One of the most inspiring things to see is older adults who are not waiting for others to meet their needs but are taking the initiative to identify needs, hear and share stories, explore the great stories in scripture and tradition, find creative ways to minister to one another and to the wider Christian community and society. Such proactive attitudes are increasingly evident and are clear expressions of baptismal covenants to be members of Christ's body in ministry today.

One of the missing links is the absence of liturgical celebrations for older adults to be in ministry. Such reaffirmations or renewals of baptismal covenants can not only strengthen individual older adults for specific forms of ministry they can highlight the commitment of the whole congregation to support and undergird such ministries. (See Chapter 12)

Specific expressions of such older adult generated and led ministries need public recognition and celebration. One of the clearest illustrations of such an older adult planned and led ministry is the ecumenical Shepherd's Center approach which was developed in the Central United Methodist Church in Kansas City, Missouri. The Shepherd's Centers, with ninety six units across the United States and Canada, are distinguished by their focus on older adults helping other older adults meet their esteem needs so that they can be empowered to live fully. While many senior centers in our communities are directed by professional staffs, Shepherd's Centers link older adults together "in conceiving, planning, making decisions, and doing services and programs that help some to survive and others to find meaning for their lives." A group of five men began a caring ministry by delivering meals to seven homebound women in 1972. They were amazed to discover how many small repairs were needed in the homes visited. They also discovered that most of the women needed transportation. Within six months, these ministries were in place and the concept of a Shepherd's Center, named after the shepherd image in the 23rd Psalm, was underway.

Dr. Paul Maves, an early director of the Shepherd's Centers International training program, says that the Center concept has a fourfold new twist. First, older people themselves should have primary responsibility for caring for each other. Second, older people themselves should control the planning, implement the programs, and own the organization by contributing to its cost. Third, delivery of services to the home should be central, thus preventing premature and inappropriate institutionalization. Finally, the Center should not be a place to which persons come, so much as it is a presence in the neighborhood or an expression of the pastoral care of the congregation. This is a commitment to the creation of a *Covenant Community*, in which persons care for each other because they care about each other![22] The services include: 1) Life maintenance such as Meals on Wheels, home health care, home repairs, companions, employment; 2) Life enrichment: adult education, volunteer service, health education, advocacy and support groups; 3) Life reconstruction: issues dealing with retirement, widowhood, Alzheimers disease, alcohol and drug abuse, and mental health; 4) Life Celebrations: gatherings and events which give meaning and purpose to life.

In an interview with the founder and acting Executive Director of Shepherd's Centers International, Dr. Albert Cole, it became clear that a new trend is on its way. Dr. Cole stated that older adult programs in general are in the process of moving from the important themes of "maintenance" and "enrichment of life" to equipping older people to make significant contributions to society. He has discovered older adults all over the country identifying a certain restlessness in themselves. They are saying, "I want to be used." And when people come to that awareness they stand up and shout with joy, "I want to be used for something meaningful." Elderhostel leaders have made this discovery as have leaders in the volunteer sector. A Cancer Hospital in Houston, Texas with 2700 volunteers is reporting a great increase in retired executives who are giving their time to research teams to seek to conquer cancer. They are saying that they have been spending their lives managing people. Now they want to work on a one to one basis with people in need or on a research project that has long-term benefits for all. Other older adults are needed to improve the quality of life for those whose only present answer is found in nursing homes.

It is apparent that older adults at all of the stages from young-old to old-old have a profound need to be needed. They can find a deep sense of spiritual empowerment and blessing in the focused renewal of their baptismal covenant. What is needed is not only *baptismal affirmation celebrations* but also *baptismal education* for older adults which helps them discover the options for ministry which are available to them. Even older, infirm adults, for instance, can enrich the lives of children who visit them. Networks of love and care can be created, as older persons and children share their lives with one another. They can share stories. They can share pictures, artifacts, treats, meals. Many surrogate grandparents are needed in our highly mobile society. Young-old adults, many with good health, much expertise, secure finances, and the desire for meaning, can make commitments to travel to other parts of the world to meet basic survival needs but also be blessed by the faith and hope of those they serve. God's spirit can be found anew, empowering and bringing new life and energy. With fidelity to the new paradigm for older adulthood it is possible to affirm with confidence the words of the poet, "Grow old along with me! the best is yet to be. . . ."

NOTES

1. Arthur H. Becker, *Ministry With Older Adults: A Guide for Clergy and Congregations* (Minneapolis: Augsburg, 1986), p. 82.
2. See Richard N. Bolles, *The Three Boxes of Life—and How to Get Out of Them: An Introduction to Life/Work Planning* (Berkeley, Cal.: Speed Press, 1981) for very helpful understandings and many practical exercises for learners.
3. Becker, *Ministry With Older Adults,* p. 83.
4. See David H. Dube, "Physical Aspects of Aging," in *Working With the Elderly,* ed. Elizabeth S. Deichman and Regina Kociecki (Buffalo, N.Y.: Prometheus Books, 1989), p. 70.
5. Lydia Bronte, *The Longevity Factor: The New Reality of Long Careers and How It Can Lead to Richer Lives* (New York: HarperCollins, 1993), p. 33.
6. Ibid., pp. 67-69.
7. Ibid., p. 71.
8. Ibid., p. 72.
9. Allison Clarke-Steward, Marion Perlmutter, and Susan Friedman, *Lifelong Human Development* (New York: Wiley, 1988), p. 560.
10. See Lynn Adler, Centenarians: *People Over One Hundred: A Triumph of Will* (Santa Fe, N.M.: Health Press, 1993). Also see Walter M. Bortz, *We Live Too Short and Die Too Long: How to Achieve and Enjoy Your Natural 100-Year-Plus Life Span* (New York: Bantam Books, 1992). Dr. Bortz forecasts that there will be one million Americans over 100 years of age by 2050. He calls for older adults to "change their clocks" concerning what is a normal life span.
11. Lewis J. Sherrill, *The Struggle of the Soul* (New York: Macmillan, 1951), pp. 10-22.
12. See Perry Gresham, *With Wings as Eagles* (Winter Park, Fla.: Anna Publishing, 1980), cited by Clarke-Steward, Perlmutter, and Friedman in *Lifelong Human Development.*
13. Clarke-Steward, Perlmutter, and Friedman, *Lifelong Human Development,* p. 560.
14. Ibid., p. 563.
15. James W. Fowler, *Stages of Faith* (San Francisco: Harper & Row, 1981), pp. 200-201.
16. Jim Fowler and Sam Keen, *Life Maps: Conversations on the Journey of Life,* ed. Jerome W. Berryman (Waco, Tex.: Word Books, 1978), pp. 91-95.
17. See Thomas H. Groome, *Christian Religious Education: Sharing Our Story and Vision* (San Francisco: Harper & Row, 1980) and *Sharing Faith* (San Francisco: HarperSan Francisco, 1991).
18. Linda J. Vogel, *The Religious Education of Older Adults* (Birmingham, Ala.: Religious

Education Press, 1984), p. 100.

19. Ibid., p. 96.

20. See Robert L. Browning and Roy A. Reed, *The Sacraments in Religious Education and Liturgy* (Birmingham, Ala.: Religious Education Press, 1985), pp. 276-281.

21. See Charles F. McCollough, *Heads of Heaven, Feet of Clay* (New York: Pilgrim Press, 1983) and Sara and Richard Reichert, *In Wisdom and the Spirit: A Religious Education Program for Those Over Sixty-Five* (New York: Paulist, 1976). These are illustrations of curricular units that finally focus on the unique ministries older adults can share with others.

22. John Gillies, *A Guide to Compassionate Care of the Aging* (New York: Nelson, 1985), pp. 159-164.

Also see Donald E. Gelfand, *The Aging Network: Programs and Services* (New York: Springer, 1993).

PART IV

LITURGICAL ISSUES AND DESIGNS

Chapter XI

LITURGIES OF BELONGING
AND COMMITMENT: PRINCIPLES
OF PLANNING AND DESIGN

We will consider the function of liturgies of belonging and commitment under five independent headings. The functions could be and have been analyzed differently. These categories appear to us to represent the many-sided dynamics of our rituals of initiation. These liturgies exist to *welcome*. They involve people uniquely as a *community* and as *individuals*. They serve to *nurture* evolving life in the church and to bring us all to commitment to Jesus Christ and his mission in the world.

1. *Hospitality*

If liturgies of initiation will work at all as real passages to Christian faith they will have to be human events of genuine hospitality. The creation of initiation as a time of real welcome is not particularly a matter of the logic of the texts of our liturgies. The words do matter and all of our liturgies, as texts, could be improved by revisions which paid attention to their character as occasions of hospitality. Nevertheless, this welcoming quality is conveyed mostly in the style of worship. The actions here speak louder than the words. Many factors contribute. What does it say when an Easter Vigil baptism/confirmation liturgy is attended by clergy, choir, families, and a scattering of the faithful? The presence of the congregation is a huge factor in the establishment of a sense of welcome. Roles of the leaders of the liturgy are significant to this sense. Do lay people have a voice important enough to say "welcome" on behalf of the congregation?

199

Are candidates introduced by lay people? Such lay introductions are congregational voices of hospitality reaching over barriers of age and station to say to newcomers that they are wanted and needed. Plans for the prompt inclusion of the newly initiated into liturgical leadership in the future, in the regular worship of the church, is another important way to say that welcome is real, not merely formal. Nothing is more vital to successful initiation than hospitality.

2. *Community*

The church is a family. It is not possible to think about and plan for events of initiation or renewal without recognition that family is a major "player" in this welcoming drama. Families are complex organisms. If the welcome is to be sincere and effective there will have to be astute judgments made and actions taken to make sure that the family knows what is happening and finds ways to invite the new members into belonging.

One pastor recently invited several church school classes to sponsor children being baptized. The infants and parents met with the classes for a portion of class time several weeks prior to the baptism, and together they considered the meaning of the sacrament and became acquainted. In the liturgy a representative of each class introduced the children to be baptized, naming them and indicating their class sponsorship. The effect of these introductions was profound, coming as they did from out of the congregation and from different places within it. It was as if the congregation as a whole had introduced the baptizands. At dinner in a local restaurant after the service a boy was asked by a guest, "What happened at your church today?" He responded, "We baptized. . . . " and he named the four names. Remarkable! This simple idea for introducing became a powerful image of community for the people to appreciate and appropriate. (See Chapter 12 for Valerie Stultz's description.)

Without doubt, the arrival of a new person into a family is a challenge to the self–understanding of the family and to the patterns of relationship within it. If the church is not really a family, the arrival of new persons can be passed off casually and these newcomers can be ignored. Anyone even vaguely familiar with what health in a family requires will recognize that the new person in the family needs considerable attention. There is nothing automatic about the kind of bonding that must take place if a family is to be a family.

What is happening in the time of initiation is in itself a particular and significant event. It is a special moment which has its own unique reasons for being. It is an end in itself. It is also a part of a process. No matter what special aspect of initiation this might be, baptism, affirmation/confirmation, eucharist, it is a step in a larger movement in the life of an evolving self. This understanding is important for communities who receive new Christians into belonging in the family of faith. The individuals received into the family are on a journey of conversion. The welcoming, loving support of the family itself is indispensable to each individual pilgrimage.

One of the important responsibilities of the community of the Christians is to tell the family stories. Passing on the tradition is what happens at the family gatherings. Ritual plays an important role in this process, because without ritual we would have no tradition. Traditions are always communicated through ritual. Without ritual there is no tradition. And without tradition there would be no identity. The identity of every individual as a Christian depends in large measure upon the capacity of the family to transmit the family tradition. This tradition is made up of many things. It is songs, poems, ideas, clothes, art, architecture, and many other things. Probably the best paradigm for all of this is "story." It all adds up to the family faith embodied in many stories. Even something so concrete as a vestment is essentially a story. The task of telling the stories is a shared responsibility in the family. When members of the family assume that this function is the responsibility solely of a patriarchy or matriarchy in the family—the pastors—then the tradition will be conveyed incompletely, and in distortion. The tyranny of authorized family leadership in these matters is a serious temptation for most families of Christians. In the nature of the case the many-sided story resides in the family itself.

Most denominations of Christians have recently created or are in the process of creating new ritual for initiation. Some of the Christian families who have completed this work are in the process of rethinking the theologies and practices of initiating believers. So there is often "fluidity" about these matters at the same time that new "settlements" in liturgy have been produced. Single units of larger families are thus sometimes faced with some dilemmas. Faithfulness to evolving tradition commits us to denominational ritual structure. It is, after all, disastrous for all the units of the family to be reinventing initiation on their own. The family itself needs to come to some agreement. At the same time evolving needs leave us wanting resources which do not exist. What is currently happening is that segments of the larger family of Christians are borrowing liberally from one another to supplement available resources. This sort of grassroots ecumenism will proceed apace. It is some of the most fruitful ecumenical work being done.

Much of what is being sought in liturgy is what might be described as "pilgrimage" liturgy. Regardless of conclusions about confirmation/affirmation of baptism as sacrament or repeatable sacrament, many Christians are today seeking liturgy that will be suitable to mark significant moments of commitment in the lifelong human journey of conversion. There are now new resources. The Catholic program of Christian Initiation of Adults contains liturgy to accompany the stages of the program. This ritual has been subject to considerable criticism, but has done a lot to establish the value of liturgy at stages of commitment. As we have noted, Gail Ramshaw provided a helpful stimulus in an essay entitled, "Celebrating Baptism in Stages: A Proposal," which appeared in the second volume of *Alternative Futures for Worship*. (See Chapter IV above.) Ramshaw risked the creation of liturgical models from "Ritual Before Birth" to "Baptismal Remembrance at Home." The models are a needed and helpful stimulus. Most denominations now provide services for the renewal of baptism and these can be adapted for specific application to unique times.[1] Some worship books contain liturgy for lay consecration to specific ministries. Materials in these services can be molded for varieties of commitment. There are collections of blessings and consecrations which can likewise be adapted to different purposes.[2] In this period of creation and adaptation care needs to be taken that our families of Christians remain faithful to the stories that themselves constitute the tradition.

3. *Individual*

Liturgies of initiation in which a family welcomes a new member into belonging inevitably come to special focus upon the individual new member. This time is a special sort of "birthday," and there are many personal dimensions. Initiation rites require significant personalization. The personalization begins considerably before the rite as the relationship is established in education, mentoring, service, etc., and it needs to come to clear symbolic expression in initiating ritual. Movement and gesture are very important to this personalization in ritual: Where people sit or stand, how they move to their places, how they are acknowledged, how addressed, how touched, how dismissed. The body language of these events says worlds. A temporal aspect is important also. Each individual must be able to "own" the whole of the belonging/community ceremony. Sometimes in confirmation the confirmands are presented with a scripture verse chosen to be special to them, with some explaining word spoken—a micro homily. This can be a very effective personalization. It needs to be brief, and it should not be a complete surprise.

4. *Nurture*

The phrase "Journey of conversion" has been used above to characterize the process of belonging to Christ and the family of Christ. In a formal sense belonging can be located both in family ceremony and in personal, emotional experience, whether or not these occasions coincide. The real belonging, however, is never truly completed. To be enrolled is still to be on pilgrimage. Knowing this, understanding this, is vital to ministries of initiation and to the sense of what is happening as rituals of commitment/acceptance are framed and performed. One of the functions of the whole people of faith is upholding. All these individuals on pilgrimage need to be held in nurture. All are at diverse places along the way, some ahead, some behind, some mature, some children, some clear, some confused, some healthy, some sick. All need to be held in nurture. There are "breakthroughs" coming, but able or not, ready or not, all need to be supported in a dynamic nurture, where they are noticed, prayed for, taught, challenged, employed, cared for. Commitments can and will come. They come in the awareness that believers are not cogs in a salvation machine, or conscripts in a celestial fire-insurance scheme, but members of a living body that holds the faithful in its embrace and feeds them when they are hungry and strengthens them when they are weak.

5. *Commitment*

In addition to being occasions of welcome, and of nurture, liturgies of initiation are events of believing. There can be no belonging without faith. The "programming" of faith is a perilous business. It cannot be programmed. Planning can make faith well articulated in the text of the liturgy. We can make space for the expression of faith on the part of the church and individuals coming to belonging, and make room for elements of inspiration in the liturgy. Doing these things is important and necessary. Even so, real faith cannot be guaranteed. The planning and preparation for genuine commitment in faith in liturgies of initiation will not be limited to the preparation of liturgies. Such planning and preparation reside more in the people themselves. This is what makes confirmation "programs" such a difficult and crucial matter. Some element of liturgy, if carefully prepared, may constitute a fruitful environment for the appearance of real faith.

It is important, in the first place, that the faith be stated clearly and compellingly in the liturgy. This is the function of no one aspect of worship. Different elements combine. Expression of faith is a function of scripture, sermon, hymns, psalms, prayers, music, art, and more. All of this should be put together with the intent of articulating the faith, dynamically, not didactically. This cannot be the sole intent of all these elements of worship, but it should be a very important single intent. There is, in fact, no complete way to say the faith, in spite of our many serious attempts to do this. Letting its articulation appear among us in liturgies of initiation is essential in planning.

A second aspect of the liturgy vital to genuine commitment is prayer. Faith has something to pray about. One way to bring expression of real faith into the initiation liturgy is to give the candidates a primary role in the creation of prayer in the service. This takes some helping participation on the part of the pastor. It can be a very effective way to bring participants into the liturgy at the level of their real acknowledgements and desires.

A third element of initiation ritual crucial to commitment is the commitment vows themselves. Sometimes, strange to say, these vows are peripheral to the whole process of initiation, appearing only at its completion in the final liturgy. Sometimes they are so unfamiliar that the candidates need to be "coached" within the service itself in the answers to questions. The commitment ought to be the primary consideration at the very outset of any program of confirmation/affirmation. Vows need full expression, exegesis, debate, prayer, etc. They need to be familiar, and understood in some simple personal terms. When they appear before us in the liturgy, it should be a high moment, an emotional and memorable moment. While this cannot be assured, it can be prepared.

The fourth element of liturgy crucial to faith in our estimation is blessing. It is necessary for the church to bestow blessing on its new members. The faith and our life in it is something good. It exists for our blessing as well as our commitment and our service. New members or members reaffirming their faith ought to receive a full sense of this in their service of belonging. Belonging in the family of Christ surely involves commitment as the gift of self, just as surely it involves blessing as a gift to self. Goodness is not just something to strive for in the faith; it is also something that falls upon us as blessing, as the goodness and love of Christ and the reflections of this in the Jesus people, reflections which fill lives with a richness of satisfactions. How can this blessing be conveyed in a liturgy of baptismal affirmation? Primarily in the ways the liturgy speaks and acts out welcome and inclusion to the person offering his or her faith, and in the various expressions of the faith as a loving, fulfilling human interaction which the liturgy affords. These elements are naturally incorporated in the texts and they can be amplified there. Blessing will mainly be conveyed though, not in the word, but in the "aura" of human activity into which words are embodied.

Creating liturgy which will function in the ways we have indicated will not happen without careful preparation and planning. Reducing the considerations we have raised—of welcome, group, individual, nurture, and commitment—to specific, effective events requires applying these categories to all the elements of liturgy in a process of evaluation. Actual planning is a subsequent step. It is possible to think of the elements of liturgy in many different ways. We attempt to characterize all of liturgy under the headings of *order*, *sound*, *environment*, *movement*, and *time*. As in our consideration of the functions of liturgy, these categories overlap one another and cannot really be considered separately. They are, nevertheless, suitably large categories under which many aspects of worship can be understood and evaluated.

1. *Order*

In the planning of worship, order is sometimes the only thing given serious consideration. The logic of a sequence of events sometimes catches our concern entirely. This is a dangerous intellectualizing of liturgy. If the other aspects are not valued and prepared, liturgy can degenerate into text and concept. This distortion not withstanding, logic is a primary and guiding element of worship. The primary, guiding logic of liturgy is its orientation in scripture. The themes and images of scripture form the logical matrix out of which liturgy is constructed. First considerations in liturgical planning involve the appropriation of the relevant Word of God. This is the logical beginning and the logical center. Scripture is not something "stuck into" a framework. It is the "stuff" which more than anything should determine the content of a liturgical framework. This is the first principle of a logic of liturgy, and it is the first thing which should be attended to; and the logic of the shape of the Word of God should inform the liturgy thoroughly.

Second, the liturgy of initiation should be evaluated in its construction in regard to the functions of such a liturgy which we have discussed above. Does it *welcome*, celebrate and involve people as *community* and as *individuals*; does it *nurture* and bring to *commitment*? These are all, among other things, basic ideas in the liturgy and belong to the logic of an order.

In addition, logical consideration needs to be given to the interplay of elements of worship. This involves much more than logic, but balance is exactly a function of logic. This includes the balance between loud and soft, between many and few and one, between ideas and emotion, between sound and silence, between proclaiming and praying, between motion and repose, between joy and repentance, etc. In part this is the logical management of another basic element of worship, time. Time for what, where and for how long? This is a matter of the logic of the whole structure.

2. *Sound*

Usually this element is thought of as a matter of music. It is that, but much more. The primary consideration is what might be called the sound of the place. A room is a resonating space for sound, among other things, and sound cannot be considered in abstraction. The sounds of worship are always the sound of the place. That always makes some things possible and some things difficult. For instance, it is hard to count on the capacity of vigorous singing of hymns to draw people together and give them a strong sense of their unity if the room where they are singing is too dry. A dry space, that is one with little natural resonance, suppresses sound and isolates individuals. Voices do not join. In a carpeted worship space, or one otherwise dampened by sound absorbent materials, you cannot count on the natural property of shared human sound to create community. This "function" of liturgy will need to be worked at on other levels.

Consideration of acoustics needs to enter in when we think about all the interplay of voices in worship. This concerns the by-play of single voice with group voice with corporate voice. Being heard, being effective, are very much matters of acoustics as well as of logical planning. The logic and the sound in fact come to us together. The story telling in lessons and sermon is the sound of meaning. Speaking singly, together, singing— all sound is the instrument of meaning. An "out of tune" instrument can seriously distort meaning. The people, the room, any means of amplification, are all sound instruments of meaning. Consider the sound.

No art of liturgy, especially in Protestant worship, is more critical than the art of music. Since initiation celebrates the group, the music of the whole congregation is especially appropriate. This music needs to be familiar to all or made familiar to all. And if the room for worship is unresonant, then the accompaniment for group singing needs to be bold enough and coming probably from enough different sources that it can somehow fill the room and carry the singing of the people. The technical resources available to us today can enable us usually to solve such problems, even if that means bringing equipment from people's homes. It should be pointed out that none of the technical sound "boosters" is really an improvement on a good resonant space.

Often times certain particular songs or hymns, or other music will become of special significance for a group affirming baptism. It is certainly desirable for such a group to share its own singing or bring a music rich in meaning for them to the whole congregation for everyone's participation.

3. *Movement*

Worship is activity. It is something, one way or another, always in motion. It would be debilitating to get bogged down in careful calculation over every gesture, posture, and movement involved in worship. Result: stilted "chancel prancing." There is rhythm in the movements of worship, though, and this rhythm is an important element. All people move in worship in some way, processing, sitting, standing, kneeling. Consider the rhythms and build them into liturgy as considered choreography. In services of initiation or the renewal of baptism movement is of special importance because there is unique movement called for on the part of a group (usually a group) of people. It is not at all uncommon for liturgies to flounder because careful prior consideration of the movement of initiates, sponsors, etc., never took place. Times which we intend to be filled with high spiritual sensibility sometimes descend to bathos in misunderstood directions and confused movement. Careful consideration and rehearsal of all involved is absolutely necessary, if a sense of "naturalness" is to be achieved. Another step in the planning concerning movement involves sight. It is intended that some of the movement necessary in these services should be seen: anointing, for instance, or the laying on of hands. Part of the thought given to movement needs to be consideration of lines of sight to the congregation. Especially the touching which takes place in initiating liturgies needs to be seen by all. This may be a matter of movement and location of a few people, but it may also be a matter of the seating of the congregation. Some of the regard for movement in our liturgies is related to things. The use of particular vessels requires movement, sometimes by several people at once, and these are motions which need to be free of awkwardness and confusion. Nothing substitutes for planning and rehearsal with the people involved.

4. *Environment*

The ecology of liturgy is sometimes an element over which we have little control. Some environments can be manipulated a great deal to create a desired sensory impact; others are inflexible. There are different sensory languages in liturgy. None of them should be ignored, for they all "speak" importantly. Sometimes the sensory language of a particular space speaks loudly in ways which contradict the language in a given liturgy. A room might convey "exceedingly formal," for instance, when what is needed and wanted is "warmly hospitable." Do something. This might mean the use of some expressive visuals. It might mean a shift of focus. It might mean a particular music. In any event, it will mean the introduction of some competing sensory language.

Even in an architectural space which one considers ideal, the question of the relationships of sensory languages needs careful attention. For instance, consider the relation between the aural and the visual. The natural bent is to consider well the aural, since that will largely be our words—and music—and discount the visual as the usual. The aural and the visual are both sensory languages, and we need to give thoughtful regard to balances between what is seen and what is said. In many situations the questions of ecology are slighted. Questions of environment, though, are utterly critical. This is no less true in the church as it is in the so-called "natural order."

5. *Time*

Have you ever "suffered" a liturgy that was organized with just the right elements in the proper sequence but failed because the time allotments were all wrong? The things that should have been long were short and vice versa. This sort of distortion is far from unusual. The question needed is, "What do we take time for?" It is time for *hospitality*, creation of *community*, and the *nurture* of *individuals* in *commitment*. Planning and critique of liturgies of confirmation and baptismal affirmation should be balanced to spend sufficient time on these functions of celebration of belonging and commitment.

Another time consideration is the revealing quality of time presented to us by the particular season of the liturgical year. Many possibilities of worship may be dictated by this special clock. All of the functions and elements of liturgy here discussed can be colored by the varied times of church seasons. What, for instance, is the difference between an Easter and Pentecost welcome? Different opportunities present themselves as we play with the possibilities of Resurrection and Spirit gift as themes in welcoming. All the aspects of services of initiation and renewal are open to this "coloring" by the revelatory times of the liturgical year.

In addition to liturgies of initiation for ceremonies of baptism and confirmation or baptismal affirmation, there is a continuing need for liturgies of baptismal renewal and commitment. Most denominations now provide, as we have indicated, some structure of worship for this purpose. The need, however, is various since there are so many possible occasions for the renewal of baptism and so many group and individual possibilities for liturgy. This means that there is need for additional creative contribution in liturgy. New published materials will be forthcoming. They will never completely meet the need, because the situations are always local and personal. Much of what is needed has to be home-grown.

NOTES

1. *The United Methodist Book of Worship* (Nashville: The United Methodist Publishing House, 1992), pp. 111-114.
   Holy Baptism and Services for the Renewal of Baptism (Philadelphia: Westminster, 1985), pp. 65-100.
   The Alternative Service Book 1980 (Cambridge: SPCK, 1980), pp. 275-278.
   Occasional Services: A Companion to Lutheran Book of Worship (Minneapolis: Augsburg, 1982), pp. 143-146.
   The Book of Occasional Services (New York: The Church Hymnal Corporation), pp. 160-176.
2. Thomas G. Simons, *Blessings for God's People* (Notre Dame, Ind.: Ave Maria Press, 1983).
   Jeffry W. Rowthorn, *The Wideness of God's Mercy* V. I, (Minneapolis: Winston, 1985), pp. 137-205.

Chapter XII

LITURGIES OF CONFIRMATION/ BAPTISMAL AFFIRMATION THROUGHOUT THE LIFE CYCLE

Returning "confirmation" to its roots in baptism and extending baptismal "renewal" into phases of life beyond and even before adolescence leaves us in want of appropriate liturgy. In this concluding section of our study we present a group of liturgies designed for confirmation and the affirmation of baptism at the crucial stages in the life cycle we have discussed above. These have been created by Kathryn Steen, a student at Methodist Theological School in Ohio and a candidate for the degree offered there in liturgical arts. Her brief liturgies are designed to be inserted into the pattern of "regular worship." They are also models of the kind of liturgy which can be created in local situations to meet local need. Three graduates of our theological school have added contributions. Sue Ralph has created an affirmation of baptism as a special "journey inward." Robert Klingler describes a baptismal liturgy which is a good and typical example of the renewal of the "unified initiation" which is being developed in the churches with and without ecclesial encouragement and sanction. To accompany Klingler's description, Valerie Stultz shares a liturgy which involves children creatively in the celebration for infant baptism, and Kathryn Steen provides a model of the unified initiation.

The following liturgies use the language "Father, Son, and Holy Spirit" recognizing the inadequacy of this language. The "father" language is not meant to be insensitive to the inclusive language concerns but rather reflects the traditional trinitarian formula used in baptism. Many people

210

trying to get around the language issue, substitute the word "God" for "Father" but this does not solve the problem, since "God, Son, and Holy Spirit" are not the trinity. With this in mind, where the traditional trinitarian formula is used you may wish to substitute another name for "Father" which would better meet the needs of your congregation.

I. GENERAL LITURGIES OF INITIATION

   A.   A Unified Liturgy of Initiation

(This example of a traditional initiation of water bath, laying on of hands, and eucharist is by Kathryn Steen.)

INFANT BAPTISM

(This infant baptism service, an example of the unified initiation with baptism, confirmation, and eucharist, is designed to be the major focus of the worship service. Because of the length of the liturgy, the sermon will need to be shortened and some parts of the normal worship service may need to be deleted. If only one infant is being baptized, insert the appropriate pronoun throughout. Some elements in this service are taken or adapted from other liturgies.)

INTRODUCTION TO THE SERVICE

Through the sacrament of Baptism, we become members of the body of Christ;
    receiving the blessings of God's continual love and grace;
    and blessing the church with our unique gifts and our presence.
We are cleansed in the baptismal river of God's love;
    transformed, empowered, and sent forth by God's Holy Spirit
    to live lives of fullness and wholeness,
    and to share this gift, revealing God's presence and power.
We are here today to affirm and celebrate that (these) precious new (lives)
    bear the mark and the unconditional love of God.
    (These children are children) of God.
We are also here to affirm and celebrate that we are the arms, hands, voice,
    ears, and love of God.
It is through our arms that (they) will find God's warmth, protection, nurture, and unsurpassing love.
We, the body of believers, are to embrace (these) tiny (children) and (their families), ministering to their needs, providing the safety, nurture, and warmth found in the arms of Jesus Christ.

PRESENTATION OF CANDIDATES

I present _____ for baptism.

RENUNCIATION OF SIN AND PROFESSION OF FAITH

(Questions addressed to the parents.)
Do you renounce evil,
and its power in the world,
which defies God's righteousness and love?

I renounce it.

Do you renounce the ways of sin
that separate you from the love of God?

I renounce them.

Do you turn to Jesus Christ
and accept him as your Lord and Savior?

I do.

Do you intend to be Christ's faithful disciple,
obeying his word, and showing his love,
to your life's end?

I do.[1]

Do you promise to be open to the Holy Spirit,
    as you read the faith stories,
    participate as a member of the church,
    raise your child(ren),
    and live your daily life?

I will.

Relying on God's grace,
do you promise to live the Christian faith
and to teach that faith to your child?[2]

I will.

(Questions addressed to the congregation.)

Do you, as Christ's body, the church,
reaffirm both your rejection of sin
    and your commitment to Christ,[3]
and in so doing,
do you promise to be the hands that will guide (these children)?

We do.

Do you promise to be the voice that will teach (these children)
the faith stories;
the voice that will speak out for (these children)?

We do.

Do you promise to be the ears that will listen to the needs and hurts and
    dreams of (these children)?

We do.
Do you promise to be the example of Christ for (these children) and (their
    families)?

We do.

Do you promise to be Christ's arms that will surround (these children)
    and (their families) with God's unsurpassing love?

We do.

Apostle's Creed

THANKSGIVING OVER THE WATER

The Lord be with you.

And also with you.

(A lay person will pour water into the font as the prayer is read.)

We give you thanks,
O holy and gracious God,

for in the beginning your Spirit moved over the water,
and you created all that is, seen and unseen.
By the gift of water you sustain all life.
In the time of Noah,
you destroyed evil in the water of the flood;
and by your saving ark, you gave a new beginning.
You led Israel through the sea,
out of slavery into the freedom of the promised land.
In the water of Jordan
our Lord was baptized by John
and anointed by your Spirit.
By the baptism of his death and resurrection,
Christ set us free from sin and death
and opened the way to eternal life.
We thank you, O God, for the gift of baptism.
In this water we are buried with Christ in his death,
From this water we are raised to share in his resurrection,
reborn by the power of the Holy Spirit.[4]
By the power of your Holy Spirit, bless this water.
Grant that (those) who (are) washed in this water
may be cleansed of sin and born anew.
Bind (them) to the household of faith
and guard (them) from all evil.
Pour out your Spirit upon (them)
that (they) may be strengthened to serve you with joy,
until that day when you make all things new.
To you, Father, Son, and Holy Spirit, one God,
be all praise, honor, and glory,
now and forever. Amen.[5]

BAPTISM WITH LAYING ON OF HANDS

_____, you are baptized in the name of the Father,
    and of the Son,
    and of the Holy Spirit. Amen.

(Pastor and parents/sponsors may lay hands on the infant—confirmation.)

"The Holy Spirit work within you,
that being born through water and the Spirit
you may be a faithful disciple of Jesus Christ. Amen.[6]

EUCHARIST
(Parents may move off to one side, or sit down—whatever is most comfortable for them and the infants, during the eucharistic prayer which follows.)

The Lord be with you.

And also with you.
Lift up your hearts.

We lift them up to the Lord.

Let us give thanks to the Lord our God.

It is right to give God thanks and praise.

Gracious God, We praise you and we bless you.
You have made us and we belong to you.
You do not hide from us. You are not distant.
You have revealed yourself
    and your great love for us.
    in all your wonderful works.
We see you in the strength of mountains,
    the solitude of deserts,
    and in gentle and refreshing rain.
We see you in the height of skies and ocean depths,
    in birds that soar and fish that swim.
We see you in the hope of sunrise,
    the relief and rest of sunset.
All your works proclaim your love.
As children, surrounded and protected
    by the warmth of your love,
    we join all creation in rejoicing, in celebrating
    your great care and concern for us.
It is in this spirit, that we raise our voices
    and praise your name:

Holy, holy, holy, Lord, God of power and might,
heaven and earth are full of your glory.
Hosanna in the highest,
Blessed is the One who comes in the name of the Lord.
Hosanna in the highest.

Gracious God, We thank you for speaking
    your greatest word of love to us: Jesus Christ.
He came to show us clearly who you are...
We are your children, your image.
We thank you that when we sinned
    you sent us Jesus Christ, our brother,
    to free the child in each of us,
    to grow in your life and spirit.
And of all he said and did
    we thank you for his greatest gift to us.
On the night before he died,
    Jesus gathered his friends together for a meal
    and shared with them his life and love.
While they were at supper, he took some bread,
    gave you thanks, broke it,
    and passed it among them saying:
Take this, all of you, and eat.
This is my body given for you.
Then he took the cup of wine, said the blessing,
    and gave it to them saying:
Take this, all of you, and drink.
This is the cup of my blood,
    poured out for people everywhere
    for the forgiveness of sins.
This is a new and everlasting covenant.
Do this in memory of me.
God, we thank you for Christ's life among us,
    the example he has left us
    of how to live a life of love.
We gratefully recall his death,
    and how he shows us a way
    to die to self and live for others.
And finally, we remember the hope we have
    in Jesus' resurrection and ascension:
    the hope of the seed that falls into the ground...
    the hope we cling to with childlike tenacity,
    the hope of new and fuller life.
Together, now, as a community of believers,
we proclaim the fullness of our faith:
Christ has died; Christ has risen; Christ will come again.
Send us your Spirit,. . .
    the Spirit Christ has promised us,

so the child in each of us can grow.
Help us rediscover creativity and imagination
and all the ways in which we can be most like you.
Give us your eyes and restore our vision.
Teach us to find you in the present moment
you have given us.
Help us to seek and find you
where you are to be found
in the ordinary, day to day living out of our lives.[7]

(Intercessory prayers for the children/parents/church.)

We thank you for (these) new gift(s) of life of _____.
Strengthen and guide (name of parents) as they nurture and raise and
love (these children).
Empower us to be your arms that will provide (them) with the safety and
love and nurture that allows (them) to experience your great and
unconditional love,
helping (them) to uncover (their) gifts and find (their) vocation.
We pray this in the name of your Son, Jesus
who is our hope.
Through him, with him, in him,
in the unity of the Holy Spirit,
all glory and honor is yours,
almighty Father, forever and ever. Amen.[8]

*(The families come forward again, as the pastor breaks the bread and
takes a very small morsel of bread, dips it in the juice and with a spoon
touches the lips of the infants and says words to the following:)*

May you grow in strength and faith, fed by the body and blood of Christ.

(A baptismal candle for each infant is lit by a sponsor or parent.)
(Pastor invites the congregation to join in celebrating the eucharist.)
Come, join our newest members and celebrate the blessings of our Oneness
in Christ.

EUCHARIST

(When all are served, conclude the eucharist with the following prayer.)

PRAYER TO REMEMBER THE SACRAMENTAL NATURE OF LIFE

Let us pray:
Today as we baptize _____ with water;
 water which cleanses,
 water which refreshes,
 water which quenches our thirst,
 water which has the power to transform and shape even the rigidity of
 rock
help us sense the power and grace of the living water hidden in the deep
 crevices of our souls.
As we celebrate this sacramental moment of baptism for _____,
 may we pause to remember and celebrate all the sacramental moments
 of our lives.
The mysterious and sacred moments when you, O God, in your infinite grace
 break through to our finite perceptions,
 and we experience Life in its fullness.
Precious moments when time seems to stop and then start up again.
Moments when the living water stirring deep within our souls rises up,
 overflowing the barriers we have constructed,
 and washes the debris from our souls,
 and then is gone.
Just a moment, but a mysterious and sacred moment with you, O most
gracious God.
 a moment that cleanses,
 a moment that refreshes,
 a moment that quenches our thirst,
 a moment that has the power to transform and shape even the rigidity
 of our lives.
O loving God, we thank you for the grace of (these) new (lives),
 and for the grace of this moment,
 and ask that we may be open to all those sacramental times,
 when your love and grace, and living water, stir within our lives.
 We pray this in the name of your son, Jesus Christ, who is the living
 water.
 Amen.

COMMENDATION AND WELCOME

*(Pastor and sponsor, or lay person, take the children out to the congre-
gation, and speak the following words.)*

It is my pleasure to introduce our newest member(s) of the body of Christ,
_____.

Love (them), guide (them), and sustain (them) as (they begin) (their) faith journey.

BENEDICTION

B. Unified Initiation

(The following is a description by Robert Klingler of a "unified" initiation of children celebrated at Sugar Grove United Methodist Church in rural western Pennsylvania.)

The service begins by including all of the children present at the morning service. At the time of the children's sermon the infant or child to be baptized is brought into the circle of children. We then spend a few minutes talking about the meaning of baptism. One morning we might focus on baptism as washing, reminding children of the way they get cleaned up to go someplace special such as a party or to church. On another day we might talk about being adopted by God so that in the church we are all part of the same special family. Yet another morning we might talk about the way we sometimes forget things and the need for reminders like a string around our finger and how baptism reminds us that we are all special to God and part of God's church.

The children then repeat the name of the child being baptized several times so that they will be able to present him/her during the baptismal liturgy. The children become the ones doing the naming, with all that naming implies.

The service then continues with the proclamation of the Word. The scriptures read and the theme of the sermon also reflect upon some aspect of baptism. An anthem by the choir follows the sermon and serves as a prelude to the baptism ritual. The ritual begins by having the family of the child join the pastor at the baptismal table, which is placed directly against the first pew. Sponsors, God-parents, etc., also join us. The children of the congregation stand directly behind the first pew where they can see well and also participate. The rest of the congregation is invited to stand in a large circle all around us, shoulder to shoulder. Because the congregations are small (maximum at worship might be 120 persons) we are able to form a comfortable circle at the front of the sanctuary.

The liturgy begins with a brief statement about baptism (from the service in the new United Methodist Hymnal). The children then present the person being baptized saying, "We present _____ _____ for baptism." To keep faith with the priesthood of all believers the congregation asks the parents the traditional questions from the liturgy. They then affirm their faith.

A prayer of thanksgiving (taken from the new Presbyterian liturgy) is offered over the water. There is a pause in the midst of the prayer to pour the water from the pitcher into the bowl. The sound of the water is very powerful in the silence. The child is then undressed and placed into the bowl. Following baptism the child is wrapped in a large white towel and shown so that all of the congregation can see him/her clearly. Then follows a prayer of blessing and the anointing with oil.

After the anointing the lay leader (or other representative of the congregation) welcomes the new member on behalf of the church. A welcome can be included on behalf of the other children. This might be spoken by one older child, or by several. Such a welcome might be:

We, the children, also welcome you into our church family. We look forward to sharing with you in Sunday School and worship. We ask God to bless you each day as you grow and learn to play.

The congregation is then invited to share signs of God's peace and love with one another as they return to their seats. The service continues with the offering followed by a celebration of the eucharist.

Whether we offer the sacrament by intinction or at the altar rail in tables, the newly baptized child is served first along with her/his family and the rest of the children in the congregation. The children come forward as a group, with their families, followed by the remainder of the congregation. In this way the children are involved in the service from beginning to end and are accorded responsibilities and privileges as members of Christ's church.

The children look forward to baptisms, perhaps even more so than adults. It's always a special day for them as much as for the person being baptized (or bap-ta-tized as my daughter calls it). They are excited, and that excitement affects the whole congregation.

C. A Service of Baptism (Valerie Stultz)

We began to prepare for the baptism of three infants a month prior to the event. At a church school teachers' meeting we discussed the various Christian traditions which were represented. Surprisingly, only two of the ten teachers present had been raised in the Methodist tradition. Relating what we knew of our own baptisms helped greatly in the preparation for the coming event.

The three candidates were "adopted" by three church school classes. The teachers developed lessons around baptism and invited the babies and their families to attend. In this way the children were acquainted with the families and were given the opportunity to ask questions such as: "Why have you decided to have your child baptized?" and "What can this mean for the child since he/she is just a baby?"

During the church school hour, the classes wrote personal letters to the children they were sponsoring, welcoming them into the church family and sharing their perceptions about the community. Two children from each class were chosen to represent the entire class in the ceremony of baptism during the service of worship. One child sat with the congregation and responded to the minister's call for the presentation of candidates. At the appropriate time he/she stood up and announced the class's candidate:

> "The sixth grade church school class presents *Gretchen Elizabeth,* seeking admission into the Body of Christ through baptism."

The second child came forward with the family and stood with them during the baptism. He/she participated with the minister and the parents in the laying on of hands and then presented the parents with the packet of class letters and a copy of *Bringing Up Children* in the Christian Faith by Westerhoff.

The sermon and preceding liturgy picked up the baptismal theme as well. For the Children's Sermon the babies were brought forward and introduced to the congregation.

The Drama

The candidates were carried forward by their families as they were introduced by the class representatives. Heretofore, the participants had always faced the chancel with their backs to the congregation. The choir had a great view of the drama, but the congregation was excluded except for a brief moment when the minister raised the child up for all to see. For this occasion the baptismal font had been brought down out of the chancel to the feet of those who sat in the front pew. The ministers and acolytes thus stood facing the congregation within touching distance, and the families formed a semicircle behind them also facing the congregation.

A = acolyte:	they loved helping! One held the certificates so the minister could read the child's name. The other held the top to the font during the service of baptism.
M = minister:	they loved seeing the faces of the congregation! One did the baptizing, lavishly washing the child's head. The other did the toweling, taking plenty of time so the con-

gregation could have a good long look. (This would be
a great job for a lay person!)

F = family: there were lots of 'em! There were aunts and uncles,
                     grand parents, siblings, godparents, and of course, the
                     class representatives.

The pitcher of water had been incorporated into the altar arrangement
for the occasion. It was brought to the font and the water was poured in with
ceremony (splashing) while the minister led the thanksgiving over the
water. The minister washed the child's head and after toweling, the minister
and family participated in the laying on of hands.
Personal Reflection (I was the toweler):
This was one of those occasions in which all time seemed to stop.
Because we were facing each other, we seemed bound together by the
experience as we became one in our baptism. My only regret was that the
choir was now behind the drama with limited vision and interaction. Next
time we'll invite them down to join us!

II.   Renewal of Baptism for Children (Kathryn Steen)

(There is every reason to want to establish baptismal identity in the
very young in events which help them to identify with their own baptisms
and prepare them for later, more mature, baptismal affirmation.)

Baptismal renewal—children—third or fourth grade

PREPARATION

1. In late spring, during church school, children will plant sunflower seeds
in small cups, two to three weeks before the Sunday of renewal. (Be sure
to plant extras so that all children in attendance on the Sunday of renewal will have a cup with plants growing in them. The plants should come up
within one week of planting.) Between the time of planting and the renewal Sunday, instructors in church school should link what they are doing
with the plants to baptism.

For example:
—Point out how the plants bend toward the light and the importance
of light, water, soil, roots. etc.
—Identify those not baptized and visit their parents and them about
being baptized for the first time.

—Invite the parents and sponsors to come to church school with their children for a discussion on baptism from the pastor. This could be a learning opportunity for the parents, as well as for the children. Parents could retell the story of their child's baptism.

—In addition to the pastor discussing baptism as a sign of our being rooted in Jesus the role of the sponsor can also be discussed, in light of baptism and of this project.

—Go over what will happen in the service, and the wording of the "prayer over the children," so that they understand the concept.

2. On the Sunday of renewal, children of the third or fourth grades will bring their plants forward for the children's sermon. (Order of worship for this Sunday—sermon, children's sermon, offering of the children/congregation, final hymn.)

Children's Sermon

(The following questions and concepts are ideas to stimulate the crafting of a children's sermon. Language may need to be simplified to suit the age of the children.)

3. For children's sermon ask the children about the plants.
   What did they do a few weeks ago with the soil and these cups?
   What do seeds/plants need in order to grow?
   What are roots? Why are they important?
   Did they notice the plant bending toward the light?

Just like plants turn toward the sun, we need to turn toward Jesus, who is called the light of the world, for warmth and nourishment.

It is important for us to be rooted firmly in Jesus, like the plant is rooted in the soil, so that we can withstand the pressures and winds of our life.

Like plants we need things to help us grow and keep us healthy—love, family, friends, the teachings of the Bible, etc.

It takes time and work to grow a plant, just like it takes time and work to grow in faith in Jesus Christ. And other people can help us grow by encouraging us, and teaching us, and sharing with us.

4. Today, during the offering, we are going to have you offer these plants you have planted, and watered, and that have started to grow.

After the service, you and someone that you have selected (mom, dad, grandpa, grandma, godparent, sponsor, sister/brother/friend), can come and get your seedling to take it home to care for it, and plant it outside, and watch it grow and produce sunflowers.

5. Baptism is a sign of our being rooted in Jesus, so when things happen in life, we can count on Jesus being there in the midst of things, always supporting us. And it is important to remember that you need things just like plants do—you need love, and encouragement, and people to teach you, and help you grow stronger in the faith.

Before we are going to offer the plants, we are going to invite those who wish to offer yourselves to Jesus. As you hold your plant in your hands, I want you to think of yourself being like that plant. For nourishment and warmth and light, you can always turn toward Jesus, the light of the world.

Offering of the Children

(If a child in the class has not been baptized, delete the word "baptized.")

6. Children come forward one by one and water is placed on their forehead in the sign of the cross while saying these words:

_____, you are a child of God, created, baptized, and nurtured by God. Be rooted and grow in the name of the Father, and in the Son, and in the Holy Spirit. Amen.

(Ushers come forward, and the offering occurs as the children are offering themselves and their plants.)

7. After the child is anointed, they can place their plants on the altar, and remain up front, with their parent/godparent/sponsor with them—possibly the one who will help them transplant and take care of the plant outdoors.

Prayer over the Children

8. Let us pray:
As a tender young plant naturally orients itself to the light,
we pray that these young lives will continue to turn themselves
   to you, O God,
   the Light which sustains all life.
We pray as they grow into adulthood, their values and lives will be
   firmly rooted in You,
so that they will be able to withstand the strong winds and pressures of

the world in which they live.
Sustain them through the winters of their life,
    and through the times of drought,
    and through the painful pruning circumstances that sometimes come with
    life.
Nurture and give them strength to bear the fruits of your Spirit—
    the fruits of love,
    and joy,
    of peace,
    and patience,
    kindness,
    and generosity,
    of faithfulness,
    gentleness,
    and self-control.
We pray all this in Jesus' name,
    who is the Light of the world. Amen.

Offerings of the Congregation

9. Questions addressed to the families/congregation:

Do you offer yourselves as nurturers of these young children?
Do you offer to provide them with love and encouragement?
Do you offer to be teachers and leaders and examples for them?
Do you offer to sustain them through the hurts of childhood,
    the struggles and questions of adolescence,
    and guide them toward a stronger faith in adulthood?

10. Offering is brought forward with the singing of the final hymn.
Hymn #664 in the Methodist Hymnal "Sent Forth By God's Blessing."

III. Renewal of Baptism for Adolescents (Kathryn Steen)

(Since many churches are bringing youth to confirmation at later ages it could be helpful to include young adolescents in services reinforcing baptismal faith. Some features of this liturgy might also be included in a service of confirmation. Some elements have been taken or adapted from other liturgies.)

Affirmation of Baptism—Adolescents

INTRODUCTION TO THE SERVICE

Through the sacrament of baptism, we become members of the body of
Christ;
    receiving the blessings of God's continual love and grace;
    and blessing the church with our unique gifts and our presence.
We are cleansed in the baptismal river of God's love;
    transformed, empowered, and sent forth by God's Holy Spirit
    to live lives of fullness and wholeness,
    and to share the Life, revealing God's presence and power.

PRESENTATION OF CANDIDATES

*(The pastor or lay person may present the candidates by saying the fol-
lowing words.)*

Today in this affirmation of baptism,
    _____, are coming before God and this community of believers
to affirm publicly (their) belief in God;
to celebrate the presence and action within (their lives)
    of God's living waters given in our baptism in Jesus Christ;
and to commit (their lives) to be lived under the guidance of the Holy
    Spirit in Christ's holy Church.
In so doing,
will you respond to the following questions?

RENUNCIATION OF SIN AND PROFESSION OF FAITH

(Questions addressed to those affirming their baptism)

Do you renounce evil,
and its power in the world,
which defies God's righteousness and love?

I renounce it.

Do you renounce the ways of sin
that separate you from the love of God?

I renounce them.

Do you turn to Jesus Christ
and accept him as your Lord and Savior?

I do.

Do you intend to be Christ's faithful disciple,
obeying his word, and showing his love,
to your life's end?

I do.[9]

Do you promise to be open to the Holy Spirit
    as you read the faith stories,
    participate as a member of the church,
    and live your daily life?

I will.

(Questions addressed to the congregation.)

Do you, as Christ's body, the church,
reaffirm both your rejection of sin
    and your commitment to Christ?[10]

We do.

And in so doing,
do you promise to nurture the body of Christ
    by offering love and encouragement to each other
    and to new members of the faith?

We will.

Will you be teachers and leaders and examples for (them),
    offering to sustain (them) through (their) struggles and questions,
    and to guide (them) toward a stronger faith?

We will.

Apostle's Creed

THANKSGIVING OVER THE WATER

(Pastor raises the pitcher of water and speaks the following words.)
Let us remember and celebrate the waters and the blessings of our Baptism!

(After the pastor pours the water into the font, those affirming their baptism will kneel.)

Gracious God, we praise you and thank you
    for the presence of your life-giving water in the (lives) of _____.
When each was growing in secret, surrounded and protected by the waters
    of a womb, you already knew (they were) there.
The baptismal waters proclaimed the love you already showered on (them)
    before (they) could even speak.
By the power of your Holy Spirit, enable (them) to recognize your continual
    presence in (their lives).
For in (their) times of thirst, you are the water
    that will quench (their) parched soul(s).
And it will be your showers of blessings which will enrich (their lives),
    and your grace, which will cleanse and renew (them).
May (they) be buoyed by your Holy Spirit,
    surrounded and protected by the ark of your people—this church,
    and carried by streams of your power and love throughout (their lives).
Amen.

(The pastor and sponsors/parents may lay hands on those who are affirming their baptism.)

_____, the Holy Spirit work with you,
that being born through water and the Spirit,
you may be a faithful disciple of Jesus Christ. Amen.[11]

(sign on forehead with water)

Remember your baptism and be thankful.[12]

(Those affirming their baptism may stand up.)

COMMENDATION AND WELCOME

(Pastor addresses the congregation)

Friends, you are the teachers, leaders, and examples for _____.
Love (them), guide (them) and sustain (them) in their faith journey.
PRAYER

Let us pray:
O God of our past, God of our present, God of our future,
    we celebrate your presence in the (lives) of (these) person(s) of faith,
for your love surrounded (them) before (they were) born,
    and continues to uphold (them) on (their) lifelong faith journey with
    you.
With the power of your Holy Spirit,
    guide (them) as (they) search for (their) way—
    as (they) struggle with doubts and frustrations,
    and the contradictions and disappointments of life.
Help (them) to uncover (their) gifts,
    find (their) true identity hidden in you,
    and dedicate (their) vocation(s) to you.
Empower (them) as (they) wrestle with the pressures of the world,
    that (they) may live (lives) of fullness and wholeness, centered in you.
May we, the church, continue to nurture and sustain (them),
    guiding (them) toward a stronger faith,
    witnessed by the fruits of your Spirit—
        the fruits of love,
        and joy,
        of peace,
        and patience,
        kindness,
        and generosity,
        of faithfulness,
        and gentleness,
        and self-control.
We pray this in the name Jesus Christ, the one body into whom we are all
baptized. Amen.

*(The pastor/sponsors greet those who have affirmed their baptism with
handshake/hug and words such as:)*
"We celebrate your journey and your gifts, and we are here for you."

THE INVITATION

*(Those who affirmed their baptism will turn and face the congregation
and invite them to affirm their baptism.)*

(We) invite anyone who wishes to remember and celebrate the waters and the blessings of your baptism, to come forward now.

(Those who affirmed their baptism will dip a small bowl, or shell, into the font and carry the water to various stations throughout the sanctuary, and there sign with water, a cross on the forehead of any who come forward using these words:)
"Remember your baptism and be thankful."

EUCHARIST

(The service may conclude with eucharist, with those who affirmed their baptism serving the elements.)

IV. Renewal of Baptism for Young Adults (Kathryn Steen)

(These liturgies were created particularly for use with young adults generally between the ages twenty to thirty. Some of the issues and life challenges discussed in the previous section surface in these services.)

A. Affirmation of Baptism—Young Adults

(Pastor addresses the congregation.)

Baptism is a sign of all our blessings found in Jesus Christ.
(These people are) coming today,
affirming (their) baptism,
celebrating (their) blessedness,
and offering (their lives) (their) vocation(s),
in thanks and dedication to Jesus Christ.

(Pastor will call out the names of those affirming their baptism. As they come forward all will join in the singing of the first verse of "What Gift Can We Bring"—Hymn #87 of the United Methodist Hymnal. The verses of the hymn will be interspersed with unison readings—in bold print—by those affirming their baptism.)

"What gift can we bring, what present, what token?
What words can convey it, the joy of this day?
When grateful we come, remembering, rejoicing,
what song can we offer in honor and praise?"
(Those affirming their baptism will face the congregation.)

(We) come today bringing the gift of (ourselves)—
    (our) uniqueness,
    (our) experiences,
    (our) talents,
    (our) hopes,
    (our) visions,
    (our) ministries.
In grateful praise, (we) bring them to you, O God, the source of these
    blessings, asking
that you will send (us) forth, empowered to do your will.

"Give thanks for the past, for those who had vision,
who planted and watered so dreams could come true.
Give thanks for the now, for study, for worship,
for mission that bids us turn prayer into deed."

(We) thank you for all who have nurtured and guided,
    for their arms that held us,
    their hands that touched us,
    their hearts that ached with ours,
    their eyes that saw (our) gifts buried deep within,
    their words that gave (us) courage to risk,
    their visions that carried (us) beyond the moment,
    to bring (us) to this point in time.

"Give thanks for tomorrow, full of surprises,
for knowing whatever tomorrow may bring,
the Word is our promise always, forever;
we rest in God's keeping and live in God's love."

(A lay person will pour water into the font at this time.)

(We) thank you for your grace offered throughout all of (our lives),
    your grace in (our) past,
    your grace in the present,
    your grace in the promises of the future,
all found in the grace of your Son,
and signified by the waters of our baptism.

"This gift we now bring, this present, this token,
these words can convey it, the joy of this day!
When grateful we come, remembering, rejoicing,

this song we now offer in honor and praise!"
The gift(s) (we) now bring, (are) the song(s) of (our lives),
   (each different, each vital, each inspired by you).
We offer (our) voice(s), (our lives), (our) vocation(s)—
   the witness (we) make in (our) work, in (our) home, in (our) church—
   in praise and service to your giving love.
(Those affirming their baptism will turn and face the pastor, who signs on their forehead with water.)

_____, You are a precious gift from God, the Father,
baptized in the grace of Jesus Christ, the Son.
Go forth in ministry, empowered by the Holy Spirit,
to celebrate and share the blessedness of your gifts.

(Pastor addresses the congregation.)

Friends, let us affirm the gifts of (these people),
and join with (them) to dedicate our lives to the One
   from whom all blessings flow. Amen.

B. Affirmation of Baptism—Young Adults

(As the pastor speaks these words, a lay person will pour water into the baptismal font—beginning with the words, "anointed us with it at our baptism". . .)

O Gracious God,
You have called us from all walks of life,
   to follow you,
   to work for you, and with you,
   to give ourselves to you—
   our lives, our trust, our gifts, our time, our talents, our love,
   our stories, our hopes, our hurts, our dreams;
And in calling, you have spoken our name—
   you have breathed it within us at our birth;
   anointed us with it at our baptism;
   thundered it above the raging storms of our life;
   whispered it from the still small voice within our souls;
   uttered it from the burning bush;
   shouted it in the lull of the pounding surf;
   and blessed it in our wrestling with you.
You have spoken our name,

as in the past, when you spoke to
Adam and Eve,
to Abraham and Sarah,
to Rachel and Jacob,
to Moses and Miriam,
to Elijah, and all the prophets,
to Mary and Joseph,
and to the disciples at the lakeshore.

(Pastor addresses those affirming their baptism.)

(Friends), how do you respond to God's call?
(Those affirming their baptism respond with the following words.)

Gracious God, from the very beginning, you have spoken (our) name(s),
    and have seen (us) wander,
    following paths of restlessness.
Lord, you have searched (us) with your eyes,
    knowing (us) better than (we) know (ourselves),
    and still you speak (our) names,
    and ask (us) to follow you.
In response to your love which never ends,
    and your call which never ceases,
    (we) offer (our lives) to you. **

**Optional—Those affirming their baptism may wish to insert a statement concerning a particular call to an occupation. For example: . . . we offer our lives to you. (My life as a teacher; my life as a parent, etc.) A similar statement may be inserted in the prayer over the people. . . . Guide the labors of our hands (Tom's vocation as a teacher; Mary's vocation as a computer programmer, etc.,) that they will be offerings of praise to you.

(Those affirming their baptism will kneel, while the choir sings the first verse of "Tu Has Venido a la Orilla—Lord, You Have Come to the Lakeshore" — #344, in the United Methodist Hymnal. The pastor will then pray over the people.)

O Lord, you have called each of us by name,
    to follow you.
Give us the courage to set aside the things that entangle us—
    keeping us from doing your will.
Guide the labors of our hands,**

that they will be offerings of praise to you.
Inspire the desires of our hearts,
    to follow you,
led by the blessings of our baptism. Amen.

(Those affirming their baptism will rise and be signed with water on their forehead, in the sign of the cross.)

_____, go out, following the One who called you into being,
and continues to call you by name,
empowered by the Holy Spirit,
to labor with the Son,
in seeking other seas. Amen.

(Conclude with the congregation singing the hymn—Lord, You Have Come to the Lakeshore"—#344.)

V. Renewal of Baptism in Middle Adulthood (Kathryn Steen)

(The four liturgies designed for middle adult years are models for some possible themes and endeavors of this period. The first deals generally with life changes, the second with faith itself and is intended particularly for a group that might have experienced together an education event or series devoted to "commitment." The other two liturgies are examples of baptismal renewal designed to help us cope in the first instance with a life tragedy, and in the second celebrating a service project.)

A. Affirmation of Baptism—Middle Age (Life Changes)

(This service is designed to meet the special needs of individuals experiencing difficult life changes. It is appropriate to be used with an individual or a couple in a private setting; at the conclusion of a retreat; or before a congregation following a study involving discussions of life changes. The wilderness is a possible metaphor on which to design the study.)

God is the God of new beginnings.
Out of darkness came the beginning of light—the dawning of a new day.
Out of chaos came order—
Out of the void came fullness and life.
Out of the rising flood waters came a new covenant with the earth and
    all its inhabitants.
Out of the bondage of Egypt came the call to leave the familiar,

to venture into unknown lands led only by the Spirit of God.
Out of the wanderings came murmurs of discontent and impatience,
     of fear and doubt.
Out of the struggle came vulnerability—the need to trust and to let go.
Out of the wilderness came the mystery of transformation—
     a new people in a new land, with new hopes and new dreams.
Out of the darkness of the tomb came new light—the dawning of a new age.
Out of the chaos of the fourth day came the gifts of the Holy Spirit.
Out of the void of his absence came the fullness of his mission—
     a mission of new paths, of new visions, of new relationships,
     of new beginnings.

Today, we affirm the struggle of all those beginnings in our lives.
And in faith we gather to celebrate the hope and promise of the new
beginnings found in Jesus Christ,
and proclaimed at our baptism.

(Questions addressed to those reaffirming their baptismal commitment.)

Do you believe that God is a God of new beginnings?

I do.

Will you entrust all your beginnings to Jesus Christ,
     in whom you were baptized,
     and with whom we make up one body?

I will.

Do you promise to be open to the prompting of the still small voice of
     the Holy Spirit,
     who in our insecurity meets us in the challenge of new beginnings?

I do.

(Those reaffirming their vows will kneel during the blessing over the oil.)

O God of new beginnings,
     come to us in the darkness and chaos of our transitions.
When the flood waters rise, threatening to overwhelm us,
     or the desert stretches before us with no sign of life,
     quiet our murmurs of discontent and impatience, our fears and ourdoubts,

with the promises of your new beginnings.
Awe us with the mystery of your transforming power
    to change darkness to light, chaos to order, voids into fullness,
    death into life, endings into beginnings.
Help us to make all our beginnings with your son, Jesus Christ,
    who is the Alpha and the Omega,
    the first and the last,
    the beginning and the end.
And now, with this oil, anoint us with your Holy Spirit—
    Your Spirit which empowers, and prepares, and transforms us.
                           Amen.

(Anointing and laying on of hands.)

_____, this is a day of new beginnings,
our God, who is the Father, and the Son, and the Holy Spirit,
is making all things new. Amen.

(Questions addressed to the congregation—omit if not appropriate.)

Do you promise to be a part of God's newness—
    bringing light to those waiting in darkness;
    bringing hope to those in despair;
    bringing courage to those who fear;
    bringing the promises of Christ to those in transitions,
    so that endings will become beginnings?

We do.

(Pastor addresses the congregation and reads the first four verses of the hymn—"This Is a Day of New Beginnings"—United Methodist Hymnal #383. This is followed by the congregation singing the hymn.)

(Friends), "this is a day of new beginnings,. . .

B. Affirmation of Baptism—Concludes a Study on Commitment

O God of grace and God of love,
    you continually give yourself to us.
From the beginning, your Spirit filled the universe,
    creating life and beauty
    out of the void and the chaos.

You brought your people out of bondage and formed them into a new people.
You pledged your faithfulness to us
in the covenant,

    expressed in the colors of the rainbow,
    inscribed in tablets of stone,
    embodied in human form in the one called Jesus—
    symbolized by the waters of baptism,
so that it would be written on our hearts—
    that you would be our God and we would be your people.
Today (these people come) offering (themselves) in response
    to your gracious self giving.

(Pastor addresses those affirming their baptism.)

(Friends), before God, in the presence of this congregation,
I ask you to witness that your life will be lived in faithfulness
    to God's covenant,
embodied in Jesus Christ, and symbolized by your baptism.

(The people affirming their baptism will respond by speaking the following words.)

O Lord, (we) offer (our lives) to you.
Guide (our) feet to follow where you lead.
Use (our) hands to build up the kingdom you proclaimed.

Take (our) possessions and make them yours.
Take (our) creativity, (our) intellect, (our) compassion and give them voice.
Take (our) heart(s), (our) love, (our) will and mold them in your hands,
    that (we) will gift the world with your grace.

(Those affirming their baptism will kneel, as a lay person pours water into the baptismal font, while the pastor speaks a blessing over the people.)

Gracious God, as your Son rose from the baptismal waters of the Jordan,
    you sent your Spirit upon him to empower and lead him.
As (these people rise), remembering and affirming (their) baptism,
    send your Spirit upon (them) to empower (them) and lead (them). Amen.

(Those affirming their baptism will rise, and be signed on their forehead with water in the sign of the cross.)

_____, rise and go forth,
loved by God, the Father,
led by Jesus Christ, the Son,
and empowered by the Holy Spirit
to live the covenant which is written on your heart. Amen.
(Pastor addresses the congregation. Those affirming their baptism will turn towards the congregation.)

Let us join with (these people), in "An Invitation to Christ."

Come, my Light, and illumine my darkness.
Come, my Life, and revive me from death.
Come, my Physician, and heal my wounds.
Come, Flame of divine love, and burn up the thorns of my sins,
    kindling my heart with the flame of thy love.
Come my King, sit upon the throne of my heart and reign there.
For you alone art my King and my Lord. Amen.

(United Methodist Hymnal—#466)

(Conclude with the congregation singing the Hymn—"Take My Life, and Let it Be"—#399 United Methodist Hymnal.)

C. Affirmation of Baptism—Experiencing a Death in the Family

(The congregation and those reaffirming their baptismal vows will read responsively Psalm 77:1-2, 11-20, p. 798 in the United Methodist Hymnal. The congregation reads the light print, with the bold print read by those who have experienced a death in their family.)

O God, we meditate on all your wondrous deeds,
    we thank you for all your gifts—
    for your special touch in the lives of loved ones who are now gone.
We celebrate your power over the waters of life—
    Your power which creates from the chaos of the waters;
    Your power which guides us through the great waters;
    Your power which causes water to flow from a rock;
    Your power which transforms the water of a river into baptismal waters;
    Your power which quenches our thirst with living water;
    Your power which stills the raging seas.
Today we come affirming your power,
    in the midst of our fear.

For with hearts heavy from our loss,
   and our vision blurred by tears,
   your footprints remain unseen.

(Blessing over the water.)
O God, pour out your Spirit upon this water,
   that it may be for us baptismal waters,
   which cleanse and heal and renew.
Cause your power to come upon us who gather at the river with sorrowing
   friends,
that your footprints will be seen in our footprints,
standing with them,
supporting them,
comforting them,
and loving them. Amen.

(Anoint with water on the forehead in the sign of the cross.)

_____, when you pass through deep waters, do not be afraid—
your troubles will not overwhelm you.
For the Father, and the Son, and the Holy Spirit are with you. Amen.

(Statement addressed to the congregation.)

People of God,
in their time of sorrow, let us gather at the river with these friends,
   to stand with them,
   to support them,
   to comfort them,
   to love them,
so that God's footprints will be made visible in our footprints.

D. Affirmation of Baptism—Commitment to Habitat for Humanity

(Those affirming their baptism and committing their energies to Habitat for Humanity, come forward at the beginning of the singing of the third verse of "When the Church of Jesus"—#592 in the United Methodist Hymnal.)[14]

(Leader or lay person will read the scripture—James 2:14-17.)

"What good is it, my brothers and sisters, if you say you have faith but do not have works? Can faith save you? If a brother or sister is naked and lacks daily food, and one of you says to them, 'Go in peace; keep warm and eat your fill,' and yet you do not supply their bodily needs, what is the good of that? So faith by itself, if is has no works, is dead."

(A second person will read an interpreted form of the text.)
What good is it, my brothers and sisters, if you say you have faith but do not have works? Can faith save you? If a brother or sister is without a home, and one of you says to them, 'Go in peace; keep warm and safe,' and yet you do not supply their bodily needs, what is the good of that? So faith by itself, if it has no works, is dead.
(As the pastor reads, a lay person will begin to pour water into the baptismal font, beginning when the pastor reads the words, "Baptized in the river Jordan . . ." and stopping with the words, "washed them clean".)

Holy are you, most gracious God,
　　for you withheld nothing from us, not even your own son.
In love and vulnerability, you entrusted your child to human parents,
　　and this worldwide human family.
Baptized in the river Jordan,
　　and empowered by your Holy Spirit,
He embodied your word of love and justice,
　　bringing light into an awaiting world.
As he walked humbly with you, O God,
　　he invited us to follow,
　　and brought sight to the blind,
　　acceptance for those excluded,
　　hope for those in despair,
　　and love for those who felt unlovable.
And in the midst of the dust, and the weariness, and their confusion,
　　he took off his outer robe, and tied a towel around his waist,
　　bent down, and with the disciples' tired, dusty feet in his hands,
　　spoke their names, and washed them clean.

(Questions addressed to those affirming their baptism.)

Do you affirm your baptism as a sign of God's love for you?
Do you promise to follow in the example set by Jesus Christ?
Do you promise to be open to the Holy Spirit to guide and empower you
　　in this role as servant?

(Those affirming their baptism will kneel during the blessing over the water.)

O God, as we affirm our baptism as a sign of your unending love for us,
 cause your Spirit to come upon this water,
 washing us clean from the dust of our lives,
 and empowering us to model your new commandment found in Jesus
 Christ,
 that we love one another, just as he loved us.
"By your Spirit make us one with Christ,
one with each other,
and one in ministry to all the world . . ." Amen.

(On the forehead, sign the cross with water.)

_____, go forth, to serve others,
called out by the gracious love of God, the Father;
empowered by God's Holy Spirit,
and led by the Son, the living Christ. Amen.
(Statement addressed to the congregation.)

As the church of Jesus Christ,
let us support (these people) in their role as servants,
and pledge not to shut our outer doors to the suffering of the world—
may our Christian worship be turned into Christian deeds.

*(Assign the speaking of the lyrics, of the hymn "When the Church of Jesus,"
to those who have affirmed their baptism. They will turn and face the congregation, and speak these words of commitment to them. The hymn may
be sung again, after the speaking of these verses.)*

"When the church of Jesus shuts its outer door,
lest the roar of traffic drown the voice of prayer,
may our prayers, Lord, make us ten times more aware
that the world we banish is our Christian care."

"If our hearts are lifted where devotion soars
high above this hungry, suffering world of ours,
lest our hymns should drug us to forget its needs,
forge our Christian worship into Christian deeds."

"Lest the gifts we offer, money, talents, time,
serve to salve our conscience, to our secret shame,
Lord, reprove, inspire us by the way you give;
teach us, dying Savior, how true Christians live."

VI. Baptismal Renewal for Older Adults (Kathryn Steen)

(The first of these two liturgies is general in character and the second seeks to affirm baptismal faith in the face of the opportunity and threat of retirement.)
A. Affirmation of Baptism—Older Adults

(Those affirming their baptism will begin by reading a verse from the scripture—II Corinthians 5:17-20.)

—"So if anyone is in Christ, there is a new creation: the former has passed away; see, everything has become new!
—All this is from God, who reconciled us to himself through Christ, and has given us the ministry of reconciliation;
—that is, in Christ God was reconciling the world to himself, not counting their trespasses against them, and entrusting the message of reconciliation to us.
—So we are ambassadors for Christ, since God is making his appeal through us; we entreat you on behalf of Christ, be reconciled to God."

(Pastor addresses those affirming their baptism.)

(Friends), before God, in the presence of this congregation,
I ask you to witness that your (lives) will be lived
    as minister(s) of reconciliation,
    as ambassador(s) for Christ,
grounding your vocation in the blessings of baptism.

(Those affirming their baptism will respond by speaking the following words.)

Lord, speak to me of new opportunities of ministry,
where my life can speak of the power of your love.

Strengthen me to share the struggles and joys of the journey,
that it may strengthen those who cannot see beyond their doubts and fears.

Teach me, Lord, that I may teach
of the ways you surprise and delight us with your unending love and grace.

Fill me with your fullness, Lord,
that it may flow out to fill those who are empty.

Use me, Lord; use me at this time,
to be your ambassador—your minister of reconciliation and love.

(Those affirming their baptism will kneel, as a lay person pours water into the baptismal font, while the pastor speaks a blessing over the people.)

Gracious God, as the Spirit moved across the baptismal waters of the Jordan
river, move across the baptismal waters of our souls,
creating in us a spirit of risk, commitment, and empowerment to
be ambassadors for Christ—
ministers of your reconciling love. Amen.

(Those affirming their baptism will rise, and be signed on their forehead with water in the sign of the cross.)

_____, go forth as an ambassador for Jesus Christ, the Son,
centered in the unending love of God, the Father,
and led by God's Holy Spirit,
to bring reconciling love to those you touch. Amen.
(Pastor addresses the congregation.)

(Friends), let us support (these people) in (their) role as minister(s),
and pledge to ground our lives in the blessings of baptism.

(Conclude with the congregational singing of the Hymn—"Lord, Speak to Me"—#463 United Methodist Hymnal.)

B. Affirmation of Baptism—Retirement (Kathryn Steen)

(Individual lines not appropriate can be omitted. If many are retiring, insert an alternative address, rather than repeating all of their names at each blank. This affirmation may be adapted for a person changing in vocational expressions in mature years.)

Profession and Recommitment of Faith

(Leader to the people, in the presence of those who are reaffirming their faith)

_____, on the occasion of (their)* retirement,
(are) coming before God and this community of believers
to reaffirm (their) belief in God;

to celebrate the presence and action within (their lives)
 of God's living waters given in our baptism in Jesus Christ;
 and to recommit (themselves) to venture toward exciting
 new horizons stretching before (them) under the guidance of God's
 Holy Spirit.

(* *Insert appropriate pronoun throughout—his/her/their, etc.*)

(*Leader addresses those reaffirming their faith.*)

_____, before God and this community of believers, reaffirm
your faith in God's presence in your life journey.

(Those retiring, reaffirm their faith by reciting the words of the psalm.)

O most gracious God,
I remember the days gone by,
I think about all your deeds,
I meditate on the works of your hands.
I stretch out my hands to you;
my soul thirsts for you like a parched land." (Psalm 143:5-6)
"You, Lord, are all I have,
and you give me all I need;
my future is in your hands." (Psalm 16:5 TEV)

Thanksgiving Over the Water

(*Those reaffirming their faith will kneel while the leader reads and congregation responds. Water may be poured into basin while the leader
reads.*)

Gracious God, we praise you and thank you
for the presence of your life-giving water in the (lives) of _____.
Growing in secret, surrounded and protected by the waters of a womb,
 you already knew (they were) there.
The baptismal waters proclaimed the love you already showered on (them),
 before (they) could even speak.
In (their) times of thirst, you were the water which quenched
 (their) parched soul(s).
Showers of blessings continued to enrich (their lives),
 and your grace cleansed and renewed (them).
(They have) been buoyed by your Holy Spirit,

surrounded and protected by the ark of your people—this church,
and carried by streams of your power and love throughout (their lives).

Leader: O most gracious God, for all of this we give you thank s . . . and cel-
ebrate.
People: We celebrate _____, gift(s) of life among us.
We celebrate the presence of your life-giving water for (their) jour-
ney.
We celebrate (their) years of service as vessels of your life-giving
Spirit.
We celebrate this time of new opportunities—of sailing toward new
horizons—of finding creative new ways to be in ministry.

Blessing Over the Water

O God of our past, God of our present, God of our future,
Cause your Spirit to move over the face of this water
transforming the promises and blessings of our past,
into visions of new horizons,
new journeys,
new opportunities,
new expressions of ministry,
new life.
Shaped and guided by one Lord,
one stream of living water,
Jesus the Christ. Amen.

*(Those reaffirming their faith will stand, and as they are addressed the
sign of the cross will be placed on their forehead with water.)*

_____, in this time of retirement, go forth buoyed by the Holy Spirit,
sustained by the living water of Christ,
and surrounded by the people of God,
in the name of the Father, and of the Son, and of the Holy Spirit. Amen.
(Leader addresses the congregation.)

_____ before God, and this community of believers,
(have) reaffirmed (their) faith journey with God.

(Questions addressed to the congregation.)
Recognizing the uncertainties of sailing toward new horizons,
do you promise to surround and protect (them) in their new ventures?

During (their) retirement, do you promise to uphold (them),
   guided by the winds of the Holy Spirit,
   and the streams of Jesus Christ, the living water?
Do you promise to accompany (them) in the recommitment of your faith
   in Jesus Christ and the journey to which he calls each one of us?
*(The pastor may ask if others from the congregation want to come for-
ward at this time for a recommitment of their faith.)*

Concluding Prayer

Gracious God, we thank you for your water
which anoints us with all your blessings.
The life-giving water that surrounds us,
and empowers us,
and guides us,
the life-giving water that meets our needs,
recreates our being,
and carries us toward exciting, yet unknown, new horizons.
Be with _____, and with each of us, as we recommit ourselves
to the awesome power and grace offered through your life-giving
baptism in Jesus, the Christ. Amen.

VII. Renewal of Baptism: Liturgies for Unspecified Occasions (Kathryn Steen)

(Sometimes affirming baptismal faith is something relevant to situations where age is not a consideration. These general services are created with such occasions in mind. The first service is for baptismal renewal in "troubled times.")

A. General Affirmation of Baptism

(Lay person begins to pour water into the font as the pastor gives the blessing over the water.)

Gracious God, out of the void, your Spirit swept over the face of waters,
Light overcame darkness, and Life emerged.
When your people were enslaved in Egypt, again your Spirit moved
across the waters, and the seas parted, and a new people emerged
out of the chaos and struggle of the wilderness.
Your own Son, anointed by your Holy Spirit, emerged from the waters
bringing light and life to an awaiting world.

Gracious God, out of the void of our lives, cause your Spirit to sweep across the face of this water anointing our barrenness,— calling forth light and life from our darkness and our chaos.

Amen.

(The pastor and congregation read the litany responsively.)

Let us pray:

Leader: For those searching for their way.
People: Come Holy Spirit sweep across our seas of doubt and frustration, uncovering our gifts and our true identity hidden beneath.
Leader: For those rocked by the contradictions of life.
People: Come Holy Spirit, sweep across our turbulent emotions, calming, renewing, and reassuring us.
Leader: For those experiencing a staleness in their days.
People: Come Holy Spirit, sweep across our barrenness, ushering in a spring breeze, fragrant with hope and transformation.

(The pastor invites anyone to come forward to affirm their baptism.)

Leader: Come, those who know a barrenness in their lives.
Come, those who know a staleness in their days.
Come, those who know the chaos of life.
Come, those who struggle with the way.
Come and be anointed with this water.
Come and let God's Holy Spirit sweep across the darkness and chaos of your life, calling forth new hope, new potential, new Life!
Come . . .

(The pastor signs with water the sign of the cross on the foreheads of those who come forward and speaks the following words.)

_____, be sustained by the gracious gifts of God, the Father, and transformed by God's recreating Spirit, to experience the New Life offered in Jesus Christ.

Amen.

B. *General Affirmation of Baptism—Thanksgiving*

(The following liturgy may be done by the pastor as indicated, or it may use total lay involvement—emphasizing the priesthood of all believers.)

Holy, holy, holy, Lord, God of power and might,
heaven and earth are full of your glory—
heaven and earth are full of your grace—
heaven and earth are full of your blessings.
At this time of thanksgiving,
we come celebrating the grace and blessings showered upon us throughout the year,
all signified by the waters of our baptism.
Come, let us remember and celebrate our blessings.

(A lay person will read from Ezekiel 34:26.)

"I will make them and the region around my hill a blessing; and I will send down the showers in their season; they shall be showers of blessing."

(A lay person may pour water into the font during the litany, as the pastor or lay person(s) read(s).)

Leader: Lord, God, we thank you for your created order which you proclaimed "Good."
People: for lakes, calm and serene, which reflect your peace.
Leader: for star–filled skies, which reflect your infiniteness.
People: for trees which stand tall, spreading out their branches which reflect your quiet strength.
Leader: for gentle breezes, which reflect your caress.
People: for birds and other animals, which reflect value without needing words.
Leader: for the seasons, which reflect change, and transformation.
People: for flowers, which radiate intricate beauty.
Leader: for seeds and young life, which reflect hope.
People: for the harvest, which reflects gift and bounty.
All: for all of these, we give you thanks and praise.
Leader: Lord, God, we thank you for covenantal relationships with you and with each other.
People: for the rich faith stories found in the Bible.
Leader: for the gift of your Son, Jesus Christ.
People: for the gift of each one of us, as channels of your grace and love

within marriage, within friendships, within our work relationships

Leader: for the gift of this Spirit - filled community to support, guide, teach, empower, forgive, and love one another.

All: **For all of these, we give you thanks and praise.**
We are living blessings—accepted, cleansed, empowered, and claimed in the baptismal river of God's love.
We, like the world, can be a sacrament of God's presence.

(Pastor or lay person(s) invite(s) any in the congregation to come forward to affirm their baptism.)

In response to the rich blessings of God, signified by our baptism,
I (we) invite anyone who wishes to come forward to do so now,
in celebration of the blessings,
and in affirmation of their desire to live as sacraments of God's presence.

(The pastor or lay person(s) sign(s) with water the sign of the cross on the foreheads of those who come forward, and speaks the following words. For a large church, various lay people may take water from the font and sign people at designated areas throughout the sanctuary.)

_____, go, blessed by God, the Father,
led by Jesus Christ, the Son,
and empowered by God's Holy Spirit,
to be a sacrament of God's presence in this world. Amen.
(Conclude by singing the hymn anthem—"Go, My Children, With My Blessing," Walter Pelz.)

VIII. Baptismal Renewal and Blessing for Groups Within a Local Church or for a Community of Faith

(This liturgy, written by Sue Ralph, might be titled, "going inward.")

Persons feeling called to enter a period of solitude may be envisioning a time of deep study and reflection, being open to the working of the Spirit in their lives. The first interaction with their community of faith, whether it be a small, ongoing spirituality group in a local church, a Women Church or house church, or a religious order or community, could be a time of reflection and discernment with a small group of guides or spiritual friends within the group. Such a meeting might last an hour to half a day, and involve (1) a short statement by persons seeking to enter solitude—how this desire has come about and what they are seeking; (2) a time of silence together, with persons speaking out of the silence as the Spirit moves them; (3) spontaneous prayers, suggestions, and offers of solidarity; and (4) plans being made for a workshop celebration to affirm and renew the community's baptismal covenant and mark the passage into a new phase of life.

What follows is a suggested worship celebration which allows opportunity for informal sharing.

Setting of Sacred Space: Chairs or pillows may be set in a circle. In the center may be placed a rug or cloth of significance to the person going inward, a large bowl of water, and objects chosen by the person to symbolize and celebrate the coming journey (such as journal and pen, Bible, road map, candle, walking stick, cushion . . .)

INVOKING AND ACKNOWLEDGING THE PRESENCE OF THE SPIRIT WITHIN US

Leader: As we enter this sacred time and space today, we remember that our gifts, possibilities, and yearnings are with us from the start, and are nurtured by the Spirit in our life of faith together.

Invocation

All: Spirit,
            You breathe softly
                in each breath we take.
            You fan to flame
                the gently-glowing coals of our yearning.
            You water
                the tender seeds of new life within us.
            You ground yourself
                in the rich soil of our giftedness.
            Open our hearts
                that we may radiate your life-giving energy.
            Amen.

WITNESSING TO THE EMPOWERING OF THE SPIRIT IN US

Leader: God's liberating grace is pure gift to us. The Spirit transforms us into new beings. We are continually being re-created.

Celebrating the "Already"

Reader One: "I have been crucified with Christ,
              and it is no longer I who live
              but it Christ who lives in me,
              and the life I now live in the flesh
              I live by the faith of Jesus Christ
              who loved me and gave himself for me."
                                  (Galatians 2:19b-20, NRSV)

Leader: Baptism is life! New Life!
People: Leaving behind our old ways,
              we are baptized into Christ,
              people of a new name,
              people of a special blessing, born from above,
              gifted with great gifts.
              Baptism is life! New life!
All: (A time of sharing informally. Tell what new name your bap
              tism has given you, or what special blessing you have received
              from your baptism.)
Leader: Let us pray.
              Christ,
              lover of us,
              whisper your name in our hearts,
              that we may remember
              by whom we live.
              Amen.

All sing Spirit chant:[15]

Ru – ah,   Ru – ah,   breath of God with   – in us —— Ru – ah,   Ru – ah,   Spir–it of our God

Celebrating What Is Stirring

Reader Two: "Jesus breathed on them and said to them,
              'Receive Holy Spirit.'"   (John 20:22, NRSV)

Leader: The Spirit is making a home in us!
People: Spirit is stirring within us,
              and is abroad in the world,
              showering us with blessing,

quickening our pulses,
lighting up our paths,
companioning us,
inspiring our creativity,
empowering newness in us.
The Spirit is making a home in us!

All: *(A time of sharing informally. Tell what the Spirit is stirring up*
             or empowering in your life.)

Leader: Let us pray.
             Breath of Christ
             within us and among us,
             blow over our heartstrings,
             that we may reverberate with your empowering.
             Amen.

All sing Spirit chant, "Ruah," above.

Celebrating What Is To Be

Reader Three: "What is born of wind is wind.
             Do not be astounded that I say to you,
             You must be born from above.
             The wind blows where it chooses,
             and you hear the sound of it,
             but you do not know where it comes from
             or where it goes.
             So it is with everyone who is born of the Spirit."
                                        (John 3:6b-8, NRSV)

Leader: We are ready, open to the gifts that the Spirit will bring.
People: The Spirit is free; it goes where it wishes.
             It moves us into unmapped territories.
             In every stirring of prayer within us
             space is created for the Spirit.
             In every wind that blows
             new grace appears, hovers, and moves on.
             In every sprinkling of water
             the fresh dew of possibility alights.
             We are ready, open to the gifts that the Spirit will bring.
All: (A time of sharing informally. Share some pieces of dreams
             you've glimpsed as you have sensed God's Spirit.)

Leader: Let us pray.
              Spirit,
              free as a bird or a wind,
              liberate our hearts from the expected,
              that we may be surprised
              by the new thing you are doing in us.
              Amen.

All sing Spirit chant, "Ruah," above.

BEGINNING TO MAP A NEW VISION FOR THE SELF AS ONE SETS OUT ON A PASSAGE INTO CHRIST

(Such a passage into Christ is "given to us as an open–ended quest"[16]; is "a leap into a new consciousness"[17]; an "intensification of the meaning of life."[18]

At this time the person going on the journey inward (a) tells the vision that has led to this moment of renewal, (b) shares with the group the reason for choosing the objects placed in the sacred space, and (c) relates a new interpretation of a name that will enlighten the upcoming phase of life journey.

Those present dip into the water bowl and sprinkle the journeying one, saying, "We bless you for your journey, Remember your baptism and be thankful!" The journeying one, in turn, sprinkles water toward the others, saying, "And *I* bless *you!* Remember *your* baptism and be thankful!"

SPIRIT BLESSING AND SENDING FORTH

Leader: Let us share in the blessing of the Spirit.
All: May the Spirit's searing fire
            purify and renew you.
        May the Spirit's fresh wind
            give you energy to soar.
        May the Spirit's gentle rain
            bless you on your way.
        May you be grounded in the Spirit
            as you renew your journey into Christ.

NOTES

1. *Holy Baptism and Services for the Renewal of Baptism.* Supplemental Liturgical Resource 2 (Philadelphia: Westminster, 1985), p. 289.
2. Ibid., p. 27.
3. *The United Methodist Hymnal.* From *Baptismal Covenants I, II and IV* © 1976, 1980, 1985, 1989 (Nashville: United Methodist Publishing House), p. 40.

4. *Holy Baptism and Services for the Renewal of Baptism,* pp. 29-30.
5. Ibid., p. 37.
6. *The United Methodist Hymnal,* p. 42.
7. The prayer is based on an eucharistic prayer by Michael Moynahan, S.J., found in a book entitled *Bread Blessed and Broken,* edited by John P. Mossi, S.J. (New York: Paulist, 1974) and adapted for the purposes of this service, pp. 20-23.
8. Ibid., p. 23.
9. *Holy Baptism and Services for the Renewal of Baptism,* Supplemental Liturgical Resource 1 (Philadelphia: Westminster, 1985), p. 28.
10. *The United Methodist Hymnal* (Nashville: The United Methodist Publishing House, 1989), p. 40.
11. Ibid., p. 42.
12. Ibid., p. 52.
13. Jane Marshall (Carol Stream, Ill.: Hope Publishing Company), © 1962. Used by permission.
14. Fred Pratt Green (Carol Stream, Ill.: Hope Publishing Company), © 1964. Used by permission.
15. From *Cry of Ramah,* songs by Colleen Fulmer. Used by permission.
16. Jeffrey VanderWilt, "Rites of Passage: Ludic Recombination and the Formation of Ecclesial Being," *Worship* (September, 1992).
17. Rosemary Radford Ruether, Women–Church (San Francisco: Harper & Row, 1985).
18. Robert L. Browning and Roy A. Reed, *The Sacraments in Religious Education and Liturgy* (Birmingham, Ala: Religious Education Press, 1985.)

APPENDIX

CONFIRMATION INVENTORY

YOUR VIEWS ABOUT CONFIRMATION:
AN INVENTORY CONCERNING ATTITUDES AND PRACTICES

Thank you for your cooperation in answering the following questions concerning what is going on in your congregation in respect to confirmation education and celebration. We are also interested in surveying how rites of baptismal renewal are being perceived and employed in relation to confirmation. Please answer the questions as fully as your time permits and return the inventory to us as soon as possible.

Church _____ Denomination _____

Church size: (check one) 25-100 _____, 100-250 _____, 250-500 _____, 500-1,000 _____, over 1,000 _____.

Location: rural ____, urban ____, suburban ____, small town ____.

Membership constituency (racial, ethnic, socio-economic)?

_____

_____

1. What confirmation education and celebrations are taking place in your congregation?

   For children_____

   _____

   For adolescents_____

   _____

   For young adults_____

   _____

   For adults_____

   _____

2. What is the length of time involved (weeks, months, years)?

3. From your perspective, at what ages and stages of life would you like to see confirmation or baptismal renewal education and celebration take place?

4. What curriculum resources do you employ?

5. Do you offer persons opportunities to participate in baptismal renewal experiences at various times? Yes _____, No _____. If so describe:

6. When adults transfer into your congregation do they experience baptismal renewal? ____
Baptismal education? ____. If so describe:

   What liturgy do you use?

7. If employed, how is baptismal renewal received by the congregation? Is it seen as an opportunity to deepen, renew, and focus commitment in specific ways?

8. Is confirmation as baptismal renewal focused on commitment of young adults or adults to specific forms of ministry through occupation or volunteer settings? Yes ____, No ____. If yes, describe:

9. Has your church established standards (attendance, knowledge of history or beliefs, service to others, etc.) for those completing confirmation programs? Yes ____, No ____. If so, what are they?

   How are they received?

10. Do you see the eucharist related to baptism or to confirmation and baptismal renewal?
Yes _____, No _____. Explain.

11. Does your church practice the unified initiation (baptism, confirmation through the laying on of hands or anointing with oil, and the eucharist, all being used to symbolize full membership in the Body of Christ)? Yes _____, No _____. Do you favor this practice?

If so, is it used with infants _____, adolescents _____, adults _____?

What is the response of the congregation?

12. Who are the persons involved in the leadership of the confirmation or baptismal renewal education? Pastors _____, laity _____, parents _____, Christian educators _____. Describe:

13. What are the major frustrations or problems you have experienced with confirmation or baptismal renewal?

14. What major changes would you like to see in confirmation or baptismal renewal education or celebration?
Why do you feel as you do?

Name _____
Position or role _____
Church _____
Telephone_____

PLEASE RETURN TO: Roy Reed and Robert Browning
The Methodist Theological School in Ohio
P.O. Box 1204
Delaware, Ohio 43015

INDEX